SIMPLY DELICIOUS

PUBLISHING

SIMPLY DELICIOUS

CONTENTS

Compiled by Judith Ferguson
and Patricia Payne
Edited by Jane Adams and Jillian Stewart
Photographed by Peter Barry
Recipes Prepared and Styled for Photography
by Bridgeen Deery and Wendy Devenish
Designed by Sally Strugnell and Alison Jewell

CLB 2460
This edition published 1990 by CLB Publishing Inc.
Airport Business Center, Kripes Road, East Granby, CT 06026
© 1990 Colour Library Books Ltd.
Typeset by Focus Photoset Ltd., London
Colour separations by Hong Kong Graphic Arts Ltd., Hong Kong
Printed and bound in Cordoba, Spain by Graficromo, S.A.
All rights reserved
ISBN 0 86283 783 9

Quick `n´ Easy

"Fast food" is a term which is becoming more and more associated with modern living. Families and individuals who no longer sit down together to eat properly are snatching hurried, pre-cooked meals, sometimes bought from the takeout or reheated from the freezer. Unfortunately, this type of food is not only expensive, but is very often of inferior quality, being high in preservatives, fat and other additives. It is also often low in fiber, essential nutrients and, most of all, variety!

The recipes in this chapter will, it is hoped, demonstrate that "fast food" need not necessarily be "junk food." All the recipes are based on fresh, natural ingredients that are easy to prepare and do not take long to cook. In addition, they are very varied, pleasing in appearance and have a high nutritional value.

GUACAMOLE
SERVES 4

This is a popular Mexican dip, usually eaten with potato chips, savory biscuits, or sticks of raw vegetables, such as cucumber, celery, or carrot.

1 ripe avocado
1 tbsp lemon juice
1 large tomato
1 large clove garlic
1 tsp salt
¼ tsp black pepper
1 tsp olive oil
2-3 sprigs fresh coriander leaves, finely chopped
1 small onion

1. Peel the avocado and cut the flesh away from the stone. Put the flesh into a bowl and mash it thoroughly with the lemon juice.

2. Cut a small cross into the skin of the tomato with a sharp knife and plunge it into boiling water for 30 seconds. Remove the tomato from the water and peel off the skin. Chop the tomato, removing any woody core, and put this into the bowl with the avocado.

Step 1 Peel the avocado.

Step 1 Put the avocado flesh into a bowl and mash it thoroughly with the lemon juice to prevent it discoloring.

Step 5 Put the avocado mixture into a liquidizer, or food processor, and blend thoroughly for about 30 seconds, until it is smooth.

3. Peel the clove of garlic and crush it with the salt.

4. Stir the garlic, pepper, oil and coriander leaves into the avocado.

5. Put the avocado mixture into a liquidizer, or food processor, and blend to a smooth pulp.

6. Transfer the avocado mixture to a small bowl and gently stir in the onion.

Cook's Notes

 TIME: Preparation will take about 5 minutes.

 VARIATION: Add 1 seeded and finely chopped green chili to the avocado purée, at the same time as the onion, for a spicy variation.

 SERVING IDEAS: Serve the dip surrounded by sticks or raw vegetables, such as cucumber, celery, pepper, carrots, or tortilla chips.

CHICKEN LIVER PÂTÉ
SERVES 4

*Deceptively quick and easy to prepare, this creamy pâté is sure to be
a firm favorite.*

2 tbsps butter, for frying
1 clove garlic, crushed
1 onion, finely chopped
Salt and pepper
8oz chicken livers, trimmed
1 tsp Worcestershire sauce
4 tbsps butter, creamed
1 tbsp brandy

Step 5 Add the creamed butter and brandy to the processed chicken livers and blend until completely smooth.

Step 2 Increase the heat and sauté the chicken livers in the hot butter and onions for about 2 minutes, stirring until they are just cooked through.

1. Heat the butter in a frying pan and add the garlic, onion, salt and pepper. Fry gently, until the onions have softened, but not colored.

2. Increase the heat and stir in the chicken livers. Sauté for about 2 minutes on each side, stirring continuously, until just cooked through.

3. Add the Worcestershire sauce and stir.

4. Put the contents of the frying pan into a food processor, or liquidizer, and blend for ½-1 minute until just smooth.

5. Add the creamed butter and the brandy to the processor and process again until the pâté is smooth.

6. Transfer the pâté to 1 large dish, or 4 individual serving dishes, and refrigerate until required.

Cook's Notes

 TIME: Preparation takes about 15 minutes and cooking a further 15 minutes.

 SERVING IDEAS: Serve with buttered French bread toast, or crusty brown bread.

 PREPARATION: If you do not have a liquidizer or food processor, the cooked chicken livers can be pressed through a wire sieve, using the back of a spoon, into a bowl; then beat in the butter and brandy to achieve the creamed pâté mixture.

 COOK'S TIP: This pâté can be prepared in advance, but if you are not eating it straight away, seal the surface with clarified butter and refrigerate until required.

 FREEZING: Chicken liver pâté freezes well for up to 3 months.

EGGS BAKED IN TARRAGON CREAM

SERVES 4

Extremely quick and easy to make, this is a very tasty way of cooking eggs for either a quick snack or an appetizer.

1 knob of butter
4 large eggs
1 tbsp chopped fresh tarragon
Salt and pepper
4 tbsps cream

1. Butter 4 individual ovenproof custard cups, and break an egg into each one.

2. In a small bowl, stir the chopped tarragon, salt and pepper into the cream and mix well.

3. Spoon 1 tbsp of the cream mixture onto each egg.

Step 1 Break an egg into each buttered custard cup, taking care not to split the yolk.

Step 2 Stir the chopped tarragon and salt and pepper into the cream and mix well.

Step 3 Carefully spoon 1 tbsp of the cream mixture onto the egg in each custard cup.

4. Put the custard cups onto a baking sheet and cook in a preheated oven, 350°F until set, about 6-8 minutes. Serve hot.

Cook's Notes

TIME: Preparation takes about 5 minutes, and cooking takes up to 8 minutes.

PREPARATION: When cooking the eggs, check them during the cooking time to see how hard they have become. If you cook them for 8 minutes, they will be very set. If you require a softer yolk, cook them for a shorter time.

SERVING IDEAS: Serve piping hot with buttered toast or crusty French bread.

CRAB AND CORN SOUP

SERVES 4-8

This unusual soup is ideal either as an appetizer or, with crusty whole-wheat bread, as a delicious lunch or supper dish.

2 tbsps cornstarch
3 tbsps water
5 cups chicken stock
12oz creamed corn
6oz crab meat, shredded
1 tsp soy sauce
Salt and pepper

Step 3 Add the corn, crab, soy sauce and seasoning to the simmering stock.

Step 1 Blend the water and the cornstarch together in a small jug, or bowl, until it forms a smooth paste.

Step 4 Remove the pan of simmering stock from the heat and gradually stir in the blended cornstarch. Return the pan to a gentle heat and bring back to the boil, stirring continuously, until the soup thickens.

1. Blend the cornstarch and water together to form a smooth paste.

2. Put the stock into a large saucepan and bring this to the boil over a moderate heat.

3. Add the sweetcorn, crab, soy sauce and seasoning to the stock. Bring to the boil again and simmer for 4-5 minutes.

4. Remove the simmering stock from the heat and gradually add the blended cornstarch, stirring all the time. Return the pan to the heat and bring the soup back to the boil, stirring, until it thickens. Serve this soup hot.

Cook's Notes

 TIME: Preparation takes about 8 minutes, and cooking also takes about 8 minutes.

 SERVING IDEAS: Whisked egg white can be stirred into the hot soup, just before serving, to create an authentic Chinese effect.

 FREEZING: This soup will freeze well, but must be thawed completely, then reheated thoroughly.

HOT AND SOUR SEAFOOD SOUP

SERVES 4

This interesting combination of flavors and ingredients makes a sophisticated beginning to an informal meal.

3 dried Chinese mushrooms
1 tbsp vegetable oil
¾ cup shrimp, shelled and deveined
1 red chili, seeded and finely sliced
1 green chili, seeded and finely sliced
½ tsp lemon rind, cut into thin slivers
2 green onions, sliced
2 cups fish stock
1 tbsp Worcestershire sauce
1 tbsp light soy sauce
2oz whitefish fillets
1 cake of fresh bean curd, diced
1 tbsp lemon juice
1 tsp sesame seeds
Salt and pepper
1 tsp fresh coriander, finely chopped (optional)

Step 1 Soak the dried Chinese mushrooms in boiling water for about 20 minutes, until they are completely reconstituted.

1. Soak the mushrooms in enough hot water to cover for 20 minutes, or until completely reconstituted.

2. Heat the vegetable oil in a large wok or frying pan, and add the shrimp, chilies, lemon rind and green onions. Stir-fry quickly for 1 minute.

3. Add the stock, the Worcestershire sauce and the soy sauce. Bring this mixture to the boil, reduce the heat and simmer for 5 minutes. Season to taste.

4. Remove the hard stalks from the mushrooms and discard them. Slice the caps very finely.

5. Cut the whitefish fillets into small dice, and add them to the soup, together with the bean curd and Chinese mushrooms. Simmer for a further 5 minutes.

6. Stir in the lemon juice and sesame seeds. Adjust the seasoning and serve sprinkled with chopped fresh coriander leaves, if desired.

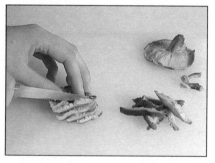

Step 4 Remove the hard stalks from the reconstituted Chinese mushrooms and discard them. Slice the caps finely.

Step 5 Cut the fish fillets into small dice, and add these to the soup mixture, together with the bean curd and shredded mushroom caps.

Cook's Notes

 TIME: Preparation takes about 20 minutes, and cooking also takes about 20 minutes.

 COOK'S TIP: Dried Chinese mushrooms and fresh bean curd cakes can be bought in most delicatessens, or ethnic supermarkets.

 WATCHPOINT: Care must be taken, when using fresh chilies, not to get the juice into the eyes or the mouth. If this should happen, rinse them with lots of cold water.

LIMA BEANS PROVENÇALE

SERVES 4

*This recipe can be used either as an interesting appetizer, or hors
d'oeuvre, or alternatively as an unusual vegetable accompaniment
to a main meal.*

1lb fresh (shelled) or frozen lima beans
2 tbsps butter
2 tsps herbes de Provence
4 tomatoes, peeled, seeded and diced
Salt and pepper

until they are just tender, about 8 minutes.

2. Drain and refresh the beans under cold water.
Peel off the outer skins, if preferred.

3. Melt the butter in a large frying pan and add the
beans, together with the herbes de Provence.

4. Add the tomatoes, salt and pepper. Heat
through, stirring continuously. Serve immediately.

Step 2 Drain the
lima beans and
refresh them under
cold water, peeling
off their outer skins,
if preferred.

1. Cook the lima beans in boiling salted water

Step 3 Toss the lima
beans and the herbes
de Provence in the
melted butter, stirring
continuously, until
they are heated
through.

Cook's Notes

 TIME: Preparation takes about
5 minutes, and cooking takes
about 8 minutes.

 PREPARATION: If you cannot
get herbes de Provence,
substitute mixed dried herbs.

 COOK'S TIP: Lima beans are an
excellent source of protein and
this recipe could be used as part of a
vegetarian meal.

VARIATION: Use cut green
beans, or runner beans, instead
of lima beans.

GINGER CAULIFLOWER

SERVES 4

This is a very simple and extremely subtle vegetable dish, deliciously spiced with ginger.

3 tbsps oil
1 medium onion, peeled and chopped
1-inch piece fresh root ginger, peeled and sliced
1-2 green chilies, cut in half lengthways
1 medium cauliflower, cut into 1 inch flowerets
Salt to taste
2-3 sprigs fresh coriander leaves, chopped
Juice of 1 lemon

1. Heat the oil in a wok or heavy-based saucepan. Fry the onion, ginger and chilies for 2-3 minutes.

2. Add the cauliflower and salt to taste. Stir to mix well.

3. Cover and cook over a low heat for 5-6 minutes.

4. Add the chopped coriander leaves and cook for a further 2-3 minutes, or until the cauliflower flowerets are just ten tender.

5. Sprinkle with the lemon juice, mix in well and serve immediately.

Step 1 Heat the oil in a wok or heavy-based saucepan until it is hot. Quick-fry the onion, ginger and chilies for 2-3 minutes.

Step 2 Stir the cauliflower and salt into the fried onion mixture. Mix well to coat the cauliflower evenly in the oil.

Cook's Notes

 TIME: Preparation takes 15 minutes and cooking also takes about 15 minutes.

 SERVING IDEAS: Serve with whole-wheat pitta bread and a tasty tomato salad.

 COOK'S TIP: Leaving the chili seeds in will produce a very hot dish. If a milder dish is required, remove the seeds from the chili.

 WATCHPOINT: Great care must be taken when preparing fresh chilies. Do not get any juice into eyes or mouth. If this should happen, rinse thoroughly with lots of cold water.

EGG CURRY

SERVES 4

*Quick and easy, this curry is a delicious way of serving
hard-cooked eggs.*

4-6 eggs
1 large onion
1 tbsp oil
1 inch stick cinnamon
1 bay leaf
4 small cardamoms
6 cloves
1 tsp garlic paste
1 tsp ginger paste
1 tsp ground coriander
1 tsp ground cumin
¼ tsp ground turmeric
1 tsp garam masala
1 tsp chili powder
8oz canned tomatoes, crushed
Salt to taste
¾ cup water or vegetable stock
2 sprigs fresh coriander leaves
2 green chilies

1. Hard-cook the eggs in boiling water for 8-10 minutes. Cool them completely in cold water, then remove the shells.

2. Peel the onion and chop it finely. Heat the oil in a large saucepan and fry the onion gently for 2-3 minutes, until it is soft, but not browned.

3. Add the cinnamon, bay leaf, cardamoms and cloves and fry for 1 minute. Stir in the ginger and garlic pastes. Add the coriander, cumin, turmeric, garam masala and chili powder. Stir together well and fry for 30 seconds.

4. Add the canned tomatoes and salt to the spices. Stir in well and simmer for 5 minutes. Add the water or stock, and bring the mixture to the boil.

5. Put the eggs into the curry sauce and simmer for 10-12 minutes.

6. Chop the coriander leaves and the green chilies finely, and sprinkle them over the cooked eggs, to garnish.

Step 3 Fry the cinnamon, bay leaf, cardamoms and cloves for 1 minute with the onion mixture.

Step 5 Put the hard-cooked eggs into the curry sauce, stir well and cook for 10-12 minutes.

Cook's Notes

TIME: Preparation takes about 10 minutes, and cooking takes 20 minutes.

SERVING IDEAS: Serve with plain boiled rice.

PREPARATION: If a milder curry is preferred, reduce the amount of chili powder to ½ tsp and carefully remove the seeds from the green chilies before you chop them.

WATCHPOINT: Great care must be taken when preparing green chilies. Try not to get juice into the eyes or mouth. If this should happen, rinse well with lots of cold water.

MEE GORENG
SERVES 4

These "celebration stir-fry noodles" are of Indonesian origin and are so easy to prepare that they make an ideal quick lunch or supper dish.

8oz fine egg noodles
4 tbsps peanut oil
1 onion, finely chopped
2 cloves garlic, crushed
1 green chili, seeded and finely sliced
1 tsp chili paste
4oz pork, finely sliced
2 sticks of celery, sliced
¼ small cabbage, finely shredded
1 tbsp light soy sauce
¾ cup shrimp, shelled and deveined
Salt and pepper

Step 4 Stir-fry the pork, celery and cabbage with the onion mixture for 3 minutes, or until the pork is cooked through.

Step 1 Soak the noodles in hot water for 8 minutes, until they are soft. Rinse in cold water and drain thoroughly in a colander.

1. Soak the noodles in hot water for 8 minutes, until they are soft. Rinse in cold water and drain thoroughly in a colander.

2. Heat the oil in a wok and stir-fry the onion, garlic and chili, until the onion is soft and just golden brown.

3. Add the chili paste and stir in well.

4. Add the pork, celery and cabbage to the fried onions, and stir-fry for about 3 minutes, or until the pork is cooked through. Season to taste.

5. Stir in the soy sauce, noodles and shrimp, tossing the mixture together thoroughly and heating through before serving.

Cook's Notes

 TIME: Preparation takes about 20 minutes, and cooking takes about 15 minutes.

 VARIATION: Substitute sliced chicken breast for the pork.

 SERVING IDEAS: Serve with plain boiled rice and shrimp crackers.

 WATCHPOINT: Great care should be taken when preparing green chilies. Try not to get juice into the eyes or mouth. If this should happen, rinse well with lots of cold water.

CHICKEN AND CASHEW NUTS

SERVES 4

Many oriental dishes are stir-fried. This simply means that they are fried quickly in hot oil, the ingredients being stirred continuously to prevent them from burning.

12oz chicken breast, sliced into 1-inch pieces
1 tbsp cornstarch
1 tsp salt
1 tsp sesame oil
1 tbsp light soy sauce
½ tsp sugar
5 tbsps vegetable oil
2 green onions, trimmed and chopped
1 small onion, diced
1-inch piece fresh root ginger, peeled and finely sliced
2 cloves garlic, finely sliced
3oz snow peas
2oz bamboo shoots, thinly sliced
1 cup cashew nuts
2 tsps cornstarch
1 tbsp hoisin sauce, or barbecue sauce
1 cup chicken stock

Step 2 Put the chicken pieces into the marinade mixture, and stir together well, to coat the pieces evenly.

Step 4 Add the snow peas and the bamboo shoots to the stir-fried onions in the wok, and continue stir-frying for about 3 minutes.

1. Roll the chicken pieces in the cornstarch. Reserve any excess cornstarch.

2. Mix together the salt, sesame oil, soy sauce and sugar in a large mixing bowl. Put the chicken into this marinade mixture and leave to stand in a refrigerator for 10 minutes.

3. Heat 2 tbsps vegetable oil in a large wok and stir-fry the onions, ginger and garlic for 2-3 minutes.

4. Add the snow peas and the bamboo shoots to the onion mixture. Stir-fry for a further 3 minutes.

5. Remove the fried vegetables, add a further 1 tbsp oil to the wok and heat through.

6. Lift the chicken pieces out of the marinade and

stir-fry these in the hot oil for 3-4 minutes, until cooked through.

7. Remove the cooked chicken pieces and clean the wok.

8. Add the remaining oil and return the chicken and fried vegetables to the wok, and stir in the cashew nuts.

9. Mix together the remaining cornstarch, the hoisin or barbecue sauce and the chicken stock. Pour this over the chicken and vegetables in the wok and cook over a moderate heat, stirring continuously, until the ingredients are heated through and the sauce has thickened.

Cook's Notes

 TIME: Preparation takes about 15 minutes, and cooking takes about 15 minutes.

 VARIATION: Stir 3oz pineapple chunks into the stir-fry mixture just before serving.

 SERVING IDEAS: Serve this stir-fry with a dish of Chinese noodles.

SHREDDED BEEF WITH VEGETABLES

SERVES 4

Stir-fried food is recognised as being extremely nutritious and wholesome. This classic Chinese stir-fry is no exception, and has the bonus of being extremely quick and easy to prepare and cook.

8oz lean beef steak, cut into thin strips
½ tsp salt
4 tbsps vegetable oil
1 red and 1 green chili, cut in half, seeded and
   sliced into strips
1 tsp vinegar
1 stick celery, cut into thin 2-inch strips
2 carrots, cut into thin 2-inch strips
1 leek, white part only, sliced into thin 2-inch
   strips
2 cloves garlic, finely chopped
1 tsp light soy sauce
1 tsp dark soy sauce
2 tsps Chinese wine, or dry sherry
1 tsp superfine sugar
½ tsp freshly ground black pepper

1. Put the strips of beef into a large bowl and sprinkle with the salt. Rub the salt into the meat and allow to stand for 5 minutes.

2. Heat 1 tbsp of the oil in a large wok. When the oil begins to smoke, reduce the heat and stir in the beef and the chilies. Stir-fry for 4-5 minutes.

3. Add the remaining oil and continue stir-frying the beef, until it turns crispy.

4. Add the vinegar and stir until it evaporates, then add the celery, carrots, leek and garlic. Stir-fry for 2 minutes.

5. Mix together the soy sauces, wine or sherry, sugar and pepper. Pour this mixture over the beef and cook for 2 minutes. Serve immediately.

Step 1 Put the finely sliced beef into a large bowl and sprinkle with salt. Rub the salt well into the meat and leave to stand.

Step 3 Add the remaining oil to the wok, and continue stir-frying the beef until it is crisp.

Step 5 Pour the soy sauce mixture over the beef and stir-fry rapidly for about 2 minutes, making sure that the beef and vegetables are well coated with the seasoning mixture.

Cook's Notes

 TIME: Preparation takes about 15 minutes, and cooking takes about 10 minutes.

 SERVING IDEAS: Serve with plain boiled rice and shrimp crisps.

 VARIATION: Use your favorite combination of vegetables in place of those suggested in the recipe.

 WATCHPOINT: Great care should be taken when preparing fresh chilies. Try not to get juice into the eyes or mouth. If this should happen, rinse well with lots of cold water.

PORK CHOW MEIN
SERVES 4

*This favorite Chinese meal is quick and simple to prepare, and
makes a refreshing change for a midweek lunch or supper.*

10oz egg noodles
1 tbsp Chinese wine, or dry sherry
1 tbsp light soy sauce
1 tsp sugar
1lb pork tenderloin, thinly sliced
3 tbsps oil
1 tsp grated root ginger
1 stick celery, sliced diagonally
1 leek, finely sliced
1 red pepper, cored, seeded and cut into strips
1 small can bamboo shoots, sliced
½ cup chicken, or other light stock
¼ cup peas
1 tsp cornstarch
1 tbsp water
Salt and pepper

1. Soak the noodles in hot water for 8 minutes, or
as directed on the packet. Rinse in cold water and
drain thoroughly.

2. Combine the wine, soy sauce and sugar in a
large bowl. Add the pork, mix together well, and set
aside to marinate for at least 15 minutes.

3. Heat the oil in a large wok, and add the ginger,
celery and leek. Stir-fry for 2 minutes.

4. Add the red pepper and bamboo shoots to the
wok, and stir-fry for a further 2 minutes.

5. Remove the vegetables from the wok. Increase
the heat and add the pork, reserving the marinade.
Stir-fry the pork over a high heat for 4 minutes, or
until cooked through.

6. Return the vegetables to the wok, mixing with the
pork. Add the chicken stock gradually, stirring well
between additions.

7. Add the peas and cook for 2 minutes.

8. Mix the cornstarch to a smooth paste with the
water. Add this to the marinade sauce and stir in
well.

9. Stir the marinade sauce into the vegetables and
pork in the wok. Mix well, until the sauce is evenly
distributed and is thickened and smooth. Add the
noodles and stir everything together thoroughly in
the wok, until it has heated through.

10. Season to taste and simmer for 3 minutes
before serving.

Step 2 Combine the
wine, soy sauce and
sugar in a large bowl.
Add the pork, and
mix together
thoroughly to ensure
that the meat is well
coated with the
marinade.

Step 4 Add the red
pepper and bamboo
shoots to the wok
and stir-fry for a
further 2 minutes.

Cook's Notes

 TIME: Preparation takes about
20 minutes, and cooking also
takes about 20 minutes.

 VARIATION: Substitute sliced
beef or chicken for the pork.

 SERVING IDEAS: Serve with
plain boiled rice.

MACARONI CHEESE WITH FRANKFURTERS

SERVES 4

A hearty family supper dish, ideal for cold winter evenings.

8 frankfurter sausages
1lb macaroni
¼ cup butter or margarine
¾ cup all-purpose flour
2 cups milk
1½ cups Cheddar cheese, grated
1 tsp dry mustard powder
Salt and pepper

Step 2 Remove the skins from the frankfurters and when they are completely cold, cut them diagonally into slices about 1 inch long.

1. Poach the frankfurters for 5-6 minutes in slightly salted boiling water.

2. Remove the skins from the frankfurters and, when cold, slice the meat diagonally.

3. Cook the macaroni in plenty of boiling salted water for about 20 minutes, or until tender.

4. Rinse in cold water and drain well.

5. Melt the butter in a saucepan. Stir in the flour and cook for 1 minute.

6. Remove the pan from the heat and add the milk gradually, beating thoroughly and returning the pan to the heat to cook between additions. When all the milk has been added, simmer for 2 minutes, stirring occasionally.

7. Stir the frankfurters, grated cheese and mustard into the sauce mixture. Season to taste.

Step 6 Add the milk gradually to the melted butter and flour mixture, reheating and beating the mixture well between additions, until all the milk is incorporated and the sauce is thick and smooth.

8. Add the drained macaroni to the sauce and frankfurter mixture, and stir well until heated through.

9. Pour the mixture into an ovenproof dish and sprinkle the top with a little extra grated cheese, if desired.

10. Cook the macaroni under a preheated moderate broiler, until the top is golden brown.

Cook's Notes

 TIME: Preparation takes about 10 minutes, and cooking takes about 20 minutes.

 VARIATION: Use 6oz of chopped broiled or fried bacon instead of the frankfurters.

 SERVING IDEAS: To serve, make a lattice of pimento strips over the top of the dish before broiling, and serve with a mixed salad.

LASAGNE ROLLS

SERVES 4

An interesting way of using sheets of lasagne.

2 tsps vegetable oil
8 lasagne sheets
½ cup button mushrooms, sliced
8oz boned chicken breast
2 tbsps butter, or margarine
¼ cup all-purpose flour
½ cup milk
1 cup Gruyère or Cheddar cheese, grated
Salt and pepper

1. Fill a large saucepan two thirds full with salted water. Add the oil and bring to the boil.

2. Add 1 sheet of lasagne, wait about 2 minutes, then add another sheet. Cook only a few at a time and when tender, after about 6-7 minutes, remove from the boiling water and rinse under cold water. Allow to drain.

3. Repeat this process until all the lasagne is cooked.

4. Wash and slice the mushrooms, and slice the chicken breast into thin strips.

5. Melt half the butter in a small frying pan and fry the mushrooms and the chicken.

6. In a small saucepan, melt the rest of the butter. Stir in the flour and cook for 1 minute.

7. Remove the pan from the heat and add the milk gradually to the melted butter and flour mixture, stirring well and returning the pan to the heat between additions, to thicken the sauce.

8. Beat the sauce well and cook for 3 minutes, until it is thick and smooth.

9. Pour the sauce into the frying pan with the

Step 5 Melt half the butter in a large frying pan and add the mushrooms and chicken. Fry these quickly, stirring continuously until the chicken is cooked, about 6-8 minutes.

Step 11 Spread the chicken mixture evenly over each sheet of lasagne and roll up jelly roll fashion, starting from a narrow end.

chicken and the mushrooms. Add half the cheese and mix well to incorporate thoroughly. Season to taste.

10. Lay the sheets of lasagne on a board and divide the chicken mixture equally between them.

11. Spread the chicken mixture evenly over each lasagne sheet and roll up lengthways, like a jelly roll.

12. Put the rolls into an ovenproof dish. Sprinkle with the remaining cheese and broil under a pre-heated moderate broiler, until the cheese is bubbly and golden brown.

Cook's Notes

 TIME: Preparation takes about 10 minutes, and cooking takes about 15 minutes.

 SERVING IDEAS: Serve piping hot with a fresh green salad and crusty French bread.

 COOK'S TIP: Precooked lasagne is now widely available at most supermarkets and does not require as much initial cooking. If available, try preparing this dish with sheets of fresh lasagne, which require the least precooking of all.

 VARIATION: For a delicious vegetarian alternative, use Stilton cheese and 4oz broccoli flowerets, instead of the chicken breasts.

CHICKEN WITH BLACKCURRANT SAUCE AND SNOW PEAS

SERVES 4

This interesting way of serving chicken is both colorful and extremely easy to prepare.

4 chicken breasts, skinned and boned
2 tbsps seasoned flour
Oil for shallow-frying
2 cups fresh blackcurrants
Juice of 1 orange
½ cup red wine
Caster sugar to taste
Chicken stock
8oz cooked snow peas
Julienne strips of orange peel
4 lemon slices
A few whole fresh blackcurrants

1. Dust the chicken lightly in the seasoned flour.

2. Heat the oil in a frying pan and fry the chicken breasts gently for about 6 minutes on each side, or until tender but cooked through.

3. Meanwhile make the blackcurrant sauce. Put the blackcurrants into a pan with the orange juice, red wine and sugar to taste. Cover and simmer gently, until the blackcurrants are soft, which will only take a few minutes.

4. Blend the blackcurrants in a liquidizer or food processor until they are smooth. Press through a wire sieve to remove the pips.

5. Reheat the blackcurrant purée in the saucepan, adding sufficient chicken stock to give it a smooth coating consistency.

6. Arrange the cooked chicken breasts on individual serving plates. Put a spoonful of the blackcurrant sauce over each breast and garnish with the snow peas, julienne strips of orange peel, lemon slices and the whole blackcurrants.

Step 1 Dust the chicken breasts lightly in the seasoned flour, making sure that they are covered all over.

Step 5 Reheat the blackcurrant purée in the saucepan and add just enough chicken stock to make the sauce coat the back of the spoon.

Cook's Notes

 TIME: Preparation takes 10-15 minutes, and cooking takes about 12 minutes.

 PREPARATION: Julienne strips of orange peel are very finely cut strips which have been blanched for 1 minute in boiling water and then drained.

SERVING IDEAS: Serve with boiled new potatoes, or brown rice.

LAMB A L'ORANGE

SERVES 4

The refreshing taste of orange complements lamb beautifully and this recipe is an ideal way of using up lamb left over from the Sunday roast.

1 tbsp oil
1 small onion, finely chopped
1 large orange
1 tbsp redcurrant jelly
1 cup stock
½ tsp dry mustard
½ tsp superfine sugar
Pinch of cayenne pepper
1 tbsp cornstarch
12oz cooked lamb

Step 2 Cut 3 fine slices from the orange, trim away the pith and discard it. Reserve the slices for garnish.

1. Heat the oil in a frying pan and fry the onion gently, until soft, but not brown.
2. Grate the orange rind, cut 3 fine slices from the orange, trim away the pith and reserve the slices for garnish.

3. Squeeze the juice from the remainder of the orange and add to the onion, with the orange rind, redcurrant jelly and stock.
4. Bring this mixture to the boil, reduce the heat and cook, stirring continuously, for 5 minutes.
5. Blend the mustard, sugar, pepper and cornstarch together with 2 tbsps cold water, and stir this into the orange sauce.
6. Slice the lamb, add this to the sauce and bring to the boil.

Step 3 Add the orange juice to the onion, together with the orange rind, redcurrant jelly and stock. Heat gently, stirring continuously, until all the redcurrant jelly has melted.

7. Reduce the heat and simmer for 15 minutes. When cooked, transfer the lamb to the serving dish, pour a little of the sauce over and garnish with the reserved orange slices.

Cook's Notes

 TIME: Preparation takes about 20 minutes, and cooking takes approximately 25 minutes.

 COOK'S TIP: The sauce in this recipe goes equally well with chicken, duck or pork.

 SERVING IDEAS: Serve the lamb with boiled rice and either a carrot, orange and watercress salad, or a green vegetable.

PEPPERED STEAK

SERVES 4

A classic way of serving steak, peppered steaks are simple to prepare and wonderful to eat.

4 rump, or fillet, steaks
Oil, for frying
2 tbsps black peppercorns, lightly crushed
4 tbsps butter
Salt
4 tbsps brandy
3 tbsps light cream
Watercress, to garnish

1. Brush the steaks on both sides with the oil, then coat with the black peppercorns. Crush these into the steak with a steak hammer.

2. Over a high heat, melt the butter in a frying pan and cook the steaks for about 1½ minutes on each side.

3. Reduce the heat and cook for a further 2 minutes for a rare steak, 3 minutes for a medium steak, or 7 minutes for a well-done steak. Season with salt.

4. Warm the brandy in a ladle near the heat. Taking great care, set the brandy alight and pour it over the steaks.

5. Remove the steaks and place on a warmed serving dish. Keep warm.

6. Stir the cream into the juices in the frying pan

Step 1 Coat the steaks with the lightly crushed black peppercorns and hammer these into the meat with a steak hammer.

Step 4 Very carefully, ignite the warm brandy in a ladle and pour it over the steaks.

and heat gently for a few minutes.

7. Pour the sauce over the steaks and garnish with the watercress.

Cook's Notes

TIME: Preparation takes about 15 minutes, and cooking takes between 5 and 15 minutes, depending on whether a rare, medium or well-done steak is required.

PREPARATION: If you prefer, the steaks can be broiled, instead of fried. The cooking times should be about the same, and the sauce can be prepared separately.

VARIATION: If you can get them, use fresh green peppercorns, in place of the black ones.

SERVING IDEAS: Serve with new potatoes, or French fries, and a large, fresh salad.

BROILED HERRINGS WITH DILL AND MUSTARD

SERVES 4

4 tbsps chopped fresh dill
6 tbsps mild Swedish mustard
2 tbsps lemon juice, or white wine
4-8 fresh herrings, cleaned but heads and tails left on
2 tbsps butter or margarine, melted
Salt and pepper

Step 1 In a small bowl mix the dill, mustard and lemon juice, or white wine, together thoroughly.

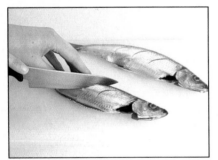

Step 2 Cut three slits, just piercing the skin, on both sides of each fish. Take care not to cut the fish too deeply, or the flesh may break when it is turned over.

1. Mix the dill, mustard and lemon juice, or wine, together thoroughly.

2. Cut three slits, just piercing the skin, on both sides of each herring and lay them on a broiler pan.

3. Spread half the mustard mixture equally over the exposed side of each fish, pushing some into the cuts.

4. Spoon a little of the melted butter over each herring, and broil the fish for 5-6 minutes.

5. Turn the fish over and spread the remaining mustard and dill mixture over them. Spoon over the

Step 3 Spread half the mustard mixture equally over the top side of each fish, pushing some of the mixture gently into each cut.

remaining melted butter and broil for a further 5-6 minutes.

6. Sprinkle the fish with a little salt and pepper before serving.

Cook's Notes

 TIME: Preparation takes about 10 minutes, and cooking takes 12-15 minutes, although this may be longer if the herring are large.

 VARIATION: Use whole fresh mackerel in place of the herring.

 SERVING IDEAS: Arrange the fish on a serving dish, garnished with lemon wedges and sprigs of fresh dill. Serve with new potatoes, if available.

SCALLOPS IN SAFFRON SAUCE
SERVES 4

Saffron is about the most expensive of all spices, but take heart -- only a few strands are needed in any recipe!

16 large scallops with coral attached
½ cup water
½ cup dry white wine
1 shallot, roughly chopped
1 bouquet garni, consisting of 1 bay leaf, 1 sprig of
 fresh thyme and 3 stalks of parsley
6 black peppercorns
A few strands of saffron
4 tbsps hot water
1¼ cups heavy cream
3 tbsps fresh chopped parsley
Salt and pepper

1. Put the scallops into a large shallow pan together with the water, wine, shallot, bouquet garni and peppercorns.

2. Cover the pan and bring the liquid almost to the boil. Remove the pan from the heat and leave the scallops to poach in the hot liquid for 10-15 minutes.

3. The scallops are cooked when they are just firm to the touch. Remove them from the liquid and keep warm on a clean plate.

Step 1 Put the scallops into a large shallow pan, along with the water, wine, shallot, bouquet garni and peppercorns.

Step 4 Reduce the cooking liquid by half by boiling rapidly over a high heat.

Step 5 Soak the saffron in the hot water for about 5 minutes, or until the color has infused into the water.

4. Strain the scallop cooking liquid into a small saucepan and bring to the boil. Allow the liquid to boil rapidly until it is reduced by about half.

5. Soak the saffron in the hot water for about 5 minutes, or until the colour has infused into the water.

6. Add the saffron with its soaking liquid, the heavy cream and the chopped parsley to the reduced cooking liquid and season to taste. Bring the sauce back to just below boiling point.

7. Arrange the scallops on a serving plate and pour a little of the sauce over them before serving.

Cook's Notes

TIME: Preparation takes about 15 minutes, and cooking also takes about 15 minutes.

PREPARATION: If you do not wish to use shellfish on the day you buy it, it should be wrapped in newspaper and stored in the bottom of the refrigerator until the next day. It should not be kept longer than overnight.

SERVING IDEAS: Serve as a starter with brown bread and butter, or as a light main course with rice or pasta.

SALADE BRESSE

SERVES 4-6

This is an extremely sophisticated salad, equally suitable as a first course, or as an accompaniment to a formal summer dinner.

1 head Belgian endive, separated and washed
1 head cos lettuce, washed
1 bunch of lamb's lettuce, or watercress, washed
4oz cherry tomatoes, halved and cored
4 chicken breasts, cooked, skinned and thinly sliced
4oz Bresse bleu, or other blue cheese, cut into small pieces
16 small pickles, thinly sliced
½ cup walnut halves
2 tbsps each vegetable and walnut oil, mixed
2 tsps white wine vinegar
¾ cup fromage frais
2 tsps chopped fresh tarragon leaves
Salt and pepper

Step 3 Mix the oils and vinegar together in a bowl and whisk well, until they are thick.

Step 3 Fold in the fromage frais and the chopped tarragon leaves, mixing them in well.

Step 1 Tear the Belgian endive into bite-sized pieces and put into a large salad bowl with the cos lettuce and lamb's lettuce, or watercress.

2. Put the tomatoes, chicken, cheese, pickles and walnuts on top of the lettuce and mix lightly.
3. Put the oils and vinegar together in a small bowl and whisk well, until they are thick. Fold in the fromage frais and the tarragon leaves. Whisk well, then season to taste.
4. Drizzle some of the dressing over the salad before serving. Put the rest of the dressing into a small jug and hand it round separately.

1. Tear the Belgian endive and cos lettuce leaves into bite-sized pieces. Pull apart the lamb's lettuce, but leave the leaves whole. If using watercress, remove any thick stems and yellow leaves. Toss the lettuces together in a large salad bowl.

Cook's Notes

TIME: Preparation takes about 20 minutes.

COOK'S TIP: If you want to prepare this salad in advance, do not put the dressing on until the last minute, otherwise the lettuces will go limp.

VARIATION: Substitute your favorite lettuces for those suggested in the recipe.

TUNA AND TOMATO SALAD

SERVES 4

Tuna and tomatoes are an ideal combination and, when prepared
with basil, are reminiscent of hot Italian summers.

1 tbsp chopped fresh basil, or marjoram
6 tbsps French dressing
12oz pasta shapes of your choice
6 tomatoes
12oz canned tuna fish, preferably in brine,
    drained and flaked

Step 4 Mix the pasta shapes with 3 tbsps of the French dressing in a large bowl. Stir well, to ensure that the pasta shapes are evenly coated.

1. Mix the basil or marjoram, with the French dressing, in a small jug or bowl.

2. Cook the pasta shapes in a large saucepan of boiling, lightly salted water, until they are tender which will take about 10 minutes.

3. Rinse in cold water and drain well, shaking off any excess water.

4. Put the pasta shapes into a large bowl and toss

with 3 tablespoons of the French dressing, mixing well to ensure that they are evenly coated. Leave to cool.

5. Slice enough of the tomatoes to arrange around the outside of the serving dish and then chop the rest.

Step 7 Add the tuna to the pasta shapes and mix together gently, so that the pasta shapes are not broken.

6. Put the chopped tomatoes into another bowl and pour over the remaining French dressing. Put this into the center of a serving dish.

7. Add the flaked tuna to the pasta shapes and toss together gently.

8. Pile the pasta shapes and tuna over the chopped tomatoes in the center of the dish.

9. Arrange the tomato slices around the edge of the serving dish and chill well until required.

Cook's Notes

 TIME: Preparation takes about 10 minutes, and cooking takes about 15 minutes.

 VARIATION: Add 2 tbsps of halved, pitted black olives for a completely different flavor.

 SERVING IDEAS: Serve this salad as part of a summer lunch, with a crisp green salad and lots of French bread.

MIXED BEAN SALAD

SERVES 4-6

This nutritious salad is made from a medley of beans, which can be varied according to preference.

Scant cup cooked red kidney beans
Scant cup cooked black-eyed beans
Scant cup cooked butter beans
¾ cup cooked lima beans, shelled
1 cup cooked green beans, sliced
Scant cup cooked chickpeas
2 tbsps brown sugar
Scant ½ cup white wine vinegar
½ tsp salt
¼ tsp black pepper
Scant ½ cup olive oil
½ tsp dry mustard powder
½ tsp dried basil
1 large Spanish, or red, onion, peeled and thinly
  sliced into rings
2 tbsps chopped fresh parsley

Step 4 Mix the dressing into the beans, stirring well to coat the beans evenly.

Step 3 In a small basin, whisk the vinegar and oil dressing together vigorously with a fork, until the mixture thickens.

1. In a large bowl mix all the beans and the chick peas together thoroughly.

2. Put the sugar and vinegar into a small bowl, together with the salt and pepper. Stir in the oil, mustard and basil.

3. Whisk the vinegar mixture vigorously with a fork, until it becomes thick.

4. Pour the dressing over the beans and mix in thoroughly, to coat the beans evenly.

5. Refrigerate until ready to serve.

6. Before serving, mix the onion rings and parsley into the bean salad, reserving a few onion rings for decoration.

Cook's Notes

TIME: Preparation will take about 15 minutes.

COOK'S TIP: If you cook the beans yourself, soak them in separate bowls overnight, and then boil them rapidly in separate pans for at least 30 minutes, until they are completely tender. Rinse in cold water and drain well.

VARIATION: Stir 4oz of tiny cauliflower flowerets into the bean salad.

GREEN AND GOLD SUNFLOWER SALAD

SERVES 4

This colorful salad makes a spectacular and delicious addition to a summer meal.

3 tbsps sunflower oil
1 tbsp lemon juice
Salt and pepper
2 large ripe avocados
8 ripe apricots
½ cup natural yogurt
2 tsps honey
Grated rind of 1 lemon
2 tsps chopped fresh parsley
1 small buttercrunch lettuce, washed and separated
    into leaves
½ cup toasted sunflower seeds

1. Put the oil and lemon juice into a small bowl with the salt and pepper. Mix together well.

2. Cut the avocados in half and remove the stones. Peel them, cut into slices and mix these into the oil and lemon juice dressing very carefully, taking care not to break them.

3. Cut the apricots in half and remove the stones. If the apricots are large, cut them in half again. Add

Step 2 Cut the avocados in half and remove the stones. Peel and cut the avocado halves into slices.

Step 4 Mix together the yogurt, honey, lemon rind and parsley.

Step 5 Place the lettuce leaves on individual salad plates and arrange the avocado and apricots on top in an attractive sunflower design.

them to the avocados in the dressing.

4. In another bowl, mix together the yogurt, honey, lemon rind and parsley.

5. Put the lettuce leaves onto individual salad plates and arrange the avocado and apricots on top in a sunflower design.

6. Spoon a little of the yogurt mixture over the salad, and sprinkle with sunflower seeds. Pour any remaining yogurt dressing into a small jug and serve separately.

Cook's Notes

 TIME: Preparation takes about 15 minutes.

 VARIATION: Use segments of ruby grapefruit in place of the apricots.

 SERVING IDEAS: Serve as an unusual first course, or as an accompaniment to a chicken or fish dish.

CRANBERRY SNOW WITH MINT

SERVES 4

*Cranberries are usually associated with turkey at Thanksgiving.
However, because these delicious berries have an interesting flavor,
they can also be used to make some mouth-watering desserts.*

½ cup fresh or frozen cranberries
2 tbsps granulated sugar
2 egg whites
4 tbsps superfine sugar
½ cup whipping cream
½ cup natural yogurt
2 tbsps chopped fresh mint

1. Put the cranberries and the granulated sugar into a small, heavy-based pan.

2. Cook the cranberries slowly over a moderate heat, until they soften and the juice begins to run.

Step 2 Cook the cranberries slowly, until the juice runs and the fruit softens. Set the berries aside, to cool completely.

3. Set the cranberries aside to cool completely.

4. Whisk the egg whites until they are stiff, but not dry.

5. Gradually whisk in the superfine sugar, whisking well between additions, until the egg whites are smooth and glossy and form stiff peaks.

6. Whip the cream until it is thick and combine this with the yogurt in a large bowl.

7. Fold the egg whites carefully into the cream and yogurt mixture.

8. Stir in the cooked, cooled cranberries and the chopped mint. Do not over-mix, as the dessert should look marbled.

9. Spoon into individual serving dishes.

Step 5 Whisk the superfine sugar gradually into the beaten egg whites. Whisk well between each addition of sugar, until stiff peaks form and the egg whites are smooth and glossy.

Step 8 Fold the cooled cooked cranberries and the chopped mint lightly into the egg white and cream mixture. Do not over-mix, as the finished dish should look marbled.

Cook's Notes

 TIME: Preparation takes about 15 minutes, and cooking takes about 5 minutes.

SERVING IDEAS: Serve garnished with whole sprigs of fresh mint and crisp cookies.

VARIATION: Any kind of soft fruit can be used instead of cranberries in this recipe. If you use blackcurrants, substitute blackcurrant leaves for the fresh mint and if you use gooseberries, try combining them with elderflowers for a refreshing change.

BRANDY BANANAS

SERVES 6

This quick and easy dessert is spectacular enough to serve at the most sophisticated of dinner parties.

6 tbsps butter
3 tbsps soft brown sugar
3 tbsps lemon juice
6 bananas
6 tbsps brandy

Step 2 Add the banana halves carefully to the sugar and butter mixture. Fry them gently, basting well with the butter sauce.

1. Put the butter, sugar and lemon juice into a frying pan. Cook over a low heat, stirring continuously, until the butter has melted and the sugar has dissolved.

2. Peel the bananas and cut them in half lengthways. Add these to the butter and sugar liquid in the pan and fry gently for a few minutes, basting them well with the liquid.

3. Add the brandy directly to the frying pan and cook for a second or two, to warm the brandy

Step 3 Warm the brandy in the frying pan for a second or two, before igniting it carefully.

through.

4. Ignite the brandy carefully and allow the flames to die down before serving the bananas. Serve with the juices and whipped cream.

Cook's Notes

 TIME: Preparation takes about 10 minutes, and cooking takes about 5 minutes.

 PREPARATION: If you have an electric frying pan, or table top cooker, prepare this dessert at the table, to impress your guests.

 COOK'S TIP: If you have difficulty igniting the brandy, warm a little extra brandy separately in a pan and ignite it, before you pour it over the bananas. Great care must be taken when using brandy to flambé a dessert.

LEMON BRANDY CREAM

SERVES 4

This rich brandy cream is prepared in minutes and tastes heavenly.

1 cup light cream
1 cup heavy cream
6 tbsps soft brown sugar
Juice and finely grated rind of 2 large lemons
3oz sponge cake
2 tbsps brandy
¼ cup toasted flaked almonds

1. Mix the light and heavy creams in a small saucepan and stir in the sugar.

2. Cook over a low heat, until the cream begins to bubble and the sugar has melted. Stir the grated

lemon rind into the cream mixture and allow it to cool in the saucepan.

3. Break the cake into fine crumbs, and divide these equally between 4 individual serving dishes.

4. Stir the brandy into the cream mixture together with the lemon juice.

5. Pour the cream mixture over the cake crumbs and refrigerate for 30 minutes, or until the cream has thickened.

6. Sprinkle the toasted almonds over the top of the cream before serving.

Step 2 Cook the cream and sugar over a low heat, stirring continuously, until the cream is almost boiling and the sugar has melted.

Step 5 Pour equal amounts of the brandy and cream mixture carefully over the cake crumbs in the dishes.

Cook's Notes

 TIME: Preparation takes about 15 minutes, and cooking takes 2-3 minutes.

 VARIATION: Use the finely grated rind and juice of 1 orange, in place of the lemons, and 2 tbsps of Cointreau instead of the brandy.

 SERVING IDEAS: Serve the creams with crisp almond cookies.

GINGER ROLLS

SERVES 6-8

This dish is best prepared the night before you require it, to allow the gingersnaps to absorb the rum.

36 gingersnaps
6 tbsps rum
2 cups heavy cream
2 tsps ground ginger
2 tsps soft brown sugar
2 tbsps ginger syrup, from jar of stem ginger
Stem ginger slices, to decorate

Step 3 Use about half of the cream to sandwich the cookies together to form either a long roll or a horseshoe shape.

Step 1 Put the cookies onto a flat dish and sprinkle with the rum.

1. Lay the gingersnaps on a flat dish and sprinkle with the rum.

2. When the rum has been completely absorbed, whip the cream with the ground ginger and sugar and add the ginger syrup.

3. Use some of the cream to sandwich together the cookies, carefully forming them into either a long roll or a horseshoe shape.

4. Cover the cookies with the remaining cream and decorate with the stem ginger. Refrigerate thoroughly before serving.

Cook's Notes

 TIME: This dish will take about 15 minutes to prepare, plus overnight soaking and final refrigerating.

 VARIATION: Use chocolate chip cookies, instead of gingersnaps, and sherry, instead of rum.

 FREEZING: This dish will freeze well, but must be eaten shortly after it is removed from the freezer.

SWEET ALMOND PUDDING
SERVES 4

A delicious variation on a traditional pudding; ground rice was never like this at school!

1½ cups blanched almonds
1½ cups water
¾ cup sugar
3 tbsps rice powder, or ground rice
½ cup milk

1. Blend the blanched almonds and the water in a liquidizer or food processor, until the almonds are well chopped.

2. Put the almond liquid into a medium-sized

Step 1 In a liquidizer or food processor, blend together the blanched almonds and water, until the almonds are thoroughly chopped.

saucepan and bring this mixture to the boil over a gentle heat.

3. Add the sugar and stir until it has completely dissolved.

4. Blend together the rice and the milk in a jug.

Step 5 Stir the blended rice and milk mixture slowly into the simmering sugar and almond mixture in the saucepan. Cook gently, stirring continuously, until the mixture thickens.

5. Add the rice mixture slowly to the simmering sugar and almond mixture, stirring continuously, until the pudding thickens.

6. Remove the rice pudding from the heat and pour into individual serving dishes.

Cook's Notes

 TIME: Preparation takes about 5 minutes, and cooking takes 6-7 minutes.

 VARIATION: Lightly toast some flaked, or chopped, almonds and sprinkle these over the top of the pudding to serve.

 SERVING IDEAS: Serve this pudding cold with fresh, or stewed, fruit.

Microwave Quick 'n' Easy

Quick and easy is what microwave cooking is all about. Adapting time-consuming conventional recipes means that you can have all the taste and variety you want in no time at all.

Quick and easy cooking doesn't simply mean opening cans and packets, although you will find recipes here that use convenience foods in creative ways. But there are also many good recipes using fresh ingredients which take an hour or more to cook conventionally, that will cook by microwaves in a fraction of the time. Home-made soups and baked potatoes are good examples of this, as are steamed puddings and meringues.

The list of healthy ingredients used in quick and easy cooking is a long one, and they're all the foods which doctors and dieticians are now telling us we should be eating more of: fresh vegetables, poultry, lean meat, fish and shellfish. The recipes in this chapter introduce many of these foods in simple, delicious dishes with the added convenience of microwave speed.

All microwave recipes were prepared in a 700 watt oven. If your microwave is of a lower output, adjust timings as follows:

500 watt – add 40 seconds for every minute stated in the recipe
600 watt – add 20 seconds for every minute stated in the recipe
650 watt – only a slight increase in the overall time is necessary

QUICK SALMON MOUSSE

SERVES 4

This very easy recipe makes such an impressive first course, and it makes a small amount of smoked salmon go a long way.

1lb salmon
1 bay leaf
4 tbsps water
½ cup low fat soft cheese
½ tsp tomato paste
2 tsps chopped fresh dill
1 tbsp lemon juice
Salt
Dash Tabasco
4 tbsps mayonnaise
4oz sliced smoked salmon
Cucumber slices
Lemon slices
Fresh dill

Step 1 Place the fish in a small casserole and cover with pierced plastic wrap before cooking for 4-6 minutes.

1. Place the fish in a small casserole with the bay leaf and the water. Cover and cook for 4-6 minutes on HIGH or until the fish flakes.

2. Remove the skin and bones and put the fish into a food processor or blender. Reserve the cooking liquid. Process the fish with the cheese, tomato paste, lemon juice, dill, salt and Tabasco until

smooth. Add the reserved liquid as necessary if the mixture is too thick.

3. Spoon into mounds on 4 small serving dishes and chill until firm. Before serving, spread 1 tbsp of mayonnaise carefully over each mound of salmon mousse.

4. Cut the slices of smoked salmon to size and press onto the mayonnaise carefully to cover the mousse completely. Leave at room temperature for about 30 minutes before serving. Garnish with the slices of cucumber and lemon and the fresh dill.

Step 3 Spread the mayonnaise over the chilled mounds of fish mousse.

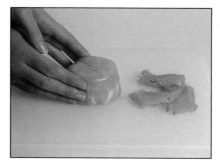

Step 4 Cover the mayonnaise with strips of smoked salmon.

Cook's Notes

 TIME: Preparation takes about 15 minutes, and cooking takes 4-6 minutes.

 SERVING IDEAS: Serve with brown bread or toast or melba toast.

 ECONOMY: Trout fillets can be used instead of salmon.

WATERCRESS SOUP

SERVES 6

Potatoes are used to thicken this pretty green soup. It makes a good dinner party appetizer, hot or cold.

4 medium-sized potatoes, thinly sliced
1 small onion, finely chopped
2 tbsps butter or margarine
3½ cups vegetable or chicken stock
1 bay leaf
Salt and pepper
2 bunches watercress, well washed and thick stems removed
½ cup heavy cream
Nutmeg

1. Place the potatoes, onion and butter in a large, deep bowl and cover loosely with plastic wrap or cover partially with a lid. Cook on HIGH for 4-6 minutes or until the potatoes and onions are beginning to soften.

2. Pour on the stock and add the bay leaf, salt and pepper. Re-cover the bowl and cook for a further 8 minutes on HIGH or until the stock just comes to the boil.

3. Allow to cool slightly and pour into a food processor or blender. Reserve 6 small sprigs of watercress for garnish and roughly chop the rest.

4. Place the watercress in the blender or food processor with the soup and purée until smooth. The soup should be lightly flecked with green. Add the cream to the soup, adjust the seasoning and add a pinch of grated nutmeg.

5. Reheat on HIGH for 2-3 minutes before serving. Garnish with the small watercress leaves.

Step 1 Place the potatoes, onion and butter in a large bowl and cover partially to allow the steam to escape.

Step 2 Cook the potatoes in the stock until they soften and the stock has boiled.

Step 4 Purée the potato mixture with the watercress, return to the bowl and stir in the cream by hand.

Cook's Notes

 TIME: Preparation takes about 20 minutes, and cooking takes 14-17 minutes.

 WATCHPOINT: Once the watercress has been added to the soup, reheat only briefly or the soup will lose its color.

 ECONOMY: If desired, omit the cream and replace half the stock with milk.

STILTON AND WALNUT SOUP

SERVES 4

This easy soup tastes as if it took twice as long to make. It makes a delicious appetizer for dinner parties.

3 tbsps butter or margarine
1 large onion, finely chopped
4 tbsps flour
1½ cups chicken stock
1 bay leaf
1 sprig thyme
Salt and pepper
2 cups Stilton cheese, crumbled
1½ cups milk
4 tbsps heavy cream
4 tbsps chopped walnuts

Step 4 Crumble the cheese and stir into the soup with the milk.

Step 2 Cook the onion in the butter for about 6 minutes or until very soft.

Step 6 Sprinkle carefully with the walnuts so that they float on top of the soup.

1. Put the butter or margarine and the onion into a large bowl and cover loosely with plastic wrap, pierced several times.

2. Cook for 6 minutes on HIGH, stirring occasionally. Stir in the flour, add the stock gradually and mix well.

3. Add the bay leaf, thyme and salt and pepper and

cook, uncovered, for 10 minutes on HIGH.

4. Remove the herbs and crumble the cheese into the soup. Add the milk and stir to mix well.

5. Cook for 1 minute on HIGH, uncovered.

6. Stir in the cream and cook for a further 1 minute on HIGH. Serve garnished with the chopped walnuts.

Cook's Notes

 TIME: Preparation takes about 10 minutes, and cooking takes about 18 minutes.

COOK'S TIP: If reheating the soup, start on a MEDIUM setting to prevent the cheese becoming stringy.

 VARIATION: Substitute half Cheddar and half blue cheese for the Stilton if desired. Celery can also be added with the onion for a slightly different flavor.

RED PEPPER SOUP

SERVES 4

Soups are easy both to make and reheat in a microwave oven.
This one has a vibrant color and taste.

3 red peppers
3 tomatoes, seeded and roughly chopped
1 medium onion, finely chopped
4 cups chicken or vegetable stock
Salt and pepper
2 tbsps cornstarch

1. Cut peppers in half and remove seeds. Slice 4 thin strips and reserve. Chop remaining peppers roughly.

2. Place the peppers, tomatoes and onion in a large bowl with the stock, salt and pepper. Stir in the cornstarch. Cover loosely and cook on HIGH for 15 minutes, stirring frequently.

3. Allow the soup to stand for 1-2 minutes and then

Step 2 Place the vegetables in a large bowl with the stock and stir in the cornstarch.

Step 4 Use the individual microproof bowls for reheating soup. Add the garnish to cook it slightly.

Step 1 Cut the peppers in half and remove the cores and seeds completely.

purée in a food processor or blender.

4. Pour the soup into individual microproof bowls and top with reserved pepper strips. Reheat for 1-2 minutes before serving.

Cook's Notes

TIME: Preparation takes about 15 minutes, and cooking takes 15 minutes.

SERVING IDEAS: Add a spoonful of natural yogurt or sour cream as a garnish just before serving. Chopped parsely or chives can be sprinkled on top for color contrast.

FREEZING: Allow soup to cool completely and pour into a freezer container. Seal well and freeze for up to 3 months. Defrost on LOW or DEFROST settings for 10 minutes, breaking up the soup as it defrosts. Reheat for 2-3 minutes and add the garnish.

GARLIC VEGETABLES

SERVES 6

Colorful vegetables create a light and different appetizer that can double as a side dish for broiled chicken or fish.

1 small head cauliflower, broken into small flowerets
4oz broccoli
2oz snow peas
½ red pepper, seeded and finely sliced
½ yellow pepper, seeded and finely sliced
4 green onions, thinly sliced on the diagonal
½ cup prepared mayonnaise
2 cloves garlic, crushed
1 tbsp chopped parsley and chives, mixed
Pinch salt and pepper
1 hard-cooked egg, finely chopped, to garnish

Step 2 Add the trimmed snow peas to the broccoli and continue cooking.

Step 2 Cook the broccoli flowerets in a few spoonfuls of water. Stir occasionally to ensure even cooking.

before the end of cooking time.

3. Drain all the vegetables and combine with the sliced red and yellow pepper and the green onions. Mix all the dressing ingredients together and stir carefully into the vegetables. Place the vegetables on serving plates and heat through for 1 minute on HIGH.

4. Garnish with the chopped hard-cooked egg before serving.

1. Place the cauliflower flowerets in a casserole with 4 tbsps salted water. Cover and cook on HIGH for 6-8 minutes.

2. Cut the broccoli spears into flowerets the same size as the cauliflower. Place in a casserole with 2 tbsps salted water and cover loosely. Cook on HIGH for 4-5 minutes. Trim the ends of the snow peas and add the pods to the broccoli 1-2 minutes

Step 3 Toss the vegetables in the dressing, before arranging them on microproof plates.

Cook's Notes

 TIME: Preparation takes about 15 minutes, and cooking takes 11-14 minutes. Allow a few minutes standing time for the vegetables before adding them to the peppers and onions.

VARIATION: Other seasonal vegetables may be used in addition to or instead of the ones suggested here.

SERVING IDEAS: Spoon the vegetables onto a bed of lettuce leaves or shredded lettuce. Serve with French bread or melba toast.

CURRIED CHICKEN KEBABS WITH CUCUMBER SAUCE

SERVES 4

_As an appetizer or main course, this is a colorful and spicy dish.
Cucumber in yogurt makes a cooling accompaniment._

Step 1 Cut the chicken into strips and combine them with the marinade, coating each piece thoroughly.

Step 2 Thread the marinaded chicken strips onto wooden skewers.

Step 2 Place the kebabs on a microwave roasting rack and cook, turning frequently.

3 chicken breasts, skinned and boned

Marinade
2 tbsps vegetable oil
1 clove garlic, crushed
2 tsps curry powder
¼ tsp cayenne pepper
1 tbsp chopped coriander leaves
Juice and grated rind of 1 lime
Salt and pepper

Sauce
½ cucumber, grated
1 cup plain yogurt
1 tbsp chopped fresh mint
1 tsp mango chutney
Pinch salt and pepper

1. Cut the chicken into 1-inch-wide strips. Combine the ingredients for the marinade and mix with the chicken to coat each piece. Leave to marinate for 1 hour.

2. Thread the chicken onto wooden skewers and place on a microwave roasting rack. Cook for 5 minutes on HIGH, turning the kebabs frequently while cooking.

3. Leave to stand, covered, for 1 minute. While the chicken is marinating, sprinkle the grated cucumber lightly with salt and leave to stand.

4. Rinse thoroughly and pat dry with paper towels. Combine with the remaining sauce ingredients and serve with the chicken kebabs.

Cook's Notes

TIME: Preparation takes about 10 minutes, plus 1 hour to marinate the chicken. Cooking takes about 5 minutes, plus 1 minute standing time.

VARIATION: Other herbs and spices may be added to the marinade. Omit the cayenne pepper for a milder flavor.

ECONOMY: The recipe can be prepared with meat from drumsticks or thighs. Add about 1 minute to the cooking time.

HOT TOMATO SALAD

SERVES 4

This recipe takes only minutes to prepare and cook, yet looks and tastes sensational, either as an appetizer or as a side dish with broiled fish or chicken.

2 large beef tomatoes (total weight about 1¼ lbs)
3 tbsps olive oil
1 tbsp cider vinegar
1 tsp chopped chives
1 tsp roughly chopped basil
½ tsp whole grain mustard

Step 2 Whisk the dressing ingredients together well in a measuring jug for easy pouring.

Step 1 Arrange the tomatoes in a circle in one large or four individual microproof dishes.

Step 3 Check the tomatoes frequently while cooking and baste them occasionally with the dressing.

1. Slice the tomatoes and arrange in a microproof serving dish or in four individual dishes.

2. Mix the oil, vinegar, chives, basil and mustard in a small jug and pour over the tomatoes.

3. Cook, uncovered, on HIGH for 2-3 minutes until

hot but not cooked. If using individual dishes, arrange these in a circle in the microwave. Serve immediately.

Cook's Notes

 TIME: Preparation takes about 5 minutes, and cooking takes 2-3 minutes.

 VARIATION: Basil is the classic herb for tomatoes, but marjoram or dill are good alternatives.

 WATCHPOINT: Tomatoes can quickly overcook and fall apart.

TARRAGON AND LEMON CARROTS

SERVES 4

*Tarragon is a lovely alternative to mint with carrots and the flavor
of lemon complements them both.*

1lb carrots, finely sliced
1 tbsp lemon juice
6 tbsps water
2 sprigs fresh tarragon
Chopped tarragon
Grated lemon zest

1. Put the carrots in a casserole with the lemon
juice, water and tarragon.

2. Cover and cook on HIGH for 10-12 minutes.

3. Drain the carrots and discard the tarragon

Step 1 Place the
carrots in a casserole
with the whole sprigs
of tarragon.

sprigs. Garnish with chopped tarragon and lemon
zest.

Step 2 Cook, covered
with pierced plastic
wrap, until the carrots
are tender.

Step 3 Sprinkle with
lemon zest and
chopped tarragon
before serving.

Cook's Notes

 TIME: Preparation takes
5 minutes, and cooking takes
10-12 minutes.

 COOK'S TIP: Cooking the stalk
as well as the leaves of both
tarragon and other herbs will
maximize their flavor.

 WATCHPOINT: If carrots
overcook in a microwave oven,
they will shrivel and toughen.

BAKED POTATOES

SERVES 4

Wrapping potatoes during standing time helps to give them a soft, even texture. Don't be tempted to omit this step.

4 potatoes, 9oz each in weight
½ cup butter mixed with one of the following
   combinations:
1 tbsp chopped chives and 2 tsps Dijon mustard, or
1 tbsp chopped parsley and 2 tsps anchovy paste or
   essence, or
1 tsp chopped basil and 2 tsps tomato paste, or
1 clove garlic, crushed and 1 tbsp crumbled blue
   cheese

Step 1 Prick the potato skins several times with a fork to allow the steam to escape while cooking.

Step 1 Place the potatoes in a circle towards the edge of the turntable. Turn over during cooking.

1. Scrub the potatoes well and pat them dry. Prick them 2 or 3 times with a fork and place in a circle towards the edge of the turntable. Cook for 18 minutes, turning over halfway through cooking.

2. Wrap each potato in foil and allow to stand for 5 minutes before serving. Make a crosswise incision in the top of each potato and press at the sides to open the cuts. Serve with one of the flavored butters.

3. To prepare the butters, place the butter in a small bowl and soften for 20 seconds on HIGH. If the butter is not soft enough to mix, heat for an additional 10 seconds on HIGH.

4. Mix in the chosen flavorings and roll the butter into a cylinder shape in plastic wrap. Chill until firm and then cut into slices to serve.

Step 2 Wrap each potato in foil and leave to stand to finish cooking.

Cook's Notes

TIME: Preparation takes about 5 minutes, and cooking takes about 18 minutes. Allow 5 minutes standing time to continue cooking the potatoes. Fewer potatoes will take less time to cook.

SERVING IDEAS: Add a green salad or vegetable for a light meal or serve as a side dish with meat, poultry or fish.

 BUYING GUIDE: Purchase potatoes that are recommended for baking. Red or new potatoes are not good for baking.

VEGETABLE STIR-FRY

SERVES 4

Chinese cooking is fast and so is microwave cooking. Why not combine the two in a crisp and colorful vegetable dish.

2 tbsps oil
4 spears broccoli
4oz miniature corn
4oz snow peas, trimmed
1 red pepper, seeded and sliced
½ cup water chestnuts, sliced
1 cup mushrooms, sliced
1 clove garlic, minced
1 tbsp cornstarch
6 tbsps vegetable stock
4 tbsps soy sauce
2 tbsps sherry
2 cups bean sprouts
2 green onions, sliced

Step 3 Add the other vegetables and toss to coat with the oil.

Step 4 Cook the sauce ingredients until the mixture thickens and clears.

Step 2 Cook the broccoli stalks and the corn in the oil first.

1. Preheat a browning dish according to the manufacturer's directions. Add the oil to the dish when hot.

2. Cut off the broccoli flowerets and reserve them. Slice the stalks diagonally. Slice the miniature sweetcorn in half lengthwise. Put the sliced broccoli stalks and the corn together in the hot oil for 1 minute on HIGH.

3. Add the red pepper, snow peas, water chestnuts, garlic, mushrooms and the broccoli flowerets and cook for a further 1 minute on HIGH.

4. Mix together the cornstarch, vegetable stock, soy sauce and sherry in a glass measure or a small glass bowl and cook for 4 minutes on HIGH, stirring occasionally after 1 minute until thickened.

5. Transfer the vegetables to a serving dish and pour over the sauce. Add the bean sprouts and spring onions and cook for a further 1 minute on HIGH. Serve immediately.

Cook's Notes

 TIME: Preparation takes about 20 minutes, and cooking takes about 7 minutes.

 COOK'S TIP: A browning dish may be a slightly expensive piece of microwave equipment, but it is extremely useful for a wide variety of microwave recipes.

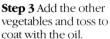 WATCHPOINT: Always follow the manufacturer's directions when using a browning dish as instructions will vary. Be sure to set the dish on a heatproof mat to protect work surfaces.

CONVENIENT VEGETABLE CASSEROLE

SERVES 4

_This is the perfect last minute dish. It can be made with ingredients
you can always keep to hand._

2 cans mushroom soup or 1 can condensed soup
   with an equal measure of water
2 tbsps cornstarch dissolved in 4 tbsps heavy cream
9-10oz frozen mixed vegetables
Pinch ground nutmeg
1 tbsp chopped parsley
1 packet crisp-fried onions

1. Mix the soup with the cornstarch and heavy
cream. Cook, uncovered, on HIGH for 6-7 minutes,
stirring occasionally after 1 minute until thickened.

2. Break up the mixed vegetables to separate and
add frozen to the sauce. Add the nutmeg and
parsley and stir well.

3. Pour into a casserole or serving dish and

Step 1 Cook the soup
and cornstarch
together, stirring
the mixture
occasionally.

Step 2 Break up the
frozen vegetables as
much as possible
before adding them
to the sauce.

Step 4 Sprinkle the
crisp-fried onions
over the surface.

microwave on HIGH for 5-8 minutes or until
heated through.

4. Sprinkle on the crisp-fried onions and heat for
30 seconds on HIGH. Serve immediately.

Cook's Notes

TIME: Preparation takes about
5 minutes, and cooking takes
about 15 minutes.

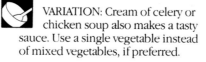
VARIATION: Cream of celery or
chicken soup also makes a tasty
sauce. Use a single vegetable instead
of mixed vegetables, if preferred.

BUYING GUIDE: Department
store food halls and
delicatessens are the places to look
for crisp-fried onions in jars, packets
or vacuum sealed containers.

SALADE DE LÉGUMES

SERVES 6

This salad is simplicity itself to prepare, yet it is special enough for a dinner party. Follow the latest trend and serve it slightly warm.

9-10oz frozen or canned artichoke hearts
1 red onion, chopped or 4 green onions, thinly sliced
1 clove garlic, minced
1 green pepper, seeded and chopped
1 tsp chopped fresh basil
1 tsp chopped fresh thyme
2 tsps chopped parsley
1lb canned navy beans, white kidney beans or
    butter beans, rinsed and drained
4 tomatoes, peeled, seeded and chopped

Dressing
3 tbsps olive oil
2 tbsps white wine vinegar
½ tsp Dijon mustard
Pinch salt and pepper

1 head Belgian endive and curly endive to garnish

Step 2 Combine all the salad ingredients.

Step 3 Pile the salad onto the prepared salad leaves and spoon over the remaining dressing.

Step 1 Cook frozen artichoke hearts, if using, until warm but not cooked through.

1. If using frozen artichoke hearts, place in a large casserole dish and cover. Microwave on HIGH for 3-4 minutes, or until slightly warm.

2. Stir in the remaining ingredients, except the dressing and garnish, and cook for 2 minutes on HIGH to warm through. Mix together the dressing ingredients, pour over the warm salad and toss to coat.

3. Arrange the Belgian endive and endive leaves on serving plates and pile on the salad. Spoon over any excess dressing to serve. Serve warm.

Cook's Notes

 TIME: Preparation takes about 15 minutes, and cooking takes 2-6 minutes.

 PREPARATION: Mix the dressing into the warm ingredients immediately to help develop their flavors.

 SERVING IDEAS: Serve as a appetizer or as a light main course salad. If desired, add drained, canned tuna.

HAM AND BEAN FRIED RICE

SERVES 4

This makes an interesting side dish for a complete Chinese meal or a light main course on its own. Ham and the egg strips give it more substance.

3 tbsps oil
2 eggs, beaten
½ cup ham, chopped
1 cup rice, cooked
4oz green beans, cut in thin, diagonal slices
1 tbsp soy sauce
4 green onions, chopped

Step 2 Turn the egg pancakes over to cook the second side.

Step 1 Pour the egg mixture onto the hot surface of the browning dish.

1. Heat a browning dish for 5 minutes on HIGH. Pour in half the oil and half the beaten egg and cook for 30 seconds on HIGH on one side.

2. Turn over and cook for 30 seconds on the second side. Repeat with the remaining egg. Keep the egg warm.

3. Add the remaining oil to the dish. Heat for 1 minute on HIGH and add the ham. Cover the dish and cook for 1 minute on HIGH. Add the rice and

cook, covered, for 5 minutes on HIGH. Add the beans, soy sauce and onions. Cook for 1 minute on HIGH and toss the ingredients to mix well.

4. Slice the eggs into thin strips and scatter over the top of the rice. Cover the dish and leave to stand for 2 minutes before serving.

Step 3 Cook the rice and other ingredients until the vegetables are tender but still crisp.

Cook's Notes

 TIME: Preparation takes about 15 minutes, and cooking takes about 9 minutes, plus 2 minutes standing time.

PREPARATION: Once the egg strips have been cooked, they can be kept warm but will toughen if reheated.

$ BUYING GUIDE: There are several different types of browning dishes available. If yours does not have a lid, the ingredients in step 3 can be cooked in any type of microproof covered dish.

ASPARAGUS AND TOMATO OMELET

SERVES 2

*A microwave oven can help you cut calories. Even omelets cook
without butter and without sticking.*

4oz chopped asparagus, fresh or frozen
2 tbsps water
4 eggs, separated
6 tbsps milk
1 tsp flour
Salt and pepper
2 tomatoes, peeled, seeded and chopped
3 tbsps grated cheese
Paprika

the dish and cook on MEDIUM for 7 minutes or
until softly set.

4. Lift the edges of the omelet as it cooks to allow
the uncooked mixture to spread evenly.

5. Sprinkle with the cheese and spread on the
drained asparagus and the chopped tomato. Fold
over and cook for 1 minute on LOW to melt the
cheese. Sprinkle with paprika and serve immediately.

Step 2 Beat the egg
whites until stiff peaks
form then fold them
into the egg yolk
mixture.

Step 3 Pour the
omelet mixture into
the pie dish.

Step 4 Lift the edges
of the omelet as it
cooks to allow the
mixture to spread and
cook evenly.

1. Put the asparagus and water into a large
casserole. Cover and cook for 5-6 minutes on
HIGH. Leave to stand while preparing the omelet.

2. Beat the egg yolks, milk, flour and salt and
pepper together. Beat the egg whites until stiff but
not dry and fold into the egg yolks.

3. Melt the butter in a 9 inch glass pie pan for
30 seconds on HIGH. Pour the omelet mixture into

Cook's Notes

 TIME: Preparation takes about
15 minutes, and cooking takes
about 15 minutes.

 VARIATION: Use your
imagination to create new filling
ideas with different cheeses,
vegetables or seafood.

 COOK'S TIP: Using the MEDIUM
or 50% setting will ensure a
light, fluffy omelet that doesn't
toughen during cooking or on
standing.

SWISS CHEESE LAYER

SERVES 4

The nutty taste of Emmental and the creamy taxture of Gruyère turn simple baked eggs into something special.

1 cup grated Emmental cheese
1 tbsp chopped borage
4 eggs
Salt and pepper
1 cup grated Gruyère cheese
2 tsps savory
¼ cup corn chips, broken

1. Mix the Emmental cheese and borage together and divide between 4 custard cups.

2. Crack 1 egg into each dish and season to taste with salt and pepper. Prick egg yolks once with a knife.

3. Mix the Gruyère cheese with the savory and use to top each dish.

4. Sprinkle with the broken corn chips, arrange in a circle and cook on LOW for 3-5 minutes until the cheese melts and the eggs are cooked.

Step 1 Mix the cheese and borage together and divide between four custard cups or individual microproof dishes.

Step 2 Prick the egg yolks once with a sharp knife to prevent them bursting.

Cook's Notes

 TIME: Preparation takes about 5 minutes, and cooking takes 3-5 minutes.

 VARIATION: Try other types of cheese and herbs for different flavor combinations.

 PREPARATION: When cooking with cheese in a microwave oven, use a LOW or MEDIUM setting to avoid toughening the cheese.

SCRAMBLED EGGS AND SHRIMP

SERVES 4

A microwave oven makes easy work of scrambling eggs. They turn out much lighter and fluffier than when conventionally cooked.

4 tsps butter or margarine
4 eggs
4 tbsps milk or light cream
1 tbsp chopped chives
1/3 cup cooked, peeled shrimp
4 large ripe tomatoes
Salt and pepper

Step 3 Stir the eggs frequently while cooking so they cook evenly.

1. Place the butter in a glass measure or a small, deep bowl and cook on HIGH for 30 seconds-1 minute.

2. Beat the eggs with the milk or cream and add a pinch of salt and pepper. Pour into the melted butter and cook on HIGH for 3-4½ minutes.

3. Stir frequently while cooking to bring the set pieces of egg from the outside of the bowl to the center.

4. When just beginning to set, remove the eggs

from the oven and stir in the chives and the shrimp. Allow to stand for 1-2 minutes to finish cooking.

5. Meanwhile, cut the tomatoes into quarters or eighths but do not cut all the way through the base. Arrange the tomatoes in a circle on the turntable and heat through for 1-2 minutes on HIGH.

6. To serve, press the tomatoes open slightly and fill each with some of the egg and shrimp mixture.

Step 4 When just beginning to set, stir in the chives and the shrimp. Cover completely before leaving to stand.

Step 6 Fill the cut tomatoes with the egg mixture.

Cook's Notes

 TIME: Preparation takes about 15 minutes, and cooking takes 5-7 minutes plus 1-2 minutes standing time.

 VARIATION: Diced ham may be substituted for the shrimp or for a vegetarian dish, use about 2oz chopped mushrooms.

 WATCHPOINT: The cooking time for the tomatoes will vary according to their ripeness.

OEUFS EN COCOTTE

SERVES 4

This is an easy appetizer, but very tasty and relatively inexpensive.
It also makes a quick and delicious lunch

1 tbsp butter or margarine
4oz mushrooms, chopped
2 tbsps flour
4 tbsps dry white wine
2 tbsps milk
2 tsps chopped mixed herbs
1 tbsp capers, chopped
Salt and pepper
4 eggs
4 tbsps heavy cream
Paprika
Nutmeg

1. Place the butter in a small casserole and melt on HIGH for 30 seconds. Add the chopped mushrooms and cook for 2 minutes on HIGH.

2. Stir in the flour and add the wine and milk. Cook for a further 1-2 minutes on HIGH, or until thickened. Add the capers, mixed herbs and salt and pepper to taste.

Step 2 Cook the sauce ingredients in a small casserole until very thick.

3. Divide the mixture into 4 custard cups and make a well in the center of the mixture in each dish.

Step 3 Spoon the sauce mixture into custard cups and make a well in the center to hold the eggs.

4. Break an egg into the center of the mixture in each cup. Pierce the yolk once with a sharp knife. Cook for 3-4 minutes on HIGH or until the white is set and the yolk is still soft.

5. Place a spoonful of cream on top of each egg and sprinkle with paprika and grated nutmeg. Cook for 1 minute on LOW to heat the cream. Serve immediately.

Step 5 When the eggs are cooked, spoon on the cream and sprinkle with paprika and nutmeg.

Cook's Notes

 TIME: Preparation takes about 10 minutes, and cooking takes about 9 minutes.

 VARIATION: Use chopped green or black olives in place of the capers. Chopped ham makes a tasty addition.

PREPARATION: Piercing the egg yolk will prevent it bursting by allowing steam to escape.

VEAL AND GARLIC CHEESE ROLLS

SERVES 4

_Tender veal needs quick cooking and a microwave oven fulfils that
while keeping all the natural juices in the meat._

4-6oz veal escalopes
2 small cloves garlic, crushed
8oz low fat, soft cheese
Small bunch chives, chopped
Salt
Freshly ground black pepper
1 tsp paprika (optional)

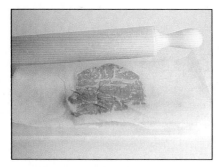

Step 1 Place each escalope between sheets of wax paper and flatten, using a rolling pin.

1. Flatten the veal escalopes between 2 sheets of wax paper using a rolling pin and taking care to keep each escalope in one piece. Set aside.

2. Combine the garlic, cheese and chives together and season with salt and pepper.

3. Spread a quarter of the mixture over each of the veal escalopes and roll up like a jelly roll. Sprinkle with paprika if desired.

4. Arrange in a circle in a dish and cook, uncovered, on HIGH for 8-10 minutes. Serve immediately.

Step 3 Spread each escalope with some of the cheese mixture, roll up and sprinkle with paprika.

Step 4 Arrange the rolls in the dish, either all together in a circle or, if large, two at a time side by side.

Cook's Notes

 TIME: Preparation takes about 10 minutes, and cooking takes 8-10 minutes.

 SERVING IDEAS: Buttered pasta and a green salad make good accompaniments.

COOK'S TIP: Paprika sprinkled onto savory food before microwaving gives it a good brown color and makes it look more appetizing.

TROUT WITH ALMONDS

SERVES 4

Whole fish cook beautifully in a microwave oven and there is less chance of the fish falling apart. They stay moist and flavorful, too.

½ cup butter
½ cup flaked almonds
4 even-sized trout, cleaned
Watercress
Lime slices or wedges

1. Preheat a browning dish according to the manufacturer's instructions. Add half the butter and heat until beginning to brown.

2. Add the almonds and stir to brown slightly. Remove the almonds and the browned butter to a dish and set aside.

3. Pat the trout dry. Reheat the browning dish. Melt the remaining butter and, when very hot, add two of the trout and cook on HIGH for 2 minutes.

4. Turn the trout over and cook for a further 2 minutes. Reposition the trout occasionally during cooking. Repeat with the remaining two trout.

5. Serve the trout topped with the almonds and any remaining butter. Garnish with watercress and lime.

Step 2 Add the almonds and cook to brown lightly, stirring constantly. If the dish is sufficiently hot, do this outside the oven.

Step 1 In a preheated browning dish, heat the butter until beginning to brown.

Step 4 When the trout have browned on one side, turn them over and cook the other side.

Cook's Notes

 TIME: Preparation takes about 10 minutes, and cooking takes about 4 minutes per fish.

 VARIATION: Use other types of nuts or substitute herbs and simply cook them for 30 seconds in melted butter.

 SERVING IDEAS: Accompany the trout with new potatoes and asparagus for an early summer meal or with rice and a seasonal vegetable.

SWEET AND SOUR FISH

SERVES 4

Fish fillets cook much better in a microwave oven than they do by conventional methods. This sauce adds zip to mild whitefish.

1lb sole or plaice fillets
4oz canned, sliced water chestnuts
8oz canned pineapple chunks, ½ cup juice reserved
1 green pepper, seeded and sliced
Juice of 1 lemon
1-2 tbsps brown sugar
1 tbsp light soy sauce
1 tbsp tomato ketchup
1 tbsp cornstarch
3 green onions, shredded
3 tomatoes, peeled and quartered
Salt and pepper

1. Skin the fish fillets and fold them in half. Place them in a large casserole, with the thinner ends of the fillets towards the middle of the dish. Pour over enough water to come ½-inch up the sides of the fillets. Cover the dish loosely and cook for 2 minutes on HIGH.

2. Set aside and keep warm. Drain the water chestnuts and place them in a small bowl with the pineapple chunks and the green pepper.

Step 1 Cover the dish with plastic wrap, piercing it several times with a sharp knife.

3. Mix the reserved juice from the pineapple with the lemon juice, brown sugar, soy sauce, ketchup, and cornstarch. Pour this over the pineapple, water chestnuts and green pepper in a small bowl and cook for 2-3 minutes on HIGH, stirring often until thickened.

4. Drain off the cooking liquid from the fish. Add the tomatoes, green onions, salt and pepper to the sauce. Cook for a further 1 minute on HIGH.

5. Arrange the fish on a serving plate and pour over the sauce.

Step 1 Place the fish fillets in a shallow casserole, thin ends to the center.

Step 2 The fish should still feel slightly firm to the touch when cooked. Cover completely and set aside to finish cooking.

Cook's Notes

 TIME: Preparation takes about 15 minutes, and cooking takes 4-5 minutes.

 \SERVING IDEAS: Rice or Oriental noodles are delicious with this dish.

 COOK'S TIP: Cornstarch sauces actually cook better in a microwave oven than they do on top of the stove. Allow to cook for 1 minute before stirring.

STUFFED BACON CHOPS

SERVES 4

A stuffing of rice and prunes flavored with fresh sage makes bacon interesting enough for dinner guests.

4 thick bacon chops
1 tbsp oil
1 small onion, peeled and finely chopped
1oz macadamia nuts, chopped
¾ cup cooked rice
¼ cup dried prunes, stoned and chopped
1 tbsp chopped sage
Freshly ground black pepper
Salt
2 tbsps butter

1. Carefully cut a slit down the side of each bacon chop. Put the oil, onion and nuts into a small bowl and cook, uncovered, on HIGH for 2 minutes.

Step 1 Cut a slit in the side of each chop to form a pocket for the stuffing.

2. Stir in the rice, prunes, sage, salt and pepper. Cover and cook on HIGH for 2-4 minutes until hot. Pack the stuffing into each chop.

Step 2 Spoon some stuffing into each pocket, spreading it out evenly.

3. Heat a browning dish according to the manufacturer's instructions. Add the butter and quickly add the chops, press down slightly and turn browned side up.

Step 3 Place the chops in the preheated browning dish and press them down to seal and brown.

4. Cook, uncovered, on HIGH for 4 minutes or until cooked through.

Cook's Notes

 TIME: Preparation takes about 10 minutes, and cooking takes 8-9 minutes.

 VARIATION: Macadamia nuts are expensive, but other nuts such as almonds may be used instead.

 SERVING IDEAS: With rice in the stuffing, these chops need only a salad or green vegetables.

HERB LAMB NOISETTES

SERVES 4

A browning dish is what gives these succulent pieces of boned lamb their appetizing color with no messy broiler pan.

1 large onion, peeled and chopped
1 tbsp oil
7oz canned chopped tomatoes
1 small clove garlic, peeled and crushed
1 tsp marjoram
1 tsp oregano
1 cup button mushrooms
4oz noisettes of lamb
Knob butter

Step 1 Cook the onion in the oil until soft and translucent.

1. Put the onion and oil in a small bowl and cook on HIGH for 3 minutes, until soft.

2. Add the tomatoes, garlic, herbs and mushrooms. Cook, uncovered, on HIGH for 3 minutes, stirring once. Set aside and keep warm.

3. Heat a large browning dish for the manufacturer's recommended time. Add the butter and quickly

place the noisettes in the dish and press each one down firmly, then turn them over and press down again. Cook on HIGH for 5 minutes.

4. Transfer the noisettes to a warm serving dish and, if necessary, reheat the sauce for 1 minute on HIGH. Remove string from noisettes. Serve the sauce poured over the noisettes.

Step 2 Combine with all the other sauce ingredients and cook until bubbling and thickened.

Step 3 Press the noisettes against the surface of the browning dish to color the meat and fat lightly.

Cook's Notes

 TIME: Preparation takes 10 minutes, and cooking takes 11 minutes.

VARIATION: Use your favorite choice of herbs – basil and rosemary are also delicious with lamb.

 SERVING IDEAS: Serve with potatoes and a green vegetable, or serve rice or pasta to go with the sauce.

$ BUYING GUIDE: The butcher will bone a best end neck of lamb for you and tie and cut noisettes. If doing this yourself, do not tie the strings too tightly.

CRISPY CHICKEN

SERVES 4-6

Chicken cooks so well in a microwave oven, and a crisp topping gives both visual and taste appeal.

3½lbs chicken pieces
1 cup crushed cornflakes
6 tbsps grated Parmesan cheese
½ tsp mustard powder
1 tsp paprika
½ tsp celery salt
½ tsp oregano
½ tsp parsley
Pepper
½ cup butter or margarine
2 eggs, beaten

1. Skin all the chicken pieces and remove any fat. Combine the cornflakes, cheese, herbs, spices and pepper and spread out evenly on a sheet of wax paper.

2. Melt the butter for 1 minute on HIGH and stir into the beaten eggs in a shallow dish. Dip the chicken into the egg and butter mixture or use a basting brush to coat each piece.

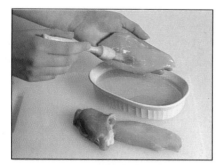

Step 2 Dip the chicken in the butter and egg mixture, or use a pastry brush to coat them with it.

3. Put the chicken pieces in the crumb mixture and lift the ends of the paper to help toss the chicken, coating each piece evenly.

Step 3 Place the chicken in the cornflake mixture, coating both sides evenly.

Step 5 Rearrange the chicken pieces halfway through cooking, keeping the thickest parts to the outside of the dish.

4. Place half the chicken in a glass dish, bone side down. Make sure the thickest pieces of the chicken are on the outside of the dish to start. Cover them loosely with wax paper. Cook on HIGH for 9-12 minutes.

5. Rearrange and turn the chicken over halfway through the cooking time, and remove the paper. Keep the cooked chicken warm while cooking the remaining chicken.

6. If necessary, cover the turntable with paper towels to reheat all of the chicken at once for 1-2 minutes.

Cook's Notes

 TIME: Preparation takes 15 minutes, and cooking takes 9-12 minutes. Allow 1-2 minutes to reheat the chicken, if necessary.

 COOK'S TIP: Keep the thickest part of the food to the outside to ensure even cooking.

 SERVING IDEAS: Serve hot with one of the vegetable dishes or refrigerate and serve cold. Good for picnics and buffets.

PLUMS IN PORT

SERVES 4

This quick dessert can be cooked at the last minute with the minimum of preparation. That's the beauty of cooking with microwaves.

3 cups granulated sugar
1½ cups ruby port or red wine
2 whole cloves or 1 cinnamon stick
1½lbs plums, halved and pitted

1. Put the sugar and port or wine into a large, deep bowl. Put in the cloves or cinnamon stick and cook, uncovered, for 4-8 minutes on HIGH, stirring occasionally to help dissolve the sugar.

Step 1 Combine the sugar, port and whole spices in a large, deep bowl. Cook uncovered, stirring occasionally.

2. Add the plums to the syrup, cover the bowl with plastic wrap and cook for 5 minutes on HIGH.

Step 2 Add the plums to the liquid and partially cover the bowl.

3. Reduce the power to MEDIUM and cook for a further 5 minutes. Uncover and allow plums to cool slightly.

Step 3 Test the plums with a knife. They should just be starting to soften when removed from the microwave.

Cook's Notes

 TIME: Preparation takes about 10 minutes, and cooking takes about 14 minutes.

 VARIATION: Use the same method for cooking peach or apricot halves. Reduce the cooking time by 2-3 minutes for apricot halves.

SERVING IDEAS: Serve either warm or cold with whipped cream or ice cream.

STEAMED RASPBERRY JAM PUDDING

SERVES 6

Steamed puddings can take hours to cook on top of the stove. Turn to your microwave oven for a traditional treat to suit modern schedules.

½ cup raspberry jam
½ cup butter or margarine
½ cup sugar
2 eggs
1 tsp vanilla extract
1 cup all-purpose flour
1 tsp baking powder
2 tbsps milk

1. Grease a 3 cup mixing bowl or decorative mold thoroughly with butter or margarine. Put the jam into the bottom of the mold and set aside.

Step 1 Spoon the raspberry jam into the bottom of a well-buttered bowl or mold.

2. Cream the remaining butter or margarine with the sugar until light and fluffy.

3. Beat in the eggs one at a time and add the vanilla extract. Sift in the flour and baking powder and then fold in. If the mixture is too stiff, add up to

2 tbsps of milk to make a soft dropping consistency.

4. Spoon the mixture carefully on top of the jam and smooth the top. Cover the bowl or mold with 2 layers of plastic wrap, pierced several times to release the steam.

5. Cook for 5-8 minutes on HIGH. Leave to stand for 5-10 minutes before turning out to serve.

Step 3 Add milk if necessary to make the batter of a dropping consistency.

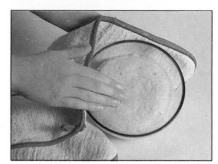

Step 5 When the pudding is done, it will still look slightly damp on top but will firm up on standing.

Cook's Notes

TIME: Preparation takes 15-20 minutes, and cooking takes 5-8 minutes plus 5-10 minutes standing time.

VARIATION: Use other flavors of jam, preserves or marmalades. Golden raisins, dates or chopped nuts can be added to the batter before cooking.

SERVING IDEAS: Serve warm with whipped or pouring cream, ice cream or custard sauce.

CHOCOLATE MOUSSE

SERVES 4

This luxurious pudding with a French accent is always a favorite for dinner parties, but when it's this easy to make, why restrict it to special occasions?

7 tbsps unsalted butter
4 tbsps sugar
4 eggs, separated
8oz semi-sweet chocolate
4 tbsps coffee liqueur
Whipped cream and coffee dragées or grated chocolate to garnish

Step 1 Heat the butter until very soft, but not melted.

1. Put the butter into a deep bowl and soften for 30 seconds on HIGH. Add the sugar and beat until light and fluffy. Gradually beat in the egg yolks.

2. Chop the chocolate roughly and place in a small bowl with the coffee liqueur. Microwave on MEDIUM for 2 minutes or until the chocolate has completely melted.

3. Combine the chocolate with the butter mixture and beat for 5 minutes or until the mixture is light and fluffy.

4. Whip the egg whites and fold into the mixture. Spoon into small dessert dishes and chill until firm. Decorate with a rosette of whipped cream and one coffee dragée or sprinkle with grated chocolate. Serve cold.

Step 2 Use a medium setting to melt the chocolate with the liqueur until smooth.

Step 3 Beat the chocolate into the butter and egg mixture until very light and fluffy.

Cook's Notes

 TIME: Preparation takes about 15 minutes, and cooking takes about 2-3 minutes plus several hours chilling time.

 VARIATION: Different liqueurs can be used to suit your own taste. You can substitute brandy, orange or raspberry liqueurs or crème de menthe.

PREPARATION: The mousse can be prepared in advance and refrigerated overnight without any change in the consistency.

MICROWAVE MERINGUES

SERVES 8-10

These are as much fun to make as they are delicious to eat. They grow magically before your eyes.

1 egg white
1lb powdered sugar (all the sugar may not be needed)
Food colorings such as red, green or yellow
Chopped toasted nuts or sifted cocoa powder
Flavoring extract
Powdered sugar
Whipped cream

1. Beat the egg white lightly and sift in the powdered sugar until the mixture forms a pliable paste that can be rolled out like pastry. Add the chosen coloring and flavoring with the powdered sugar. The mixture may also be divided and several different colorings and flavoring used.

Step 1 Mix the egg white with enough sifted powdered sugar to make a pliable dough.

2. Roll the dough to a thin sausage shape about ½ inch thick. Cut into small pieces and place well apart on wax paper on a plate or microwave cookie sheet. Flatten the pieces slightly.

3. Cook for 1 minute on HIGH or until dry. The meringues will triple in size. Leave to cool on a wire rack.

4. When the meringues are cool, sandwich them together with whipped cream and sprinkle lightly with powdered sugar.

Step 2 Roll the dough into a thin sausage shape.

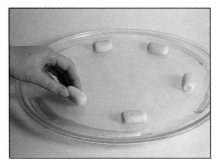

Step 2 Cut each sausage into small pieces and arrange them in a circle, leaving ample space for the meringues to triple in size. Do this in batches, if necessary.

Cook's Notes

TIME: Preparation takes about 15 minutes, and cooking takes about 6 minutes.

VARIATION: The meringue mixture may be rolled to a ½-inch thickness and a very small pastry cutter used to cut out different shapes. These meringues will be slightly larger than those made by the first method.

SERVING IDEAS: Serve with a fresh fruit salad, fruit or chocolate sauce, if desired.

CHOCOLATE RING CAKE

SERVES 6-8

Cakes bake in about a quarter of the time they take in a conventional oven. This one has an easy topping, too.

1½ cups all-purpose flour
1½ tsps bicarbonate of soda
4 tbsps cocoa
1 cup sugar
¾ cup evaporated milk
1 tbsp white vinegar
⅔ cup butter or margarine
2 eggs, beaten
Few drops vanilla extract
4oz white chocolate

1. Lightly grease a 6 cup cake ring. Sift the flour, soda and cocoa into a mixing bowl and add the sugar. Combine the evaporated milk and vinegar and set aside.

2. Melt the butter or margarine on HIGH for 2-3 minutes or until liquid. Pour into the milk and vinegar and gradually add the beaten eggs. Stir in the vanilla extract. Pour into the cake ring and smooth down the top to level.

3. Cook on HIGH for 10 minutes or until top of the cake is only slightly sticky. Cool in the ring for 10 minutes then turn out onto a wire rack to cool completely.

Step 3 When the cake is done, the top will still be slightly sticky to the touch.

4. Melt the white chocolate in a small dish for 1-2 minutes on HIGH or until liquid. When the cake is cool, drizzle over the still warm white chocolate and allow to set completely before cutting the cake to serve.

Step 2 Pour the liquid ingredients into the dry ones and mix together quickly. The vinegar and soda will bubble.

Step 4 When the cake has cooled completely, drizzle with melted white chocolate to make a lacy pattern.

Cook's Notes

TIME: Preparation takes about 20 minutes, and cooking takes about 10 minutes, plus 10 minutes standing time.

VARIATION: For a completely dark chocolate cake decorate with the same amount of semi-sweet chocolate or use milk chocolate.

FREEZING: Plain cake can be frozen for up to 2 months. Defrost at room temperature or use the DEFROST setting for 2 minutes then set aside at room temperature to finish defrosting. Decorate with chocolate once the cake has defrosted.

FIG AND APRICOT CHARLOTTES

SERVES 6

Try this deceptively easy pudding for your next dinner party. It looks impressive and as if it took hours to make!

1¼ cups dried figs
1¼ cups dried apricots
½ cup brandy
1lb cream or curd cheese
½ cup thick natural yogurt
3 tbsps honey
Halved toasted almonds
½ cup heavy cream
Nutmeg

1. Place the figs and the apricots in a deep bowl with the brandy and heat for 30 seconds-1 minute on HIGH. Leave to stand, covered, for 2-3 minutes. Drain off the brandy and reserve.

2. Place a circle of wax paper in the bottom of 6 custard cups. Cut the figs in half and press them flat. Press the apricots to flatten slightly. Use the fruit to line the sides of the dishes, with the seed side of the fig to the inside.

3. Soften the cream or curd cheese for 30 seconds-1 minute on MEDIUM. Stir in the yogurt, honey and the reserved brandy.

4. Spoon the mixture into the custard cups, pressing it down firmly against the base and the fruit lining the sides. Fold any fruit ends over the cheese filling and chill.

5. Turn the charlottes out onto a serving plate and pour cream carefully around the base of each. Remove the paper circles from the top and decorate with toasted almonds and freshly grated nutmeg.

Step 1 Heat the figs and apricots in the brandy to flavor and soften them.

Step 2 Cut the figs and apricots to fit the dishes and use alternately to line the sides.

Step 4 Fill the dishes with the softened cheese mixture, pressing it in well.

Cook's Notes

TIME: Preparation takes about 20 minutes, and cooking takes 1-2 minutes.

PREPARATION: Charlottes can also be prepared in advance and refrigerated overnight in their individual dishes.

FREEZING: Wrap well and freeze in the individual dishes for up to 1 month. Defrost overnight in the refrigerator and then leave at room temperature for 1 hour before serving.

Fish`n`Seafood

Fish and shellfish must surely be one of the most versatile types of food there is, with seemingly endless variations in type, texture, flavor and color.

Fish is also one of the most nutritious foods available, and an answer to the modern cook's concern for fresh, healthful ingredients. It is low in saturated fat, high in protein and contains many vitamins and minerals, some of which are not readily available from other sources, such as iodine. It seems a pity, therefore, that most people stick firmly to cod, plaice, smoked haddock or shrimp when choosing fish for a meal, and never try the many other delicious types of fish or shellfish that are available.

The recipes in this chapter demonstrate a variety of preparation and cooking methods, using a wide range of fish and shellfish. With the help of these recipes you will discover the exciting tastes of different varieties of seafood as well as discovering a new form of healthy, delicious and elegant eating.

SHRIMP IN MELON

SERVES 4

Deliciously cool and refreshing for a summer lunch, this recipe could also be served as an unusual appetizer for eight people.

2 small melons
4 medium tomatoes
1 small cucumber
1 orange
Juice of half a lemon
4 tbsps light vegetable oil
3 tbsps heavy cream
2 tbsps chopped fresh mint, reserve 4 sprigs for garnish
Pinch of sugar
Salt and pepper
1 tsp chopped fresh lemon thyme, optional
1¼ cups peeled shrimp
¾ cup toasted slivered almonds

Step 2 Prepare the fruit and vegetables so they are a convenient size to eat.

Step 3 Mix the dressing in a large bowl and add the rest of the ingredients to it, stirring well to coat thoroughly.

Step 1 Leave a ¼-inch border of flesh on the inside of each shell, so they are rigid enough to hold the salad.

1. Cut the melons in half through the middle, remove the seeds and scoop out the flesh with a melon baller, or spoon. Leave a ¼-inch border of fruit on the inside of each shell.

2. Cut the melon flesh into ½-inch cubes, or leave in balls. Peel the tomatoes and remove the seeds. Cut the flesh into strips. Peel the cucumber, cut into half lengthways and then into ½-inch cubes. Peel and segment the orange.

3. In a large bowl, mix together the lemon juice, oil and heavy cream. Stir in the mint, sugar, salt and pepper and thyme, if using. Add the shrimp and the fruit and vegetables, and mix thoroughly to coat evenly with the dressing.

4. Pile equal quantities of the fruit and shrimp mixture into the two shells and chill well.

5. Serve garnished with the reserved mint sprigs and the almonds.

Cook's Notes

 TIME: Preparation takes about 25 minutes. Allow at least 2 hours for chilling the salad, before serving.

PREPARATION: If the melon shells will not stand upright, cut a thin slice off the bottom of each one to make them more stable.

 SERVING IDEAS: Serve with a mixed green salad and new potatoes.

SMOKED SALMON STUFFED CUCUMBERS

SERVES 4

This exquisite appetizer will soon become a firm favorite.

1 large cucumber
Salt for sprinkling
4oz smoked salmon
1 cup curd cheese
2 tsps finely chopped fresh chives
½ cup natural yogurt
2 tsps finely chopped fresh dill
2 tbsps whipping cream
Squeeze of lemon juice
Salt and pepper
1 head of iceberg lettuce
Red caviar, to garnish

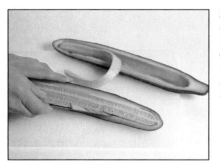

Step 1 Cut the cucumber in half lengthways and carefully scoop out the seeds using a serrated grapefruit spoon or knife.

1. Cut the cucumber in half lengthways and scoop out the seeds. Sprinkle the surface with salt and leave to stand for 1 hour.

2. Work the smoked salmon and the cheese in a blender until smooth. Stir in the chives.

3. Mix the yogurt, cream and dill together, adding lemon juice and seasoning to taste.

4. Rinse the cucumber thoroughly and pat as dry as possible. Using a pastry bag, fitted with a ½-inch plain nozzle, pipe the smoked salmon mixture into the hollow left in the cucumber, sandwich the two halves together firmly, wrap tightly in polythene or plastic wrap and chill for at least 1 hour.

5. Arrange the lettuce leaves on serving plates. Unwrap the cucumber, trim away the ends and slice carefully into ¼-inch slices. Arrange these on top of the lettuce.

6. Spoon a little of the yogurt mixture over, and garnish with a little red caviar.

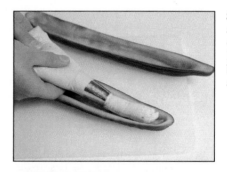

Step 4 Pipe the salmon mixture evenly into the hollow left in the cucumber by the removal of the seeds.

Step 5 Use a sharp knife to cut the chilled stuffed cucumber carefully into ¼-inch slices.

Cook's Notes

 TIME: Preparation takes about 15 minutes, but allow at least 1 hour for chilling, before serving.

 VARIATION: Use halved, hard-cooked eggs, with the yolks removed, instead of the cucumber. The yolks can be sieved over the dressing instead of the caviar, if preferred.

SERVING IDEAS: Use the slices of stuffed cucumber, without the yogurt dressing, as part of a tray of hors d'oeuvres.

MUSSELS À LA GRECQUE

SERVES 4

Fresh mussels are a real treat during the autumn and winter and the sauce in this recipe is a reminder of warmer days!

4 cups mussels
1 onion, chopped
½ cup white wine
Lemon juice
2 tbsps olive oil
1 clove garlic, crushed
1 shallot or 2 green onions, chopped
1½lbs fresh tomatoes, chopped
1 tsp fennel seeds
1 tsp coriander seeds
1 tsp crushed oregano
1 bay leaf
1 tbsp chopped fresh basil
Pinch cayenne pepper
Salt and pepper
Black olives, to garnish

Step 5 Boil the tomato mixture rapidly, until the sauce has reduced and is thick and pulpy.

Step 2 Cook the mussels quickly, until all the shells are open, about 8 minutes. Discard any with shells that stay shut after this time.

1. Scrub the mussels and discard any with broken shells, or which do not shut when tapped with a knife.

2. Put them into a large saucepan with the onion, wine and lemon juice. Cover and cook quickly until the mussels open, discarding any that do not.

3. Remove the mussels from their shells and leave to cool. Reserve the cooking liquid.

4. Heat the olive oil in a saucepan and add the garlic and the shallot, or green onions. Cook gently, until golden brown.

5. Stir in the tomatoes, spices and herbs. Season to taste and blend in the reserved liquor from the mussels. Bring this mixture to the boil and allow to boil rapidly, until the tomatoes are soft and the liquid is reduced by half. Remove the bay leaf.

6. Allow the sauce to cool, then stir in the mussels. Chill well and serve garnished with black olives.

Cook's Notes

 TIME: Preparation takes about 20 minutes, including cleaning the mussels. Cooking will take about 20 minutes.

 SERVING IDEAS: Serve with a green salad and French bread.

 PREPARATION: The shells of fresh mussels must be tightly closed and intact. Any that are cracked or do not shut tight when tapped with a knife should be thrown away. Any mussels that stay shut after being cooked, should also be discarded.

 COOK'S TIP: To keep mussels fresh overnight, wrap them in a thick layer of damp newspaper. Put this inside a polythene bag and store them in the bottom of a refrigerator. DO NOT KEEP FRESH SHELLFISH FOR ANY LONGER THAN OVERNIGHT.

SHRIMP PASTRY PUFFS

SERVES 4

These light pastry puffs are excellent savory snacks for a picnic or informal party.

6 tbsps butter
1/3 cup water
Generous 3/4 cup all-purpose flour, sieved
3 eggs, beaten
3 tbsps butter
6 tbsps flour
1 cup milk
2 tbsps white wine
1 bay leaf
1 cup peeled shrimp, chopped
2 hard-cooked eggs, chopped
Pinch nutmeg
1 tsp chopped fresh dill
Salt and pepper

1. Put the 6 tbsps butter and the water into a saucepan. Bring to the boil. Tip in the 3/4 cup flour all at once and beat, until the mixture is smooth and leaves the sides of the pan clean. Leave to cool slightly.

2. Add the eggs gradually to the flour mixture, beating vigorously, until they are well incorporated and the mixture forms a smooth, shiny paste.

3. Line a cookie sheet with silicone paper and drop heaped teaspoonsful of the mixture onto it, spaced well apart. Bake in a preheated oven, 400°F, for 25 minutes, or until the pastry puffs are firm to the touch and golden brown.

4. Melt the remaining butter in a saucepan and stir in the remaining flour. Blend in the milk gradually,

Step 2 Beat the eggs vigorously into the flour and water mixture, adding them gradually, until a smooth, shiny paste is formed.

Step 6 Cut the puffs almost in half through the middle and fill each cavity with the shrimp and egg mixture.

beating well between additions. When all the milk is mixed in, add the wine and bay leaf and bring to the boil, stirring constantly.

5. Remove the bay leaf and stir in the remaining ingredients.

6. Cut the pastry puffs almost in half through the middle and fill with the shrimp and egg mixture.

Cook's Notes

 TIME: Preparation will take about 15 minutes and cooking takes about 30-35 minutes.

 VARIATION: Use whole-wheat, instead of all-purpose, flour to make the pastry puffs.

PREPARATION: The eggs can be mixed into the flour and water mixture, using a food mixer or processor.

 COOK'S TIP: To make sure that the pastry puffs stay crisp, after cooking is complete, make a small slit in the side of each puff and return them to the oven, with the heat switched off, for 5 minutes, so that they dry out completely.

FISH TEMPURA

SERVES 4

This is a traditional Japanese dish, which can be served
as an unusual appetizer.

12 uncooked large shrimp
2 whitefish fillets, skinned and cut into 2 x ¾-inch
  strips
Small whole fish, e.g. smelt or whitebait
2 squid, cleaned and cut into strips 1x3 inches long
2 tbsps all-purpose flour, for dusting
1 egg yolk
Scant ½ cup iced water
1 cup all-purpose flour
Oil for frying
6 tbsps soy sauce
Juice and finely grated rind of 2 limes
4 tbsps dry sherry

1. Shell the shrimp, leaving the tails intact. Wash
the fish and the squid and pat dry. Dust them all
with the 2 tbsps flour.

2. Make a batter by beating together the egg yolk
and water. Sieve in the 1 cup of all-purpose flour
and mix in well with a table knife.

3. Dip each piece of fish into the batter, shaking
off any excess.

4. In a wok or deep-fat fryer, heat the oil to 350°F.
Lower in the fish pieces a few at a time and cook for
2-3 minutes. Lift them out carefully and drain on
paper towels, keeping warm until required.

5. Mix together the soy sauce, lime juice, rind and
sherry and serve as a dip with the cooked fish.

Step 2 The batter will
be lumpy and look
under mixed.

Step 3 Do not batter
too many pieces of
fish at a time. Only
coat those you are
about to cook.

Step 4 Cook only
3 or 4 pieces and only
one kind of fish at
a time.

Cook's Notes

 TIME: Preparation takes about
30 minutes and cooking time
varies from 2 to 3 minutes
depending on the type of fish.

 COOK'S TIP: If the batter seems
to drain off too quickly, leave
each batch of fish in the bowl of
batter, until you are ready to lower
them into the hot oil.

VARIATION: Use a few
vegetables, as well as fish, for
an interesting change. Whole button
mushrooms are especially good.

SHRIMP AND CASHEWS IN PINEAPPLE WITH TARRAGON DRESSING

SERVES 4

Served in the pineapple shells, this impressive salad is ideal for a summer lunch or buffet.

2 small fresh pineapples, with nice green tops
1¼ cups cooked, peeled shrimp
1 cup roasted, unsalted cashew nuts
2 sticks of celery, thinly sliced
4 tbsps lemon juice
1 egg
2 tbsps superfine sugar
1 tbsp tarragon vinegar
2 tsps chopped fresh tarragon
½ cup whipping cream

1. Cut the pineapples carefully in half lengthways, leaving their green tops attached.

2. Cut out the pineapple flesh carefully, leaving a ¼-inch border of flesh on the inside of the shell. Remove the cores and cut the flesh into bite-sized pieces.

3. Put the chopped pineapple into a bowl, along with the shrimp, cashew nuts and celery. Pour in the lemon juice and mix well. Divide the mixture equally between the pineapple shells, and chill them in the refrigerator.

4. In a heat-proof bowl, whisk together the egg and sugar. Stand the bowl over a pan of simmering water, and whisk in the vinegar and tarragon. Continue whisking until the mixture has thickened.

5. Remove the bowl from the heat and allow to cool completely, whisking occasionally.

6. When completely cold, whip the cream until it is just beginning to thicken, then fold it into the dressing mixture.

7. Pour the cream dressing over the salad in the pineapple shells and serve.

Step 1 Cut the pineapples in half lengthways, making sure that the leafy tops stay intact.

Step 4 Whisk the egg and sugar mixture, together with the vinegar and the tarragon, over a pan of simmering water, until it is pale and thick.

Step 6 Fold the lightly whipped cream carefully into the tarragon and egg dressing, before pouring it over the individual salads.

Cook's Notes

 TIME: Preparation takes about 30 minutes, and cooking about 10-15 minutes.

 PREPARATION: Whisking the egg and sugar dressing can be done with an electric mixer. It will not then be necessary to whisk the dressing over a pan of hot water.

COOK'S TIP: If you cannot buy unsalted cashew nuts, wash salted ones in water, but make sure they are completely dry before adding them to the salad.

SALADE NIÇOISE

SERVES 4

This classic French salad is a meal in itself when served on a bed of crisp mixed lettuce leaves with some crusty bread.

2 large, or 6 small, new potatoes, cooked and cut into ½-inch dice
6oz green beans, trimmed and cooked
¼ cup black olives, halved and pitted
1 small cucumber, diced
4 tomatoes, cut into eight
7½oz can tuna, in brine for preference
¾ cup peeled shrimp
4 hard-cooked eggs, shelled and quartered lengthways
2oz can anchovies, drained and chopped
6 tbsps olive oil
2 tbsps white wine vingar

3 tbsps chopped fresh mixed herbs
2 tsps French mustard
Salt and pepper

1. In a large bowl, mix together the potatoes, beans, olives, cucumber and tomatoes.

2. Drain the tuna and flake it with a fork. Mix this, along with the shrimp, eggs and anchovies into the salad mixture.

3. In a small bowl, mix together the oil, vinegar, herbs and mustard. Whisk with a fork until thick.

4. Pour the dressing over the salad ingredients and stir gently to coat evenly. Season to taste.

Step 3 Whisk together the dressing ingredients until they are thick.

Step 4 Combine the dressing carefully with the salad ingredients, tossing gently, to ensure they are all evenly coated.

Cook's Notes

 TIME: Preparation takes about 20 minutes, and cooking takes about 20 minutes.

 PREPARATION: If you have a screw top jar, the dressing ingredients can be put into this and shaken vigorously, until they have thickened.

 COOK'S TIP: The dressing used in this recipe is delicious and will keep for up to 2 weeks in a refrigerator. So make double quantities and keep some to enliven other salad meals.

LOBSTER AND CAULIFLOWER SALAD
SERVES 6

This salad has a touch of elegance that makes it the sophisticated choice for a stylish meal.

1 large cauliflower, washed
½ cup vegetable oil
3 tbsps lemon juice
1 tbsp dry mustard
Salt and pepper
1 large cooked lobster
1 cup mayonnaise
2 tsps Dijon mustard
4 hard-cooked eggs, coarsely chopped
16 black olives, halved and pitted
2 bunches watercress, washed
Red caviar

1. Break the cauliflower into small flowerets and mix with the oil, lemon juice, dry mustard and seasoning, stirring well, to ensure that all the cauliflower is well coated. Chill for at least 2 hours.

2. Crack the lobster and remove all the meat from the shell and claws. Put the lobster meat into a bowl and stir in the mayonnaise and Dijon mustard.

3. Mix the eggs and olives into the cauliflower, tossing gently so as not to break up the eggs.

4. Trim the watercress and arrange it on a serving plate. Spoon over the cauliflower mixture and top with the lobster and mayonnaise mixture. Sprinkle with the caviar and serve at once.

Step 1 Coat the cauliflower flowerets thoroughly with the oil, lemon juice and dry mustard, before marinating it for at least 2 hours.

Step 2 Crack open the lobster and pick out all the meat from the shell and claws.

Cook's Notes

 TIME: Preparation takes about 30 minutes.

 VARIATION: Fresh crab could be used instead of the lobster, to make an equally delicious dish.

 SERVING IDEAS: Serve with small new potatoes and well-chilled white wine.

SPANISH RICE AND SOLE SALAD

SERVES 4

A complete meal in itself, this salad is ideal for a summer lunch.

2 large lemon sole, each filleted into 4 pieces
4-6 peppercorns
Slice of onion
1 tbsp lemon juice
¾ cup long grain rice
1 small eggplant
2 tbsps olive oil
1 red pepper, seeded and chopped into ¼-inch dice
1 shallot, finely chopped
1 green pepper, seeded and chopped into ¼-inch dice
3 tbsps French dressing
1 tbsp chopped fresh mixed herbs
1 cup prepared mayonnaise
1 clove garlic, crushed
1 level tsp tomato paste
1 level tsp paprika
Salt and pepper
2 bunches watercress, to garnish

Step 1 Allow the fish to cool, then cut each fillet into 1-inch pieces.

Step 4 Mix the eggplant into the rice along with the peppers.

1. Lay the sole fillets in an ovenproof dish, together with the peppercorns, slice of onion, lemon juice and just enough water to cover. Sprinkle with a little salt and cover the dish with foil or a lid. Poach in a preheated oven, 350°F, for 8-10 minutes. Allow the fish to cool in the liquor, then cut each fillet into 1-inch pieces.

2. Cook the rice in boiling water, until soft. Rinse in cold water and separate the grains with a fork.

3. Cut the eggplant in half and sprinkle with 2 tsps salt. Allow to stand for ½ an hour, then rinse very thoroughly. Pat dry and cut into ½-inch dice.

4. Heat the oil in a large frying pan, and fry the eggplant, until it is soft. Allow the eggplant to cool, then mix it into the rice along with the shallot, peppers, half the chopped herbs and the French dressing.

5. Mix together the mayonnaise, garlic, tomato paste, paprika, remaining herbs and seasoning.

6. Arrange the rice on one side of a serving dish and the sole pieces on the other. Spoon the mayonnaise over the sole and garnish the dish with watercress.

Cook's Notes

 TIME: Preparation will take about 20 minutes. Cooking takes about 15-20 minutes.

 COOK'S TIP: Cooked rice usually weighs about twice its dry weight.

 FREEZING: Rice can be cooked and frozen in convenient amounts. To use, the frozen rice should be put straight into boiling water and allowed to cook for 3-4 minutes, then rinsed in cold water.

RICE AND TUNA STUFFED EGGPLANTS

SERVES 4

An interesting way of serving eggplant, this recipe could also serve eight as an appetizer.

4 small eggplants
3 tbsps olive oil
Salt and pepper
1 small onion, finely chopped
1 clove garlic, crushed
6 tbsps cooked brown or wild rice
1 tbsp mayonnaise
1 x 7oz can tuna, drained and flaked
4 tomatoes, skinned, seeded and chopped
1 tsp chopped fresh parsley
1 tsp curry powder

1 tsp of the oil and sprinkle with salt.

2. Place the eggplants on a lightly greased cookie sheet and cook in a preheated oven, 375°F, for 15 minutes. Allow to cool slightly.

3. Scoop the flesh carefully from each half eggplant, leaving about ¼-inch around the edge, to form a shell. Chop the flesh.

4. Fry the onion in the remaining 2 tbsps of the olive oil. Add the garlic and the chopped eggplant flesh. Cook for 2 minutes, then stir in the rice, mayonnaise, tuna, tomatoes, parsley and seasonings. Mix together thoroughly.

Step 1 Score the cut surfaces of the eggplants with a knife at regular intervals, making sure that you do not break the skin.

Step 3 Carefully scoop out the cooked eggplant flesh from the skins, leaving a ¼-inch rim, to form a shell.

1. Cut the eggplants in half lengthways. Score the cut surfaces lightly, with a sharp knife, making sure that you do not break the skin. Brush lightly with

5. Divide the rice mixture equally between the eggplant shells. Place the filled eggplants in an ovenproof dish and bake for 25 minutes.

Cook's Notes

TIME: Preparation takes about 40 minutes, and cooking takes about 50 minutes.

PREPARATION: A serrated spoon, or grapefruit knife, is useful for scooping out the eggplant flesh.

SERVING IDEAS: Serve with crusty French bread and a bean and cauliflower salad.

SHRIMP EGG RICE
SERVES 6

Serve this on its own for a tasty lunch or supper dish, or as part of a more elaborate Chinese meal.

1lb long grain rice
2 eggs
½ tsp salt
4 tbsps oil
2 green onions, chopped
1 large onion, chopped
2 cloves of garlic, chopped
¾ cup peeled shrimp
¼ cup shelled peas
2 tbsps dark soy sauce

Step 4 Cook the eggs with the onions gently, until set and softly scrambled.

Step 3 Rinse the rice in cold water and separate the grains with a fork.

1. Wash the rice thoroughly and put it in a saucepan. Add water to come 1 inch above the top of the rice.

2. Bring the rice to the boil, stir once, then reduce the heat. Cover and simmer the rice for 5-7 minutes, or until the liquid has been absorbed.

3. Rinse the rice in cold water and fluff up with a fork, to separate the grains.

4. Beat the eggs with a pinch of salt. Heat 1 tablespoon of the oil in a wok and cook the onions until soft, but not brown. Pour in the egg and stir gently, until the mixture is set. Remove the egg mixture and set it aside.

5. Heat a futher tablespoon of the oil and fry the garlic, shrimp, peas and green onions quickly for 2 minutes. Remove from the wok and set aside.

6. Heat the remaining oil in the wok and stir in the rice and remaining salt. Stir-fry, to heat the rice through, then add the egg and the shrimp mixtures and the soy sauce, stirring to blend thoroughly. Serve immediately.

Cook's Notes

 TIME: Preparation takes about 20 minutes and cooking takes about 15 minutes.

 VARIATION: Use chopped red peppers or corn kernels, instead of the peas.

 FREEZING: Rice can be cooked and frozen for up to 6 weeks. Frozen rice should be defrosted and rinsed, before being used in this dish.

HALIBUT AND CRAB HOLLANDAISE

SERVES 4

Rich and creamy, the Hollandaise sauce adds an air of sophistication to this lovely dish.

4 large fillets of halibut
1 bay leaf
Slice of onion
5 tbsps white wine
2 egg yolks
1 tbsp lemon juice
Pinch cayene pepper
Pinch paprika pepper
½ cup butter, melted
1 tbsp butter
2 tbsps flour
2 tbsps heavy cream
Salt and pepper
8oz crab meat

Step 2 Add the melted butter very gradually to the egg yolks, lemon juice and seasoning in the liquidizer, to ensure a smooth, thick Hollandaise sauce.

Step 1 Lay the halibut fillets in an ovenproof dish and poach with the wine, bay leaf, onion slice and just enough water to cover.

1. Put the fish with the bay leaf, onion slice, wine and just enough water to cover the fish, into a baking dish. Cover and cook in a preheated oven, 325°F, for 10 minutes.

2. Put the egg yolks, lemon juice, cayenne and paprika into a liquidizer, or food processor. Turn the machine on and gradually pour in the melted butter. Continue processing, until the Hollandaise sauce is thick. Set aside.

3. Put the 1 tbsp unmelted butter into a saucepan, melt over a gentle heat and stir in the flour. Cook gently for 1 minute.

4. Remove the fish from the baking dish and strain the cooking liquor onto the flour and butter in the saucepan, stirring well, to prevent lumps from forming. Cook this sauce gently, until it is smooth and has thickened. Stir in the cream, but do not allow to boil. Season to taste.

5. Stir the crab meat into the fish stock sauce and pour this mixture into an flameproof dish. Lay the halibut fillets on top and cover these with the Hollandaise sauce.

6. Brown under a hot broiler before serving.

Cook's Notes

TIME: Preparation will take about 15 minutes and cooking takes about 20 minutes.

PREPARATION: If you do not have a liquidizer or food processor, Hollandaise sauce can be prepared by hand. This should be done by whisking the egg yolks, lemon juice and seasoning in a bowl over a pan of simmering water, then very gradually whisking in the melted butter. This will take about 10 minutes.

SERVING IDEAS: Serve with new potatoes and broccoli.

DRESSED CRAB

SERVES 2-3

No book on fish cookery would be complete without instructions on how to dress a crab. Crabs are in season between May and September. They should have rough shells, large claws and feel heavy for their size. Do not buy a crab which sounds to have water in, when shaken.

1 large cooked crab
Chopped fresh parsley, to garnish

Step 2 Lay the crab on its upper shell and pull the underbody firmly away from the main shell.

Step 3 Remove and discard the stomach bag which lies behind the head, and the gray, finger-like gills, as these must never be eaten.

1. Pull off the crab claws, and crack these with a small hammer or nutcrackers. Pull out the meat and put into a basin for light meat.

Step 5 Carefully crack away enough of the edges of the upper shell to form a flat case, in which to serve the crab meat.

2. Turn the crab onto its back or uppermost shell, and pull the underbody firmly away from the main shell.

3. Remove and discard the stomach bag and gray, feathered gills, or fingers, as these must not be eaten. Scoop out the dark meat from the shell with a spoon and put into a basin.

4. Crack open the underbody and remove all the white meat with a skewer or fork. Put into the appropriate basin.

5. Remove enough of the top shell to make a flat case, in which to serve the meat. Scrub the shell thoroughly.

6. Arrange layers of dark and light meat alternately in the shell, and garnish with the parsley.

Cook's Notes

 TIME: Preparation takes about 35-45 minutes.

 SERVING IDEAS: Serve with new potatoes and a simple, mixed lettuce salad.

 COOK'S TIP: Use fresh crabs on the same day that you purchase them. Always buy them from a reputable source. If you must store them until the next day, wrap them in damp newspaper and keep them in the bottom of a refrigerator.

 VARIATION: To make the crab serve 4 people, hard-cook 2 eggs, chop the whites and sieve the yolks and arrange these in stripes with the dark and light crab meat.

SOUR FRIED SEAFOOD

SERVES 4

A fragrant sour fried curry from the Far East. This can be served on its own, or as one of a combination of dishes.

1lb mixed fish and seafood, to include any of the following: large shrimp; scallops; squid, cleaned and cut into rings; oysters, shelled; clams, shelled; crab claws, shelled; small whole fish, e.g. whitebait or smelt.
½ cup oil
1 tbsp grated fresh ginger
4 shallots, finely chopped
3 cloves garlic, crushed
4 red chili peppers, seeded and finely chopped
1 tsp ground mace
½ tsp shrimp paste
1 piece tamarind, soaked in 4 tbsps hot water OR
2 tbsps lemon juice
Pinch brown sugar
Salt

1. Heat the oil in a frying pan, until it begins to smoke. Fry the fish in several batches for 2-3 minutes per batch, or until lightly browned and cooked through. Drain on paper towels and keep warm.

2. Grind the shallots, ginger, garlic, chilies and mace to a smooth paste in a pestle and mortar. Add the shrimp paste and blend together well.

3. Put 1 tbsp of oil into a wok and add the spice paste. Cook gently for 2-3 minutes. Strain in the tamarind and water, or lemon juice. The sauce

Step 1 Fry the fish in hot oil, in several batches, to prevent it from breaking up.

Step 2 Grind the shallots, ginger, garlic, chilies and mace to a smooth paste in a pestle and mortar.

should be of a thin coating consistency, add a little more water, if it is too thick.

4. Stir in the sugar, the cooked fish and salt to taste. Cook for 2-3 minutes, or until the fish is heated through.

Cook's Notes

 TIME: Preparation takes about 20 minutes, and cooking takes about 12-15 minutes.

 COOK'S TIP: Great care should be taken when preparing fresh chilies. Always wash hands thoroughly afterwards, and avoid getting any neat juice in the eyes or mouth. Rinse with copious amounts of clear water, if this happens.

SERVING IDEAS: Serve with a mixed salad, rice and shrimp crackers.

SARDINE AND TOMATO GRATINÉE

SERVES 4

Fresh sardines are becoming more widely available and this recipe makes the most of these delicious fish.

3 tbsps olive oil
2lbs large fresh sardines, descaled and cleaned
2 leeks, cleaned and sliced
½ cup dry white wine
8oz tomatoes, skinned and quartered
Salt and pepper
2 tbsps each chopped fresh basil and parsley
½ cup Parmesan cheese, grated
½ cup dry breadcrumbs

1. Heat the oil in a frying pan and fry the sardines, until they are brown on both sides. It may be necessary to do this in several batches, to prevent the fish from breaking up.

2. When all the sardines are cooked, set them aside and cook the leeks gently in the sardine oil. When the leeks are soft, pour in the wine and boil rapidly, until it is reduced by about two thirds.

3. Add the tomatoes, seasoning and herbs to the leeks and cook for about 1 minute. Pour the vegetables into an ovenproof dish and lay the sardines on top.

4. Sprinkle the cheese and breadcrumbs evenly over the sardines and bake in a preheated oven, 425°F, for about 5 minutes.

Step 1 Fry the sardines a few at a time, to prevent them from breaking up during cooking.

Step 4 Sprinkle the Parmesan cheese and breadcrumbs evenly over the sardines, before baking them.

Cook's Notes

 TIME: Preparation takes about 20-25 minutes. Cooking takes about 15 minutes.

VARIATION: Try substituting herrings or mackerel for the sardines. They will take a little longer to fry.

SERVING IDEAS: Cut a few anchovy fillets in half lengthways and arrange them in a lattice on top of the gratinée, before serving with hot garlic bread.

 FREEZING: Sardines can be frozen for up to 2 months, but remember to clean and descale them first.

PROVENÇALE FISH STEW
SERVES 4

A hearty Mediterranean lunch or dinner, this dish is a real delight for fish lovers.

1 medium onion, finely chopped
2 cloves garlic, crushed
3 tbsps olive oil
1½lbs tomatoes, skinned, seeded and chopped
2 cups dry red wine
2 tbsps tomato paste
Salt and pepper
4 cups fresh mussels in their shells, scrubbed and debearded
8 large Mediterranean shrimp
¾ cup peeled shrimp
4 crab claws, shelled but with the claw tips left intact

Step 3 Cook the mussels in the tomato sauce, until all the shells have opened.

Step 1 Gently fry the tomatoes with the onions and garlic, until they are beginning to soften.

1. In a large pan, fry the onion and garlic together gently in the olive oil, until they are soft but not brown. Add the tomatoes and fry until they are beginning to soften.

2. Stir in the red wine and the tomato paste. Season to taste, then bring to the boil, cover and simmer for about 15 minutes.

3. Add the mussels, re-cover the pan and simmer for 5-8 minutes, or until all the mussel shells are open. Discard any that are not.

4. Stir in the remaining ingredients and cook, uncovered, for about 5-8 minutes, or until the shell fish has thoroughly heated through.

Cook's Notes

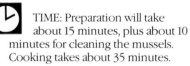

TIME: Preparation will take about 15 minutes, plus about 10 minutes for cleaning the mussels. Cooking takes about 35 minutes.

SERVING IDEAS: Deep-fry chunks of crusty bread, then sprinkle with garlic salt and parsley, to serve with the fish stew.

PREPARATION: To make sure the mussels are fresh, whilst scrubbing them, tap any open ones sharply with a knife. If they do not shut tight, quite quickly, discard them. Also discard any with broken shells or that do not open after cooking.

COOK'S TIP: If you have to keep the mussels overnight, wrap them in damp newspaper and store them in the vegetable tray at the bottom of the refrigerator.

RED SNAPPER NIÇOISE

SERVES 4

*Red snapper is now widely available and its attractive appearance
lends itself to this colorful dish.*

2 tbsps red wine vinegar
8 tbsps olive oil
¼ tsp French mustard
Handful of chopped fresh mixed herbs
1 shallot, finely chopped
1 clove garlic, crushed
Salt and pepper
1 cup button mushrooms, quartered
4 red snapper, descaled and cleaned
Seasoned flour
Lemon juice
1lb tomatoes, quartered and cores removed
1 green pepper, seeded and sliced
¼ cup pitted black olives, halved
2 hard-boiled eggs, quartered
Small can anchovy fillets

1. In a screw top jar, shake together the vinegar, 6 tablespoons of the olive oil, the mustard, herbs, shallot, garlic and seasoning, to make a French dressing.

2. Put the mushrooms into a bowl and pour over the French dressing. Stir to coat the mushrooms evenly and refrigerate for about 1 hour.

3. Toss the snapper in the seasoned flour to coat lightly. Heat the remaining oil in a frying pan and fry the fish on both sides for 2-3 minutes per side, taking care not to break the fish. Sprinkle lightly with lemon juice and salt and pepper, and allow to go cold.

Step 2 Put the mushrooms into a bowl with the dressing and stir to coat them evenly.

Step 3 Toss the snapper in just enough seasoned flour to coat lightly, before cooking.

4. When ready to serve, add the tomatoes, pepper, olives and eggs to the mushrooms. Stir together gently, to coat the salad with the dressing.

5. Pile the salad onto a serving dish and arrange the red snapper on top. Garnish with the drained anchovy fillets.

Cook's Notes

TIME: Preparation takes about 15 minutes. Cooking takes about 15 minutes.

COOK'S TIP: The French dressing is delicious with other salads, so make extra. It will keep in a screw top jar in the refrigerator for up to 2 weeks.

SERVING IDEAS: Serve with hot French bread or crusty rolls.

STEAMED FISH ROLLS

SERVES 4

*Rolled fish looks elegant and makes a dish that is slightly
out of the ordinary.*

2 large sole or plaice, cut into 4 fillets
1 cup peeled shrimp, chopped
2 tsps cornstarch
1 tsp dry sherry
4 green onions, green only, chopped
2 eggs, beaten with a pinch of salt

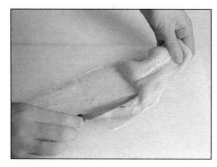

Step 1 Lay the fillets with the skin side down and carefully ease the meat away from the skin with a very sharp knife. Pull the skin towards you and roll the meat away, as you cut.

Step 3 Cook the eggs in a wok or frying pan over a gentle heat, stirring continuously, until they are softly scrambled.

Step 4 Carefully roll up the fillets from the thickest end and secure them with a wooden pick, while they cook.

1. Skin the fish fillets carefully and lay them "skin" side up on a flat surface.

2. Mix the shrimp with the cornstarch, sherry and onions. Divide this mixture equally between the plaice fillets.

3. Cook the eggs in a wok or frying pan, until they are softly scrambled. Spread equal quantities of this over the shrimp mixture.

4. Roll up the fish fillets jelly roll fashion, folding

the thicker end over first. Secure with wooden picks.

5. Put the fish rolls in the top of a steamer or fish kettle and fill the bottom with boiling water. Steam for 10-15 minutes, until the fish is cooked. Remove the wooden picks and serve immediately.

Cook's Notes

TIME: Preparation takes 25 minutes and cooking takes 10-15 minutes.

SERVING IDEAS: Serve with new potatoes and a fresh mixed salad.

PREPARATION: Whilst skinning the fillets, take care to angle the sharp blade of the knife down towards the skin, to prevent cutting the flesh.

COOK'S TIP: Spread more of the filling towards the thicker end of the fillets, to help prevent it falling out as you roll.

VINEGARED CRAB

SERVES 4

An unusual way of serving fresh crab. You should be able to buy the rice vinegar from a delicatessen or health food shop. If not, substitute white wine vinegar.

1 small cucumber, grated
Salt, for sprinkling
1 large cooked crab
1 small piece fresh ginger, grated
Chinese cabbage, for serving
3 tbsps rice vinegar
2 tbsps dry sherry
2 tbsps soy sauce

1. Sprinkle the cucumber with salt and leave for 30 minutes.

2. Crack the legs and claws off the crab. Remove the meat from the claws and legs, but leave four thin legs whole as a garnish.

3. Separate the underbody from the shell. Remove

and discard the stomach sac and the gray, feathered gills.

4. Scrape the brown meat from the shell and crack open the underbody. Use a skewer to pick out the meat.

5. Rinse the cucumber, drain well and squeeze out excess moisture. Mix together the cucumber, crab meat and ginger.

6. Arrange the Chinese cabbage on serving plates, to represent crab shells. Pile equal quantities of crab mixture onto the Chinese cabbage, leaving some of the leaf showing. Garnish with a whole crab leg and some grated, pickled ginger, if you can get it.

7. Mix together the vinegar, sherry and soy sauce. Serve with the crab in little bowls.

Step 2 Remove meat from claws and legs.

Step 4 Crack open the underbody of the crab and use a skewer to remove the white meat inside.

Cook's Notes

 TIME: Preparation takes about 30 minutes.

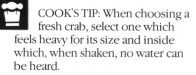 COOK'S TIP: When choosing a fresh crab, select one which feels heavy for its size and inside which, when shaken, no water can be heard.

 SERVING IDEAS: A rice or pasta salad would be excellent with this dish.

COD IN PAPRIKA SAUCE

SERVES 4

*Creamy paprika sauce complements the flavor of cod magnificently
in this tasty recipe.*

1lb cod fillets
Lemon juice
1 bay leaf
Slice of onion
6 peppercorns
2 tbsps butter
½ cup button mushrooms, trimmed and sliced
1 small red pepper, seeded and sliced
1 shallot, finely chopped
2 tsps paprika pepper
1 clove garlic, crushed
¼ cup all-purpose flour
1 cup milk
1 tbsp chopped fresh parsley
1 tsp chopped fresh thyme
1 tsp tomato paste
Salt and pepper
8oz fresh pasta, cooked
2 tbsps sour cream, or natural yogurt

1. Cut the fish into 1-inch chunks. Put these into an ovenproof dish with the lemon juice, bay leaf, onion, peppercorns and just enough water to cover. Cover with a lid and poach for about 10 minutes in a preheated oven, 350°F.

2. Melt the butter in a saucepan and stir in the mushrooms, pepper, shallot, paprika and garlic. Cook gently, until the pepper begins to soften.

3. Stir the flour into the mushrooms and peppers. Gradually add the milk, stirring until the sauce has thickened.

Step 1 Put the cod chunks into an ovenproof dish, along with the bay leaf, lemon juice, onion slice and peppercorns. Pour in just enough water to cover the fish.

Step 4 Stir just enough of the strained fish liquor into the sauce for it to coat the back of a spoon.

4. Remove the fish from the dish and strain off the liquor. Stir enough of this liquor into the pepper sauce to make it of coating consistency. Add the parsley, thyme and tomato paste to the sauce and simmer for 2-3 minutes. Season to taste.

5. Arrange the hot, cooked pasta on a serving plate and place the cod on top. Coat with the paprika sauce, and spoon over the sour cream, or yogurt, to serve.

Cook's Notes

 TIME: Preparation takes about 20 minutes, and cooking takes about 16 minutes.

 VARIATION: Use any other firm-fleshed whitefish, e.g. monkfish, instead of the cod.

 SERVING IDEAS: A mixed salad would be ideal to serve with this dish.

SHRIMP CRESPELLE

SERVES 4

A delicious dish from Italy, crespelle are simply rich, wafer-thin pancakes.

3 eggs, beaten
¾ cup all-purpose flour
Salt
1 cup water
1 tsp olive oil
3 tbsps butter or margarine, melted
2 tbsps butter
2 tsps all-purpose flour
1½ cups milk
Juice 1 lemon
Salt and pepper
1¼ cups shrimp
Lemon slices, to garnish

Step 2 Heat and lightly grease a 7-inch frying pan. Put 1 tablespoon of batter into the center and roll and tilt the pan, to coat the base thinly with the batter.

1. Sift the ¾ cup flour into a bowl, whisk the eggs into the flour gradually, until the mixture is smooth. Stir in the water and oil and leave the batter to stand for 30 minutes.

2. Heat a frying pan and brush it lightly with the melted butter. Put 1 tablespoon of the batter in the center and roll and tilt the pan to coat the base evenly.

3. Fry until the pancake is golden brown underneath, then carefully turn over, to brown the other side. Stack and keep warm until required. Repeat until all the batter has been used up.

4. Melt the 2 tbsps of butter in a saucepan and stir in the 2 tablespoons of flour. Gradually add the milk, beating well, and returning the pan to the heat between additions, until all the milk has been incorporated. Simmer the sauce for 2-3 minutes. Stir in the lemon juice and season to taste.

5. Mix together half of the sauce and the shrimp. Put one pancake into an ovenproof dish and spread a spoonful of the shrimp sauce over this. Cover with

Step 5 Put alternate layers of pancake and sauce into an ovenproof dish. Finish with a pancake and bake.

another pancake and repeat the sauce/pancake procedure until all the pancakes have been used up, finishing with a pancake. Bake in a preheated oven, 375°F, for 10 minutes.

6. Cover with the remaining sauce and garnish with lemon slices. Cut the crespelle like a cake, to serve.

Cook's Notes

TIME: Preparation takes about 40 minutes. Cooking takes about 30 minutes.

SERVING IDEAS: Serve this dish with a colorful mixed salad.

 FREEZING: Pancakes can be made in advance and frozen in stacks, with a piece of wax paper between each one. To use, allow the pancakes to defrost, then reheat as required.

MONKFISH AND PEPPER KEBABS WITH BEARNAISE BUTTER SAUCE

SERVES 4

Monkfish is a firm, succulent whitefish, ideal for kebabs.

8 strips bacon, bone and rind removed
2 pieces lemon grass
2lbs monkfish, cut into 2-inch pieces
1 green pepper, seeded and cut into 2-inch pieces
1 red pepper, seeded and cut into 2-inch pieces
12 button mushrooms, washed and trimmed
8 bay leaves
Oil for brushing
½ cup dry white wine
4 tbsps tarragon vinegar
2 shallots, finely chopped
1 tbsp chopped fresh tarragon
1 tbsp chopped fresh chervil or parsley
1 cup butter, melted
Salt and pepper

1. Cut the bacon in half lengthways and then in half across. Peel the lemon grass and use only the core. Cut this into small shreds.

2. Place a piece of fish on each strip of bacon and top with a shred of lemon grass. Roll up the bacon around the fish. Thread each fish and bacon roll onto kebab skewers, alternating with the peppers, mushrooms and bay leaves. Brush well with oil.

3. Cook under a moderate broiler for 15 minutes, turning frequently and brushing with more oil, if necessary, until the fish is cooked.

4. Heat together the wine, vinegar and shallots in a

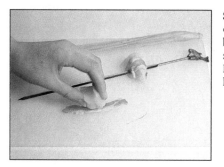

Step 2 Place a piece of fish onto a strip of bacon and top with a shred of lemon grass. Roll and thread onto kebab skewers.

Step 5 Stir the herbs into the reduced wine mixture. Lower the heat and beat in the butter, bit by bit, until the sauce is thick and creamy.

small saucepan until they are boiling. Cook rapidly until reduced by half.

5. Stir in the herbs and lower the heat. Beat in the butter, a little at a time, until the sauce is the thickness of an Hollandaise. Season to taste and serve with the kebabs.

Cook's Notes

 TIME: Preparation takes about 30 minutes, and cooking takes about 25 minutes.

 PREPARATION: These kebabs are ideal for cooking over a barbecue.

 SERVING IDEAS: Serve with a large mixed salad and rice, or pasta.

PAELLA

SERVES 4

A reminder of sunny Spanish holidays, this traditional dish is easy to prepare.

1lb Mediterranean shrimp, or scampi
2 cups mussels in their shells
2 cups shrimp in their shells
½ cup dry white wine
4 tbsps olive oil
1 small onion, chopped
1 clove garlic, crushed
4oz chorizo, or other cooked, spicy sausage, sliced
1 cup long grain rice
Few strands of saffron
4 tomatoes, cores removed and chopped
2 green peppers, seeded and chopped
Small bunch green onions, chopped
Salt and pepper
Lemon juice, to taste

1. Wash the shrimp and scrub the mussels well, discarding any with broken shells or which do not shut tight when tapped.

2. Cook the mussels in the wine over a high heat, until the shells open. Discard any that do not. Strain the liquid, to use for cooking the rice, and put the mussels to one side. Peel half the washed shrimp.

3. Heat the oil in a large frying pan and cook the onion and garlic until they are golden brown. Stir in the chorizo and the rice. Cook gently, until the rice looks clear.

4. Add the shellfish liquor, the saffron and enough water to cover the rice. Cook for about 15 minutes, stirring occasionally, to prevent sticking.

5. Stir the tomatoes and peppers into the rice and cook for a further 5-10 minutes.

6. Stir in all the shellfish, adjust the seasoning, sprinkle with the green onion and serve hot.

Step 1 Scrub the mussel shells thoroughly and cut away the beard with scissors or a knife. Discard any mussels with broken shells or those which do not shut when tapped with a knife.

Step 3 Cook the rice in the oil, until it begins to turn transparent.

Cook's Notes

TIME: Preparation takes about 25 minutes. Cooking takes about 30-35 minutes.

SERVING IDEAS: Serve with a large mixed salad, garlic bread and a full-bodied red wine.

PREPARATION: Great care must be taken when preparing mussels. The shells of mussels must be tightly closed and intact. Any that are cracked or do not shut tight when tapped with a knife, must be discarded. Any mussels that stay shut after being cooked over a high heat for about 6-8 minutes, should also be discarded.

COOK'S TIP: Saffron is very expensive. If you do not have any, use ½ teaspoon of turmeric in its place.

SHRIMP AND GINGER

SERVES 6

Quick and easy to prepare, this dish is really delicious and also very nutritious.

2 tbsps oil
1½lbs peeled shrimp
1-inch piece fresh root ginger, peeled and finely chopped
2 cloves of garlic, peeled and finely chopped
2-3 green onions, chopped
1 leek, white part only, cut into strips
¾ cup peas, shelled
3 cups bean sprouts
2 tbsps dark soy sauce
1 tsp sugar
Pinch salt

1. Heat the oil in a wok and stir-fry the shrimp for 2-3 minutes. Set the shrimp aside.

2. Reheat the oil and add the ginger and garlic. Stir quickly, then add the onions, leek and peas. Stir-fry for 2-3 minutes.

3. Add the bean sprouts and shrimp to the cooked vegetables. Stir in the soy sauce, sugar and salt and cook for 2 minutes. Serve immediately.

Step 2 Stir-fry the onions, leek and peas for 2-3 minutes.

Step 3 Cook all the ingredients together for 2 minutes before serving.

Cook's·Notes

TIME: Preparation takes about 10 minutes, and cooking takes 7-9 minutes.

PREPARATION: The vegetables can be prepared in advance and kept in airtight plastic boxes in the refrigerator for up to 6 hours before needed.

SERVING IDEAS: Serve this on its own with rice or pasta, or as part of an authentic Chinese meal.

COCONUT FRIED FISH WITH CHILIES

SERVES 4

A real treat for lovers of spicy food.

Oil for frying
1lb sole or plaice fillets, skinned, boned and cut
   into 1-inch strips
Seasoned flour
1 egg, beaten
¾ cup shredded coconut
1 tbsp vegetable oil
1 tsp grated fresh ginger
¼ tsp chili powder
1 red chili, seeded and finely chopped
1 tsp ground coriander
½ tsp ground nutmeg
1 clove garlic, crushed
2 tbsps tomato paste
2 tbsps tomato chutney
2 tbsps dark soy sauce
2 tbsps lemon juice
2 tbsps water
1 tsp brown sugar
Salt and pepper

1. In a frying pan, heat about 2 inches of oil to 375°F. Toss the fish strips in the seasoned flour and then dip them into the beaten egg. Roll them in the shredded coconut and shake off the excess.

2. Fry the fish, a few pieces at a time, in the hot oil and drain them on paper towels. Keep warm.

3. Heat the 1 tbsp oil in a wok or frying pan and

Step 1 Toss the strips of fish in the flour and then dip them in the beaten egg. Roll them finally in the shredded coconut. Do not coat the fish too soon before frying.

Step 2 Fry the fish in the hot oil, a few pieces at a time, to prevent it from breaking up.

fry the ginger, red chili, spices and garlic, for about 2 minutes.

4. Add the remaining ingredients and simmer for about 3 minutes. Serve the fish, with the sauce handed round separately.

Cook's Notes

 TIME: Preparation takes about 30 minutes, and cooking takes about 30 minutes.

COOK'S TIP: Great care should be taken when preparing fresh chilies. Always wash your hands thoroughly afterwards, and avoid getting any juice in your eyes or mouth. Rinse with copious amounts of clear water, if you do.

VARIATION: Substitute a firm-fleshed fish like haddock, or monkfish, for the plaice.

 SERVING IDEAS: Serve with plain boiled rice, a cucumber relish and plenty of salad.

COD CURRY

SERVES 4

The fragrant spices used in this recipe are now readily available at most supermarkets.

3 tbsps vegetable oil
1 large onion, peeled and chopped
1-inch piece cinnamon stick
1 bay leaf
1 tsp ginger paste
1 tsp garlic paste
1 tsp chili powder
1 tsp ground cumin
1 tsp ground coriander
¼ tsp ground turmeric
½ cup natural yogurt OR
8oz can tomatoes, chopped
1-2 fresh green chilies, chopped
2 sprigs fresh coriander leaves, chopped
1 tsp salt
1lb cod cutlets, or fillets, cut into 2-inch pieces

1. In a large heavy-based saucepan, fry the onion in the oil until golden brown. Add the cinnamon, bay leaf and the ginger and garlic pastes and fry for 1 minute.

2. Add the ground spices and fry for a further minute, then stir in *either* the yogurt, *or* the canned tomatoes and the chopped chilies and coriander leaves.

3. Only if you have used yogurt, stir in ½ cup water and simmer the mixture for 2-3 minutes. Do not add any water if you have used the canned tomatoes.

4. Stir the cod into the sauce, and add the salt. Cover the pan and simmer for 15-18 minutes before serving.

Step 1 Fry the cinnamon, bay leaf and the ginger and garlic pastes with the onions for 1 minute.

Step 4 Add the cod pieces to the sauce in the pan, stir well to coat thoroughly, before covering and simmering for 15-18 minutes.

Cook's Notes

TIME: Preparation takes about 15 minutes, and cooking takes about 20 minutes.

COOK'S TIP: Great care should be taken when preparing fresh chilies. Always wash hands thoroughly afterwards, and avoid getting any juice in the eyes or mouth. Rinse with copious amounts of clear water if this happens. For a milder curry, remove the seeds; for a hotter curry, leave them in.

SERVING IDEAS: Serve with boiled rice and a cucumber raita.

SMOKED HADDOCK AND EGG QUICHE

SERVES 6

This classic quiche is a firm favorite for lunches, buffets and suppers alike.

8oz whole-wheat dough
12oz smoked haddock fillet
½ cup chicken stock
2 hard-cooked eggs, chopped
1 tbsp chopped fresh chives
¾ cup cheese, grated
3 eggs
1 cup milk
Salt and pepper

Step 1 Press the dough into a flan dish and ease a piece of wax paper over the base and against the sides of the dough case. Half fill with dried beans or peas, to bake blind. The

1. Roll out the dough to fit a 9-inch deep fluted pie pan. Press the edges up well and push the base well down. Prick the base with a fork and bake blind for 15 minutes in a preheated oven, 375°F.

2. Poach the fish gently in the chicken stock for about 8 minutes, or until just tender. Drain the fish and flake it into a bowl, discarding any skin or bones.

3. Mix the chopped eggs, chives and cheese into the fish, and spread this mixture evenly into the part-baked dough case.

4. Beat together the eggs and milk and season to taste. Pour over the fish mixture in the dough case.

5. Bake for 25-30 minutes, or until the filling is set, at the same oven temperature as before.

Step 3 Mix the chopped eggs, chives and cheese into the fish and spread this mixture evenly into the dough case.

Step 4 Carefully pour the beaten egg and milk over the fish in the dough case.

Cook's Notes

TIME: Preparation will take about 25 minutes, and cooking takes about 40 minutes.

VARIATION: Use flaked canned tuna fish, in place of the smoked haddock.

SERVING IDEAS: Serve with new or jacket potatoes and a crisp salad.

PLAICE AND MUSHROOM TURNOVERS

SERVES 4

These delicious individual pies make a warming family lunch or supper dish.

4 plaice fillets, skinned
Salt and pepper
Scant ½ cup milk
1 cup button mushrooms, trimmed and thinly sliced
2 tbsps butter
Juice 1 lemon
3 tbsps hazelnut, or lemon, stuffing mix
12oz puff paste
Beaten egg, for glazing
Poppy seeds, for sprinkling

1. Season the plaice fillets and roll them up jelly roll fashion. Secure each roll with a wooden pick and poach gently in the milk for about 10 minutes in a preheated oven, 350°F.

2. Drain the fish and allow it to cool. Remove the wooden picks. Increase the oven temperature to 400°F.

3. Put the mushrooms and butter into a pan with the lemon juice. Cook over a moderate heat for about 5 minutes.

4. Allow the mushrooms to cool and then stir in the stuffing mix.

5. Roll out the paste, quite thinly, into 4 circles, each 6 inches in diameter. Brush the edges with beaten egg.

6. Put a fish roll into the center of each pastry circle and top with a quarter of the mushroom mixture. Pull the paste edges up and over the fish and pinch

Step 4 Allow the cooked mushrooms to cool and then stir in the stuffing mixture, making sure they are well combined.

Step 6 Pull the paste edges up and over the fish filling. Pinch the edges together firmly to seal completely.

together to seal.

7. Place the turnovers on a greased cookie sheet and glaze with the beaten egg. Sprinkle with a few poppy seeds.

8. Bake in the reset oven for about 25 minutes, or until well risen, puffed and golden. Serve piping hot.

Cook's Notes

 TIME: Preparation will take about 25 minutes, plus the cooling time. Cooking will take about 35 minutes.

 VARIATION: Make these turnovers with whole-wheat puff paste for an even more nutritious dish.

 SERVING IDEAS: Serve with new or mashed potatoes and a salad or green vegetable.

Microwave Fish`n`Seafood

A microwave oven is a must if you like fish and seafood. Whether you choose expensive salmon or economical cod, it's perfect cooked in a microwave oven. Fish fillets cook in a few minutes, whole fish take a little longer, but retain their shape and all their delicious flavor and, because microwave cooking preserves all the natural moisture in food, the flesh does not dry out. Shellfish is also ideal for microwaving, as it needs only the briefest cooking.

Our recipe collection of appetizers, soups, main dishes and snacks, introduces you to a whole range of fish and seafoods, both old favorites and more unusual varieties. You"ll find special first courses like Oysters à la Crème and elegant soups such as Smoked Salmon Cream Soup. There is a super-quick recipe for Spicy Potted Shrimps and one for a hearty Cream of Smoked Haddock Soup. Try Poisson Suprême for a lovely dinner party dish, or serve Scampi Provençale in the fastest possible time. If you're doubtful about fish and seafood, these luscious dishes should change your mind.

All microwave recipes were prepared in a 700 watt oven. If your microwave is of a lower output, adjust timings as follows:

500 watt — add 40 seconds for every minute stated in the recipe
600 watt — add 20 seconds for every minute stated in the recipe
650 watt — only a slight increase in the overall time is necessary

OYSTERS À LA CRÈME

SERVES 4

Opening oysters is no trouble when you use your microwave oven to help.

2 dozen oysters on the half shell or unopened
4 tbsps heavy cream
4 tbsps cream cheese
1 tbsp chopped fresh parsley
Salt and pepper
Nutmeg
Coriander leaves to garnish

Step 1 Scrub oyster shells well with a stiff brush.

1. Scrub the oyster shells well, if unopened, and leave to soak in clean water for 2 hours.

2. Arrange in a circle on the microwave turntable and cook on HIGH for 45 seconds to 2 minutes.

3. After 45 seconds insert a short-bladed knife near the hinge and prise open. If the oysters do not open easily, they need further cooking for up to 2 minutes.

4. Remove any pieces of broken shell from the inside and place the oysters in a circle on the turntable.

5. Mix together the heavy cream, cream cheese, parsley and salt and pepper. Top each oyster with some of the cream mixture.

6. Sprinkle with nutmeg and heat through for 2-3 minutes on MEDIUM. Garnish with coriander leaves and serve immediately.

Step 3 Heat for 45 seconds and then open using a short-bladed knife inserted at the hinge.

Step 5 Top each of the oysters with some of the cream mixture.

Cook's Notes

 TIME: Preparation takes about 15 minutes, and cooking takes about 5 minutes.

 PREPARATION: Add a handful of flour to the soaking water for the oysters. The oysters will expel any sand and take up the flour which will plump them up.

COOK'S TIP: If oyster shells will not sit firmly, place in a microproof dish with ½ inch coarse salt. Press shells into the salt to steady them.

MARINATED SALMON

SERVES 6

This delicious appetizer of fresh salmon "cooks" in the refrigerator in its spiced marinade.

½ cup dry white wine
2 tsps white wine vinegar or lemon juice
1 cinnamon stick
1 tsp coarsely ground white peppercorns
1 tbsp crushed coriander seeds
2 whole cloves
1 onion, finely chopped
2 tsps sugar
4 tbsps oil
1lb salmon, filleted and skinned
Curly endive or watercress

1. Combine the white wine, vinegar, spices, onion and sugar in a glass measure.

2. Cook for 6-8 minutes on HIGH. Stir in the oil and allow to cool slightly.

3. Cut the salmon across the grain into thin slices and arrange in a large, shallow dish.

4. Pour over the white wine and spice mixture and leave to cool at room temperature.

5. Cover and put into the refrigerator for at least 4 hours. Serve arranged on a bed of curly endive with a little of the marinade spooned over.

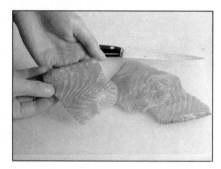

Step 3 Cut the salmon into thin slices across the grain.

Step 4/5 Pour the marinade over the salmon pieces and refrigerate. Turn the pieces in the marinade occasionally.

Cook's Notes

 TIME: Preparation takes 20 minutes, although the salmon must marinate for at least 4 hours. The marinade takes 6-8 minutes to cook.

 PREPARATION: The salmon pieces are best laid flat to ensure that the marinade "cooks" the salmon evenly.

SERVING IDEAS: If desired, mix 2 tsps Swedish mustard with ⅔ cup mayonnaise and add 2 tsps chopped fresh dill to use as a dressing.

MASALA SHRIMP

SERVES 4

This is a perfect appetizer for an Indian meal. It's spicy, but not spicy hot.

1½lbs large shrimp
2 tbsps oil
1 small onion, finely chopped
2 cloves garlic, crushed
1 tsp ground coriander
1 tsp ground cumin
1 tsp ground mustard
1 tsp ground ginger
1 tsp ground turmeric
¼ tsp ground cinnamon
Pinch cayenne pepper
4 tomatoes, peeled, seeded and diced
2 tsps tomato paste
Juice of ½ lime
Salt and pepper
6 tbsps natural yogurt
2 tsps garam masala
Lime wedges and coriander leaves to garnish

1. Remove the shells from the shrimp but leave on the very tail ends. Wash, devein and pat dry.

2. Put the oil, onion, garlic and spices into a bowl. Cover loosely with plastic wrap and cook on HIGH for 2 minutes.

Step 1 Remove all but the very tail ends of the shrimp shells.

Step 3 Cook the tomatoes until they become soft and pulpy.

3. Mix in the tomatoes, tomato paste, lime juice and seasoning. Cook on HIGH for 3-4 minutes until the tomatoes have pulped.

4. Add the shrimp and cook on HIGH for 3-4 minutes, or until the shrimp are tender and pink.

5. Stir in the yogurt and leave to stand for about 2 minutes before serving.

6. Divide the shrimp between 4 serving dishes and sprinkle each serving with some of the garam masala. Garnish with lime wedges and coriander leaves.

Step 4 Add the shrimp to the dish and cook until pink and tender.

Cook's Notes

 TIME: Preparation takes 15 minutes, and cooking takes 11-12 minutes. Allow 2 minutes standing time.

VARIATION: If raw shrimp are not available cook sauce separately and add cooked shrimp during the last minute of cooking time.

 SERVING IDEAS: This dish may be prepared in advance and served cold, if desired. Accompany with poppadums.

SALMON AND GREEN PEPPERCORN TERRINE

SERVES 6-8

This elegant fish terrine cooks in only a fraction of the time it would take in a conventional oven.

12 large spinach leaves
1 shallot, finely chopped
12oz plaice or sole fillets, skinned
1lb salmon
1 cup fresh white breadcrumbs
5 tbsps light cream
1 egg white, lightly beaten
Salt
1 cup heavy cream, lightly whipped
1 tbsp green peppercorns

1. Wash the spinach leaves and remove the stalks. Place the leaves in a bowl, cover loosely with plastic wrap and cook on HIGH, in the water that clings to the leaves, for 30 seconds to 1 minute.

2. Rinse with cold water and pat dry with paper towels. Use the leaves to line the base and sides of a terrine or loaf pan, leaving the ends of the leaves overhanging the sides of the dish.

Step 2 Line a glass loaf pan with the cooked spinach leaves.

3. Place the shallot in a small bowl and cover loosely. Cook for 1 minute on HIGH to soften.

4. Cut the plaice or sole fillets into long, thin strips.

5. Skin the salmon and remove any bones. Cut into small pieces. Place in a food processor or blender with the breadcrumbs, light cream, egg white, shallot and salt.

6. Process to a smooth purée. Fold in the heavy cream and green peppercorns by hand.

7. Spread one third of the salmon mixture over the bottom of the terrine dish on top of the spinach leaves. Arrange half of the plaice or sole strips on top and then cover with another third of the salmon mixture.

8. Repeat with the remaining fish strips and salmon mixture. Fold the spinach leaves over the top of the mixture and cover the dish loosely with plastic wrap.

9. Place the terrine in a shallow dish half filled with hot water. Cook on MEDIUM for 14-16 minutes.

Step 7 Layer the fish strips and puréed salmon mixture on top of the spinach.

10. Remove the terrine and leave to cool slightly. Loosen the edges carefully with a knife and invert the terrine onto a serving plate.

Cook's Notes

 TIME: Preparation takes 25 minutes. Cooking takes 16-18 minutes.

 COOK'S TIP: Rinse the green peppercorns several times in cold water to remove some of their hotness whilst retaining the peppery taste.

 SERVING IDEAS: Serve hot with hollandaise sauce or choron sauce from the recipe for Salmon Steaks with Sauce Choron. Serve cold with mayonnaise.

GARLIC SHRIMP AND MUSHROOMS

SERVES 4

*Seafood appetizers are always a popular choice and shrimp with
mushrooms make an excellent combination.*

4-8 oyster or wild mushrooms, depending on size
½ cup butter
1 large clove garlic, chopped
Salt and pepper
Lemon juice
1½ lbs raw shrimp, peeled
2 tbsps chopped parsley

4. Cook for 30 seconds more on HIGH, if required, to cook the shrimp thoroughly.

5. Mix in the parsley and add more seasoning if necessary. Arrange the mushrooms in individual dishes and spoon over the shrimp and any remaining butter in the dish.

Step 2 Cook the mushrooms in the melted butter with the garlic, seasoning and lemon juice.

Step 3/4 Cook the shrimp thoroughly.

1. Leave the mushrooms whole, but remove the stalks. Rinse, if necessary.

2. Melt the butter in a shallow casserole for 30 seconds on HIGH. Add the mushrooms, garlic, salt, pepper and lemon juice. Cook for 2 minutes on HIGH. Remove and set aside.

3. Add the shrimp to the casserole and cook on HIGH for 1 minute, stirring several times.

Step 5 Mix in the parsley and add more seasoning, if necessary.

Cook's Notes

 TIME: Preparation takes about 10 minutes, and cooking takes 3-4 minutes.

 VARIATION: If oyster or wild mushrooms are not available use large flat mushrooms.

 SERVING IDEAS: Accompany with hot French bread.

SPICY POTTED SHRIMP

SERVES 4

This favorite seafood appetizer gets a new flavor with the addition of ground spices to the butter.

12oz cooked fresh or frozen shrimp
¾ cup butter
1 tsp grated nutmeg
½ tsp ground ginger
½ tsp freshly ground pepper
½ tsp paprika
Lemon wedges and small parsley sprigs or dill to
  garnish

Step 2 Skim any salt from the surface of the melted butter and discard it.

1. If using frozen shrimp, defrost and dry well on paper towels. To clarify the butter, heat on MEDIUM for 2 minutes. Leave the butter to stand for about 15 minutes.

2. Skim the salt from the top of the butter and carefully pour or spoon off the clear butter oil. Discard the milky sediment in the bottom of the dish.

3. Combine the clarified butter and the spices in a clean bowl and cook for 1 minute on HIGH.

4. Stir in the shrimp and spoon the mixture into 6 small custard cups pressing it down firmly.

Step 4 Combine the butter, spices and shrimps and press the mixture into individual custard cups.

5. Spoon over any remaining butter, cover and chill until firm.

6. To serve, turn out the shrimp onto small plates and garnish with lemon wedges and sprigs of parsley or dill.

Cook's Notes

 TIME: Preparation takes about 5 minutes, however, the shrimp will need at least 2 hours to chill until firm. Cooking takes 3 minutes.

 PREPARATION: This dish may be prepared a day in advance and kept in the refrigerator.

SERVING IDEAS: Melba toast or hot whole-wheat toast triangles make good accompaniments.

POTTED SMOKED FISH

SERVES 4

*This smooth fish pâté can be prepared well in advance and will keep
fresh under a layer of clarified butter.*

2 smoked or kippered fish fillets
1 tbsp butter or margarine
1 tbsp all-purpose flour
1/3 cup cream cheese
1/3 cup milk
6-8 pimento-stuffed olives, sliced
2 tsps Dijon mustard
Salt and pepper
1 cup butter for clarifying
Pimento-stuffed olives and black peppercorns to
  garnish

1. Skin the fish fillets and break up into small
pieces. Melt butter for 1 minute on HIGH.

2. Stir in the flour and cook for 2 minutes on
HIGH. Blend in the cheese, milk, half the olives,
mustard and seasoning.

3. Add fish and mix until well blended. Put into
four custard cups and smooth the tops of each.

4. Cover individually with plastic wrap and cook
for 1 minute on HIGH to set the mixture.

5. Put butter into a medium bowl and heat for
3-4 minutes on HIGH, or until boiling. Leave to
stand for 10-15 minutes.

6. Skim the salt off the top and spoon the butter oil
carefully over each pot of fish. Fill nearly to the top,
and leave until almost set.

7. Place the remaining olives and peppercorns on
top of the butter. Chill until set, then cover the
decoration with another thin layer of clarified
butter and refrigerate again.

Step 2 Make a very
thick roux and add
the cheese, milk, half
the olives, the
mustard and
seasoning.

Step 3 Stir in the fish
and pack the mixture
into small dishes.

Step 6 Carefully
spoon a layer of
clarified butter over
the top of each
portion.

Cook's Notes

TIME: Preparation takes about
15 minutes, and cooking takes
about 8 minutes. The pâté needs at
least 2 hours chilling time.

SERVING IDEAS: Serve as a
starter or snack with hot
ordinary or melba toast or savory
biscuits.

COOK'S TIP: Clarified butter
can be used to seal pâtés and
this will keep them fresh in the
refrigerator for several days if the
seal is unbroken. It can also be used
in conventional cooking for sautéing
without the usual danger of burning.

SPARKLING SHRIMP

SERVES 4

Sparkling wine peps up this special occasion appetizer.

Juice and grated rind of half an orange
1 tbsp green peppercorns in brine, rinsed
½ cup sparkling dry white wine
Salt and pepper
1½lbs peeled shrimp
½ cup heavy cream

1. Put orange rind and juice, peppercorns, wine and seasoning into a bowl. Heat for 30 seconds on HIGH.

2. Stir in the shrimp and heat for 1 minute on HIGH.

3. Lightly whip the cream, fold in, and heat for a further 1 minute on HIGH.

4. Adjust seasoning before putting into serving dishes. Garnish with the orange slices.

Step 1 Cook the orange juice and rind with the wine, peppercorns and seasoning.

Step 3 Fold in the lightly whipped cream.

Cook's Notes

 TIME: Preparation takes about 5 minutes and cooking takes 2½ minutes.

 SERVING IDEAS: This starter can also be served cold. Allow the wine mixture to cool before folding in the shrimp and cream.

$ BUYING GUIDE: Green peppercorns in brine are available from large supermarkets or delicatessens. Dried and fresh green peppercorns are also available.

BOUILLABAISSE
SERVES 4

This classic fish soup usually takes a lot longer to cook.
The microwave version is just as delicious and so much faster.

12oz assorted fish (e.g. monkfish, red snapper, cod)
8oz assorted cooked shellfish (shrimp, lobster, scallops, crab)
2 leeks, cleaned and thinly sliced
1 small bulb fennel, sliced
1 clove garlic, crushed
2 tbsps olive oil
1 strip orange rind
Few shreds saffron
1 bay leaf
1 tsp lemon juice
3 cups water
½ cup white wine
1 tbsp tomato paste
Salt and pepper
2 tomatoes, skinned, seeded and roughly chopped
1 tbsp chopped parsley
¼ cup prepared mayonnaise mixed with 1 clove garlic, crushed, and a pinch of cayenne pepper
4 slices French bread, toasted

1. Cut fish into 1-inch pieces. Remove shells from shellfish and cut crab and lobster into small pieces.

2. Put the leeks, fennel, garlic and olive oil into a large casserole. Cover and cook for 3 minutes on HIGH.

3. Add the orange rind, saffron, bay leaf, lemon juice, water and wine. Stir in the tomato paste and seasoning and mix well.

4. Add fish and tomatoes and cook for 5 minutes, covered, on HIGH.

5. Add shellfish and parsley, and cook for 2 minutes on HIGH. Leave to stand, covered, for 2 minutes before serving.

6. Mix the mayonnaise, garlic and cayenne pepper and spread on the pieces of toasted French bread. Place the bread in the bottom of the serving dish and spoon over the soup.

Step 1 Cut the fish into even-sized pieces. Remove the crab and the lobster meat from the shells and chop.

Step 6 Place a piece of French bread in the bottom of each serving bowl and spoon over the soup.

Cook's Notes

 TIME: Preparation takes about 15 minutes, and cooking takes 10 minutes.

 VARIATION: If fresh fennel is unavailable, add 1 tbsp fennel seed.

 SERVING IDEAS: If desired, the bread croûtes and garlic mayonnaise may be omitted and the soup served with hot bread.

CREAM OF SMOKED HADDOCK SOUP

SERVES 4

*This soup is rich and wonderfully creamy. It makes a delicious lunch
or light supper with French bread.*

1lb smoked haddock fillets, skinned
2 cups hot fish or vegetable stock
8oz potatoes, peeled and diced
1 large onion, peeled and chopped
2 sticks celery, peeled and diced
Salt and pepper
1 tbsp lemon juice
2 cups milk
2 hard-cooked eggs, chopped
2 tbsps chopped parsley

1. Place the fish in a shallow pan and pour over a few spoonfuls of stock. Loosely cover the dish and cook for 4-5 minutes or until the fish is cooked through.

2. Flake the fish finely, discarding any bones. Set aside.

3. Place the potatoes, onion, celery and remaining stock in a bowl. Cover loosely and cook for about 10 minutes, stirring occasionally during cooking.

Step 3 Cook the potatoes with the onion, celery and stock until fork tender.

4. Add the fish to the potato mixture, season with salt and pepper and stir in the lemon juice. Add the milk.

Step 4 Stir the fish, seasoning and lemon juice into the potato mixture. Do not break up the potatoes too much.

5. Cover loosely and cook for a further 5 minutes on HIGH.

6. Allow the soup to stand for about 2 minutes before serving. Garnish with the chopped hard-cooked egg and parsley.

Step 6 Sprinkle evenly with the chopped egg and parsley.

Cook's Notes

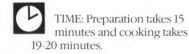 TIME: Preparation takes 15 minutes and cooking takes 19-20 minutes.

 VARIATION: Smoked cod can be used instead of haddock.

 WATCHPOINT: Smoked fish is usually quite salty so season with care.

SMOKED SALMON CREAM SOUP

SERVES 4

*This soup is perfect for a dinner party because it tastes so special but
is very easy to make.*

8oz whitefish, cut into 1-inch chunks
½ cup white wine
3 tbsps butter or margarine
2 tbsps flour
3 cups milk
Pepper
8oz smoked salmon, cut into 1-inch pieces
½ cup light cream
Salt
Sour cream
Chopped chives

frequently, until thickened.

4. Add the pepper, smoked salmon and cream.
Blend in a food processor until smooth.

5. Reheat for 1 minute on HIGH loosely covered
and add salt to taste. Garnish each serving with a
spoonful of sour cream and a sprinkling of
chopped chives.

Step 3 Cook the
flour, milk, fish and
cooking liquid
together until
thickened.

Step 1 Cook the fish
and wine in a loosely
covered bowl.

Step 5 Return the
puréed soup to the
rinsed bowl to reheat.

1. Cook the whitefish and wine for 2 minutes on
HIGH.

2. Melt the butter for 30 seconds on HIGH. Stir in
the flour, milk, whitefish and its cooking liquid.

3. Cook for 5-6 minutes on HIGH, stirring

Cook's Notes

 TIME: Preparation takes 15
minutes and cooking takes
7-8 minutes.

 SERVING IDEAS: For special
dinner parties add a spoonful
of salmon caviar as a garnish.

 ECONOMY: Whilst this soup is
expensive, the cost can be cut
slightly by using offcuts of smoked
salmon.

WATERZOI

SERVES 4-6

This Dutch fish soup adapts well to microwave cooking. The stock can be made in advance and frozen for later use.

1lb whitefish such as turbot, monkfish, cod or freshwater fish such as pike or perch, skin and bones reserved
Bouquet garni (1 bay leaf, sprig thyme, parsley stalks)
6 black peppercorns
1 tbsp lemon juice
2 shallots, finely chopped
½ cup dry white wine
4oz carrots, cut into thin rounds
2 sticks celery, thinly sliced
2 leeks, well washed and cut into thin rounds
Salt and pepper
Scant 1 cup heavy cream
3 tbsps chopped parsley

Step 1 Combine the fish bones and trimmings with the water, bouquet garni, black peppercorns and lemon juice to make a fish stock.

1. Combine the fish bones and trimmings with 1¾ cups water, the bouquet garni, black peppercorns and lemon juice in a large, deep bowl. Cook for 10 minutes on HIGH and then strain.

2. Discard the bouquet garni and the fish bones and trimmings.

3. Combine this fish stock with the shallots, wine, carrots, celery and leeks in a large, deep bowl. Cover loosely and cook for about 6 minutes on HIGH, or until the vegetables are nearly tender.

4. Cut the fish into 2-inch pieces and add to the bowl. Season with salt and pepper, re-cover the bowl and cook for a further 6-8 minutes on HIGH or until done.

5. Stir in the heavy cream and leave the soup to stand for 2 minutes before serving.

6. Top each bowl with a sprinkling of chopped parsley before serving. The soup should be thin.

Step 3 Cook the vegetables in the stock until nearly tender.

Step 4 Add the fish and cook until all the ingredients are done.

 Cook's Notes _____

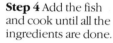 TIME: Preparation takes 20 minutes and cooking takes 12-14 minutes plus 2 minutes standing time.

 SERVING IDEAS: Waterzoi is often served with boiled potatoes.

$ BUYING GUIDE: Ready-made bouquets garnis, some especially for fish cooking, are available in the herbs and spices section of supermarkets and delicatessens.

CHEESE AND CLAM CHOWDER

SERVES 4

Chowders are quick creamy soups that are as filling as a main course. This one gets its color and flavor from Red Leicester cheese.

2 tbsps butter or margarine
1 onion, finely chopped
2 sticks celery, chopped
1 green pepper, chopped
2 tbsps flour
½ tsp dry mustard
3½ cups milk
2lbs canned clams, liquid reserved
2 cups potatoes, diced
¼ tsp thyme
Salt and pepper
1 bay leaf
1 cup Red Leicester cheese, grated
Dash Worcestershire sauce
Light cream
2 tbsps chopped parsley

1. Put the butter or margarine, onion, celery and pepper into a large bowl. Cover loosely and cook on HIGH for 2 minutes.

2. Stir in the flour, mustard, milk and clam liquid. Blend well and add potatoes, thyme, salt and pepper.

3. Put in the bay leaf, and cook on HIGH for 10 minutes, stirring occasionally.

4. Remove the bay leaf and add the clams, cheese and Worcestershire sauce. Heat for 2 minutes on MEDIUM to melt the cheese.

5. Add light cream to thin the soup if it is too thick. Garnish with the parsley and serve immediately.

Step 2 Stir the flour and mustard together well before adding the liquid ingredients gradually.

Step 4 Add the clams, cheese and Worcestershire sauce to the soup before heating to melt the cheese.

Cook's Notes

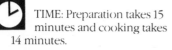

TIME: Preparation takes 15 minutes and cooking takes 14 minutes.

PREPARATION: This soup does not reheat well, as the cheese will become stringy and the clams will toughen.

VARIATION: Octopus, mussels or cockles may be substituted for the clams. Scrub mussel shells well removing seaweed "beards". Steam open and and discard any mussels with unopened shells.

CURRIED SHRIMP SOUP

SERVES 4

A quick and colorful soup with the spicy taste of curry and the sharp flavor of apple.

3 tbsps butter or margarine
1 tbsp curry powder
1 shallot, finely chopped
1 apple, peeled, quartered, cored and cut into dice
3 tbsps flour
2 cups fish or vegetable stock
2 cups milk
12oz-1lb cooked, peeled shrimp
½ cup natural yogurt

1. Melt the butter, add the curry powder and cook for 1 minute on HIGH.

Step 2 Stir the shallot and diced apple into the curry powder and butter.

2. Stir in the shallot and apple and cook for a further 2 minutes on HIGH.

3. Stir in the flour and when well blended pour on the stock. Stir well and cook for a further 4 minutes on HIGH, or until thickened.

Step 4 Purée the soup until smooth before adding the milk.

Step 6 Add the yogurt, which can be swirled through the soup using the blade of a knife to make an attractive pattern.

4. Leave to cool. Pour into a food processor or blender and purée until smooth.

5. Add the milk and cook for 1-2 minutes on HIGH.

6. Add the shrimp and leave to stand for 2-3 minutes before serving. Top with natural yogurt.

Cook's Notes

 TIME: Preparation takes 15 minutes and cooking takes 8-9 minutes, plus an extra 2-3 minutes standing time.

 COOK'S TIP: Cooking curry powder or other spices before adding liquid gives them a mellower flavor.

 SERVING IDEAS: If desired, cooked rice may be added to each serving. Heat through before adding the shrimp.

ORANGE BAKED FISH

SERVES 4

Quick to prepare, this dish uses the tangy taste of orange to offset the richness of the herring.

4 herrings
4 bay leaves
4 tbsps butter
Juice and grated zest of ½ orange
1 tbsp chopped dill
Orange slices

Step 1 Place a bay leaf inside each fish, before placing on a sheet of non-stick parchment.

1. Rinse the fish and dry well. Place a bay leaf inside each fish. Place each fish on a sheet of non-stick baking paper.

2. Put the butter in a small bowl and cook on HIGH for 30 seconds to 1 minute to soften slightly.

3. Beat in the orange juice, zest and dill. Divide the butter into four and spread some over each of the fish.

4. Wrap each parcel separately, making sure the fish is totally enclosed.

5. Cook on HIGH for 6-8 minutes, until the fish is cooked, turning the fish parcels halfway through the cooking time. Serve in the paper garnished with orange slices.

Step 3 Spread the orange butter mixture over the outside of each fish.

Step 4 Seal up the parcels of fish twisting the edges of the parchment together.

Cook's Notes

 TIME: Preparation takes 10 minutes and cooking takes 6-8 minutes.

 PREPARATION: If preferred, or if the fish is large, the head and tail of the fish may be removed before or after cooking.

 VARIATION: Other herbs such as tarragon or chives may be used instead of the dill.

SERVING IDEAS: Green beans and almonds or snow peas make a good accompaniment to this dish.

SIMPLE FISH CURRY

SERVES 4

A delicious curry sauce spices up mild-flavored cod or haddock.

2 tbsps butter or margarine
1 onion, chopped
½ tsp ground turmeric
1 tsp ground cumin
1 tbsp ground coriander
1 tsp paprika
Pinch mace
1 tsp fennel seed
1 tbsp flour
1 cup water
1 bay leaf
1 tbsp chopped parsley
1 tbsp shredded coconut
1lb haddock or cod, cut in large chunks
Chopped coriander leaves

1. Melt the butter in a shallow pan or casserole and add the onion, spices and fennel seed and cook for 2 minutes on HIGH.

Step 1 Cook the fennel seed with the onion and spices in a shallow dish.

2. Add the flour and water and blend well. Add the bay leaf and cook for 5-6 minutes on HIGH to thicken.

Step 2 Add the flour and water and blend together well to make a smooth sauce.

3. Add the parsley, coconut and fish and cook for 3-5 minutes or until the fish is tender.

Step 3 Cook the fish in the sauce until if flakes easily.

4. Remove the bay leaf and garnish with chopped coriander leaves.

Cook's Notes

 TIME: Preparation takes about 20 minutes and cooking takes 10-13 minutes.

 VARIATION: This dish is also delicious made with shrimp. If using cooked shrimp, prepare sauce and reheat with the shrimp for about 1 minute.

SERVING IDEAS: Serve with plain rice or rice pilaff and a choice of chutney or pickle.

RAIE AU BEURRE NOIR

SERVES 4

*Delicious meaty skate cooks so easily in a microwave oven that you
can enjoy it in its classic brown butter sauce more often.*

4 skinned wings of skate, about 1½lbs in total weight
6 tbsps butter
2 tbsps capers
Juice of 1 lemon
2 tsps chopped parsley
Salt and pepper
Parsley sprigs

Step 1 Arrange the skate wings, thin edges to the center, in a microproof baking dish.

1. Arrange the skate wings in a casserole dish with the thin edges towards the middle. Cover and cook on HIGH for 8-10 minutes.

2. Leave covered while preparing the butter sauce. Heat a browning dish according to the manufacturer's instructions.

3. Add the butter and cook until golden. Add the capers and stir them in the butter for 1 minute.

4. Reheat until the butter is a nut-brown color.

5. Add the lemon juice, parsley, salt and pepper and pour over the fish to serve. Garnish with whole sprigs of parsley if desired.

Step 3 Add the capers to the melted butter in the browning dish.

Step 4 Reheat the butter until nut-brown in color.

Cook's Notes

 TIME: Preparation takes 10 minutes and cooking takes 12-14 minutes.

 COOK'S TIP: When using a browning dish, always wear oven gloves to handle the hot dish. Also place it on a heatproof mat to protect work surfaces.

VARIATION: Capers are the classic ingredient but, if desired, finely chopped shallot or onion can be substituted and cooked in the butter.

POISSON SUPRÊME

SERVES 4

*A classic French dish easily made in your microwave oven — perfect
for a fish lovers' dinner party.*

4 large plaice fillets, skinned
4 tbsps dry white wine
1 bay leaf
2 parsley stalks
4 black peppercorns
2 tbsps butter or margarine
1 shallot, finely chopped
2 carrots, peeled and cut into thin 2-inch strips
3 sticks celery, cut into thin 2-inch strips
¾ cup mushrooms, sliced
2 tbsps flour
1 cup milk
2 tsps chopped fresh thyme or tarragon
2 tbsps heavy cream
Salt and white pepper

1. Fold the fish fillets in half and place in a shallow dish, thin ends towards the middle. Pour over the white wine and add the bay leaf, parsley stalks and peppercorns.

2. Cover loosely and cook for 5-6 minutes, or until the fish is tender. Pour off and reserve the cooking juices. Leave the fish covered while preparing the sauce.

3. Place the butter in a deep bowl and melt for 30 seconds on HIGH. Stir in the shallot and cook for 2 minutes on HIGH, stirring occasionally until softened.

4. Add the carrots and celery and loosely cover the bowl. Cook for 6 minutes on HIGH, stirring frequently until the carrots and celery are almost tender.

5. Add the mushrooms and stir in the flour carefully. Add the milk gradually, stirring constantly. Re-cover the dish and cook for a further 2 minutes on HIGH, stirring occasionally to keep the sauce smooth.

6. Add the thyme, cream and salt and pepper. Place the fish in a serving dish, cover with the sauce and reheat for 1 minute on HIGH.

Step 1 Fold the fillets in half and place in a round dish with the thickest part to the outside of the dish.

Step 6 Cover the fish with the sauce and reheat in a microproof serving dish.

Cook's Notes

 TIME: Preparation takes about 20 minutes and cooking takes 12-13 minutes.

 COOK'S TIP: Positioning food so that the thin ends are towards the center of the dish prevents them overcooking.

 SERVING IDEAS: Cooked, peeled shrimps makes a good addition to the sauce for dinner parties. Serve the dish with rice or new potatoes.

COD STEAKS WITH MUSHROOMS AND PINK PEPPERCORNS

SERVES 4

A creamy sauce studded with bright pink peppercorns lifts everyday fish like cod out of the ordinary.

4-8 cod steaks, depending on size
½ cup white wine
1 bay leaf
2 shallots, finely chopped
2 tbsps butter or margarine
1½ cups mushrooms, sliced
2 tbsps flour
½ cup milk
2 tsps pink peppercorns
2 tsps chopped parsley
Grated nutmeg
Salt and pepper

1. Put the cod and wine into a casserole with the thin ends of the steaks pointing towards the middle.

2. Add the bay leaf and shallot. Cover loosely and cook for 6 minutes on HIGH. Leave covered and set aside.

3. Melt the butter in a small bowl for 30 seconds on HIGH. Add the mushrooms, cover loosely and cook for 1 minute on HIGH to soften slightly.

4. Stir in the flour and milk and strain on the cooking liquid from the fish. Add the peppercorns, parsley, a pinch of grated nutmeg and salt and pepper.

5. Cook, uncovered, for 2-3 minutes on HIGH, stirring often until thickened.

6. Remove the skin and bone from the cod steaks if desired and spoon over some of the sauce to serve. Serve the remaining sauce separately.

Step 2 Loosely cover the fish with plastic wrap or with a lid set at a slight angle.

Step 4 Add the peppercorns, parsley, nutmeg and seasoning to the sauce and cook to thicken.

Cook's Notes

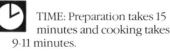 TIME: Preparation takes 15 minutes and cooking takes 9-11 minutes.

SERVING IDEAS: Serve with rice or new potatoes and a green vegetable such as beans, broccoli or snow peas.

 BUYING GUIDE: Pink peppercorns, also called pink berries, are available in the spice section of specialist shops and delicatessens.

SALMON STEAKS WITH SAUCE CHORON

SERVES 4

This Hollandaise-type sauce is not difficult to make when you have a microwave oven, and it's delicious with salmon.

---

4 salmon steaks, about 1½lbs in total weight
½ cup butter
3 egg yolks
Juice and rind of 1 orange
1 tbsp lemon juice
Salt and pepper
2 tbsps heavy cream

---

1. Pin the ends of the salmon steaks together with wooden picks.

Step 1 Pin the ends of each salmon steak together with wooden picks.

2. Arrange in a round dish with the secured ends towards the middle. Cover loosely and cook on MEDIUM for 8-12 minutes, or until just cooked. Turn the fish over halfway through the cooking time. Leave covered whilst preparing the sauce.

3. In a glass measure, melt the butter for 1 minute on HIGH. Beat the egg yolks with the orange juice and rind, lemon juice and salt and pepper. Stir the mixture gradually into the butter.

Step 3 Gradually add the egg yolk mixture to the hot butter, whisking constantly.

4. Cook on LOW for 15 seconds and whip. Repeat every 15 seconds until the sauce thickens, about 3 minutes. Place the bowl in iced water if the sauce starts to curdle. Stir in the cream.

Step 4 After about 30 seconds, the sauce will begin to thicken. Whisk often to ensure a smooth consistency.

5. Arrange the salmon steaks on a serving dish and pour over some of the sauce. Serve the rest of the sauce separately.

Cook's Notes

 TIME: Preparation takes 15 minutes and cooking takes 11-15 minutes.

 COOK'S TIP: Hollandaise-type sauces are best cooked on a low setting. Medium settings can be used, but watch the sauce carefully. Do not reheat.

SERVING IDEAS: Serve with asparagus and new potatoes.

WHOLE SALMON

SERVES 6-8

When you have a microwave oven you can very easily cook a whole fish with delicious results.

3½lb salmon, cleaned, with head and tail
    left on
Whole fresh herbs, such as dill or tarragon
Oil for brushing
Lemon slices or wedges
Sliced cucumber
Fresh herbs

1. Wash the salmon and pat dry. Place the fresh herbs inside the cavity of the fish and brush the skin on both sides with oil.

2. Use foil to cover the thin end of the tail and the head to prevent overcooking. Wrap the whole fish in several thicknesses of plastic wrap.

3. Make an incision along the skin on either side of the dorsal fin to allow steam to escape and prevent the skin bursting.

4. Lay the fish flat on the turntable, if it will fit, or curve it to fit the shape of the turntable. If curving the fish, tie loosely with string to hold the shape.

5. Cook for 8-9 minutes per 1lb on LOW or DEFROST. About halfway through the cooking time, remove the string and uncover the head and tail to allow them to cook through.

6. To see if the salmon is cooked, slip a sharp knife through one of the slits made on either side of the dorsal fin. If the blade passes through without resistance, the fish is cooked.

7. Allow the fish to cool slightly and then peel away the skin carefully. Start at the dorsal fin with a sharp knife and carry on peeling with a round-bladed table knife which should slip easily between the skin and the flesh.

8. Transfer the fish carefully to a serving plate, removing the herbs from the cavity.

9. Garnish with cucumber, lemon slices or wedges and fresh herbs to serve.

Step 3 Make an incision along the dorsal fin on both sides of the salmon to allow the steam to escape.

Step 4 Tie the head to the tail with a loop of string to keep the fish in a curved shape.

Cook's Notes

 TIME: Preparation takes 20 minutes and cooking takes 8-9 minutes per 1lb of salmon.

 PREPARATION: Skinning fish is much easier whilst it is still warm.

COOK'S TIP: The foil will deflect the microwaves and the plastic wrap will keep the foil from arcing.

 SERVING IDEAS: Serve hot with new potatoes and Hollandaise sauce or cold with mayonnaise and a green salad.

SCAMPI PROVENÇALE

SERVES 4

Sit down to this classic seafood dish in double-quick time with the help of your trusty microwave oven.

2 tbsps olive oil
1 onion, finely chopped
1 clove garlic, crushed
14oz canned plum tomatoes, juice reserved
5 tbsps dry white wine
¼ tsp thyme
1 tsp basil
1 tbsp chopped parsley
1 bay leaf
Salt and pepper
2 tsps cornstarch
1½lbs scampi, shelled

1. Combine the olive oil, onion and garlic in a deep bowl and cook for 5 minutes on HIGH, stirring frequently.

2. Add the tomatoes, wine, herbs, bay leaf, salt and pepper and stir together well. Heat for 2 minutes on HIGH.

Step 2 After adding the tomatoes to the sauce, break them up using a fork or potato masher.

3. Mix the reserved tomato juice with the cornstarch and add to the sauce. Cook for 3 minutes on HIGH and stir well.

Step 3 Stir the cornstarch mixture into the hot sauce to blend smoothly.

4. Add the scampi to the sauce and cook for 2-4 minutes on HIGH or until they are tender and the sauce has thickened. Remove the bay leaf before serving.

Step 4 Cook the scampi in the sauce until they are tender and the sauce has thickened.

Cook's Notes

 TIME: Preparation takes 15 minutes and cooking takes 10 minutes.

VARIATION: If scampi are not available, substitute large shrimp.

 SERVING IDEAS: Rice is the usual accompaniment, but why not try pasta for a change?

STUFFED TROUT

SERVES 4

Whole fish cook quickly and evenly in a microwave oven and remain moist and flavorful.

4 tbsps butter
1½ cups fresh white breadcrumbs
2 tsps chopped fresh basil
2 tsps chopped parsley
1 clove garlic, crushed
4oz cooked peeled shrimp, roughly chopped
Salt and pepper
1 egg, beaten
4 trout, cleaned and boned
Juice of 1 lemon
Lemon slices
Whole fresh basil leaves

2. Stir in the breadcrumbs, herbs, garlic, shrimp, salt and pepper and enough egg to bind the mixture together.

3. Sprinkle the insides of the trout lightly with salt and pepper and fill each with some of the stuffing.

4. Place the trout in a large, shallow dish and sprinkle with lemon juice. Cover loosely with plastic wrap and cook for 6 minutes on HIGH.

5. Carefully reposition the trout, re-cover the dish and cook for another 7 minutes on HIGH.

Step 2 Add only enough egg to bind the stuffing ingredients together.

Step 5 Carefully reposition the trout halfway through cooking.

1. Place the butter in a small bowl and heat for 30 seconds on HIGH to melt.

6. Allow to stand for 3 minutes before serving. Garnish with lemon slices and basil leaves.

Cook's Notes

 TIME: Preparation takes 20 minutes and cooking takes 14 minutes.

 COOK'S TIP: Leave the large dorsal fin on each fish. When it pulls out easily, the fish is cooked.

 SERVING IDEAS: This makes an elegant dinner party dish for fish lovers. Serve with new potatoes and asparagus.

PICKLED HERRING

SERVES 4

Herring in a piquant marinade is a delicious choice for a light lunch.
A microwave oven cooks in all the flavor.

4 herrings, gutted and boned
1 onion, sliced in rings
½ cup white wine vinegar
½ cup water
4 peppercorns
4 allspice berries
2 tsps mustard seed
1 bay leaf
1 large sprig fresh dill
Salt
1 head lettuce
Fresh dill

glass measure and cook for 6-8 minutes on HIGH.

3. Allow to cool slightly and then pour over the fish. Leave the fish to cool in the liquid, cover and leave in the refrigerator overnight.

4. Serve the fish with some of the onions on a bed of lettuce, and garnish with sprigs of fresh dill if desired.

Step 2 Cook the vinegar mixture until boiling and then allow to cool slightly.

Step 1 Place the herring fillets in a single layer in a shallow dish.

Step 3 Pour the vinegar mixture over the fish, cover and leave to marinate.

1. Separate all the fish into whole fillets removing the heads, tails and fins. Place the fillets in a shallow dish, scatter over the onion and set aside.

2. Mix the vinegar, water, peppercorns, allspice berries, mustard seed, bay leaf, dill and salt in a

---

Cook's Notes

 TIME: Preparation takes 20 minutes, plus overnight marinating time. Cooking takes 6-8 minutes.

 VARIATION: Mackerel fillets may be prepared in the same way.

 SERVING IDEAS: Top with sour cream or natural yogurt. Accompany with a salad of fresh beet if desired.

SMOKED HADDOCK WITH PEAS AND PASTA

SERVES 4

This colorful fish and pasta dish tastes as good as it looks. It's ideal for a quick lunch or supper.

8oz smoked haddock fillets
1 cup milk
2 tbsps butter or margarine
2 tbsps flour
3 tbsps frozen peas
1 tbsp chopped chives
1 tbsp chopped parsley
1 hard-cooked egg, chopped
Salt and pepper
8oz pasta shells, cooked

1. Place the smoked haddock in a large, shallow dish and pour over 6 tbsps of the milk, reserving the rest.

2. Cook for 4-5 minutes on HIGH and leave to stand, covered, while preparing the sauce.

3. Melt the butter or margarine for 30 seconds on HIGH in a deep bowl or glass measure.

4. Stir in the flour and pour on the reserved milk. Strain the fish cooking liquid into the bowl and stir well. Cook on HIGH for 3 minutes, stirring once or twice.

5. Add the frozen peas to the sauce along with the chives and parsley. Cook for a further 2-3 minutes on HIGH, or until the sauce is thick and the peas are cooked.

6. Skin and flake the fish, removing any bones. Add to the sauce with the chopped hard-cooked egg and salt and pepper. Stir carefully.

7. Stir in the drained pasta shells. Heat through for 1 minute on HIGH before serving.

Step 7 Combine all the ingredients and return to the microwave to heat through.

Cook's Notes

TIME: Preparation takes about 15 minutes and cooking takes 10-12 minutes.

COOK'S TIP: Pasta can be cooked in a microwave oven. Combine 8oz pasta shapes with 3 cups boiling water. Cook for about 7-10 minutes on HIGH. Cover and let it stand for 5 minutes. Drain and rinse in hot water.

SERVING IDEAS: Serve with a tossed green salad for a light meal.

CRAB AU GRATIN

SERVES 4

Crabmeat in a creamy sauce gives a luxuriously rich flavor to this quick snack.

2 tbsps dry white wine
1 stick celery, finely chopped
1 shallot, finely chopped
7oz jar Cheddar cheese spread
4 tbsps heavy cream, lightly whipped
6oz fresh or frozen crabmeat
4 slices brown bread toast, crusts removed
Paprika
Salt and pepper

further 2 minutes on MEDIUM until piping hot.

4. Arrange the toast in a microproof baking dish and spoon over the cheese and crabmeat mixture.

5. Sprinkle with paprika and heat through on HIGH for 30 seconds to 1 minute. The toasts may be browned under a broiler before serving.

Step 3 Add the cream and crabmeat to the softened vegetables and cheese spread.

Step 4 Arrange the toast in a circle in a microproof baking dish. Spoon over the crabmeat mixture.

Step 5 Sprinkle the top of the toasts with paprika.

1. Place the white wine in a deep bowl and add the celery and shallot. Loosely cover the bowl and cook for 2-3 minutes on HIGH, stirring once or twice, until the vegetables are softened.

2. Stir in the Cheddar cheese spread and heat on MEDIUM for 30 seconds or until softened.

3. Stir in the cream and the crabmeat and heat for a

Cook's Notes

TIME: Preparation takes 15 minutes and cooking takes 6-8 minutes.

COOK'S TIP: Cheddar cheese spread can be used any time as a quick cheese sauce. It heats well in a microwave oven without curdling or becoming stringy. Putting the toast on a piece of kitchen paper ensures that the toast stays crisp.

SERVING IDEAS: Serve as a snack or light lunch. Serve with a salad, or put cooked broccoli or asparagus on the toast before topping with the sauce.

SMOKY CHEESE AND SHRIMP DIP

SERVES 4

Delicious as a snack and with drinks, this dip will be a popular addition to your recipe file.

1 tbsp butter
1 shallot, finely chopped
1½ cups Cheddar cheese, shredded
1 cup smoked or smoky cheese, shredded
1 tbsp all-purpose flour
¾ cup light cream
Salt and pepper
¾ cup cooked shrimp, chopped
Raw vegetables

1. Melt the butter in a small, deep bowl for 30 seconds on HIGH.

2. Add the shallot and cook for 1 minute on HIGH to soften.

3. Toss the cheeses and flour together and add to the bowl with the shallot. Stir in the cream, salt and pepper.

4. Cook for 4 minutes on MEDIUM or until the cheese has melted. Stir the mixture twice whilst cooking. Stir in the shrimp.

5. Serve hot with raw vegetables for dipping.

Step 1 Cover the bowl loosely while melting the butter to prevent it spattering.

Step 3 Add the cream to the cheese and butter mixture.

Cook's Notes

 TIME: Preparation takes 15 minutes and cooking takes about 5 minutes.

 PREPARATION: Serve as soon as the dip is made. It does not reheat well.

 VARIATION: If smoked cheese is not to your taste, add extra Cheddar or 1 cup Gruyère cheese.

SMOKED FISH IN A POTATO

SERVES 4

*This recipe only looks complicated. Once prepared and assembled,
these stuffed potatoes are quickly cooked.*

4 large baking potatoes
4 small smoked haddock fillets
4 tbsps water
½ cup milk
1 tbsp butter or margarine
1 tsp mild curry powder
2 tbsps butter or margarine
2 tbsps flour
Pinch dry mustard
Pinch cayenne pepper
1 cup milk
½ cup shredded cheese
Salt and pepper
1 tbsp chopped chives
Paprika

1. Wash the potatoes and prick the skins several times with a fork. Bake the potatoes for 10-12 minutes on HIGH.

2. Wrap them in foil and leave to stand for 5 minutes.

3. Place the smoked haddock fillets in a shallow dish with the 4 tbsps water. Cover loosely and cook for 5 minutes on HIGH, or until the fish is tender.

4. Set the fish aside whilst heating the ½ cup milk on HIGH for 5 minutes.

5. Melt the 1 tbsp butter or margarine in a deep bowl for 30 seconds on HIGH. Stir in the curry powder and cook for a further 1 minute on HIGH.

6. Cut a slice off the top of each potato and scoop out the flesh, leaving a border inside the skin.

Step 7 Fill each potato equally with cooked haddock.

7. Skin and flake the smoked haddock, removing any bones. Put an equal portion of fish inside each potato shell.

8. Add the scooped out potato to the curry powder and butter in the bowl and mash well with a fork.

9. Gradually pour in the hot milk and continue mashing until smooth. It may not be necessary to add all the milk, but the potato must be soft yet still hold its shape. Set aside whilst preparing the sauce.

10. Melt the remaining butter or margarine in a small, deep bowl. Stir in the flour, mustard and cayenne pepper.

11. Gradually beat in the 1 cup milk and cook for 3-5 minutes on HIGH, stirring frequently, until thickened. Add the grated cheese, chopped chives and salt and pepper to taste and stir well.

12. Spoon an equal amount of the sauce mixture over the smoked haddock in each potato shell.

13. Pipe or spoon the potato mixture on top and sprinkle with paprika. Cook for 3-4 minutes on HIGH to heat through completely before serving.

Cook's Notes

 TIME: Preparation takes 20 minutes and cooking takes 26-32 minutes.

 PREPARATION: The potatoes may be cooked and filled in advance. If reheating from cold, add 1-2 minutes to the final cooking time.

 VARIATION: If preferred, the curry powder may be omitted.

PIZZA MARINARA

SERVES 4

*In only a few minutes you can cook these delicious seafood pizzas to
eat as a snack or as a light meal with a salad.*

4 tbsps tomato paste
1 tbsp dry white wine
1 tbsp water
2 green onions, chopped
½ tsp oregano
1 clove garlic, crushed
¾ cup shrimp, canned or frozen mussels, canned
   or fresh clams or cockles, or a combination of
   all three
8 anchovy fillets
4 black olives, pitted and sliced
2 tsps capers
¾ cup Mozzarella cheese, shredded
2 tbsps Parmesan cheese, shredded
Salt and pepper
4 English muffins, split

1. Mix the tomato paste with the wine, water,
green onion, oregano, garlic, salt and pepper.
Spread the halved muffins with this mixture.

2. Arrange the shellfish on top with a cross of
anchovies. Add the olives and capers and sprinkle
with the Mozzarella cheese.

3. Sprinkle the Parmesan cheese on last and
arrange the pizzas on a paper towel on a plate on
the oven turntable.

4. Cook for 2-4 minutes on HIGH, changing the
position of the pizzas once or twice during
cooking.

5. Leave to stand for 1 minute before serving.
Pizzas may be browned quickly under a preheated
broiler, if desired. Serve hot.

Step 1 Spread the
tomato mixture onto
the muffin halves.

Step 3 Place topped
pizzas on paper
towels and arrange
on a plate in a circle.

Step 4 Cook on
HIGH to melt the
cheese and heat the
pizzas through.
Finish by browning
under the broiler, if
desired.

Cook's Notes

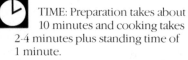 TIME: Preparation takes about
10 minutes and cooking takes
2-4 minutes plus standing time of
1 minute.

 VARIATION: Chopped peppers
or sliced mushrooms may be
included in the pizza topping.

 FREEZING: The pizzas may be
prepared in advance and
frozen. If freezing, use fresh shellfish
or canned tuna fish. Open freeze
and wrap individually.

Hot `n´ Spicy

Spices have been used in cookery for centuries. In the early days they were costly and were therefore a symbol of wealth in the East. During the Crusades, spices started to filter back to Europe and by the Middle Ages were already being used in British cookery. It was the opening of the spice routes in the nineteenth century which reduced the price of spices and made them available to rich and poor alike.

The popularity of spicy food has continued to grow, and although people still tend to associate spices with curries, there are many other dishes which use them to great advantage.

This chapter features recipes from all over the world which use a great variety of spices, some well known, others more unusual and exotic. In all the recipes, the spices lend their own particular characteristics to the dishes, introducing new and exciting flavors to stimulate and transform your cooking.

Thanks to the pioneers of old, there is no need for you to travel to far-off places to experience their spicy exotic food. With the help of this collection, you can create delicious hot and spicy dishes in the comfort of your own home.

SPICED FRIED SOUP

SERVES 4

Spicy and fragrant, this warming Indonesian soup is a meal in itself.

4-8 tbsps oil
1 clove garlic, peeled but left whole
1lb chicken breast, skinned, boned and cut into
small pieces
1 cake tofu, drained and cut into 1 inch cubes
½ cup raw cashew nuts
4 shallots, roughly chopped
1 carrot, very thinly sliced
3oz snow peas
2oz Chinese noodles, soaked for 5 minutes in hot
water and drained throughly
5 cups vegetable or chicken stock
Juice of 1 lime
¼ tsp turmeric
2 curry leaves
1 tsp grated fresh ginger
1 tbsp soy sauce
Salt and pepper

Step 2 Stir the chicken pieces into the hot oil, and stir-fry them until they begin to brown.

Step 6 Fry the noodles on one side, until they have browned. Turn them over to brown the other side.

1. Heat some of the oil in a wok or large frying pan. Add the garlic and cook until brown. Remove the garlic from the pan and discard.

2. Add the chicken pieces and cook in the oil, until they begin to brown. Remove the pieces and drain well.

3. Add a little more oil and cook the tofu until lightly brown. Remove and drain well.

4. Add the cashews and cook, stirring constantly until toasted. Remove and drain well.

5. Add a little more oil and fry the shallots and carrots until lightly browned. Stir in the snow peas and cook for 1 minute. Remove from the pan and drain.

6. Heat the oil in the wok until it is very hot, adding any remaining from the original amount. Add the noodles and cook quickly until brown on one side. Turn over and brown the other side.

7. Lower the heat and pour in the stock. Stir in the lime juice, turmeric, curry leaves, ginger, soy sauce and seasoning. Cover and simmer gently for 1¼10 minutes, stirring occasionally, to prevent the noodles from sticking.

8. Add the fried ingredients and heat through for 5 minutes. Serve immediately.

Cook's Notes

 TIME: Preparation takes about 20 minutes and cooking takes about 20-25 minutes.

 COOK'S TIP: If it is not possible to buy raw cashew nuts, use well rinsed and dried salted cashew nuts, and do not fry them in the oil.

 VARIATION: Substitute 8oz of button or, if obtainable, wild mushrooms and 4oz shredded Chinese leaves in place of the chicken and vegetable stock, to make a delicious vegetarian meal.

DAAL SOUP

SERVES 6

Thick and hearty, this soup can be made with either red or yellow lentils.

1½ cups red or yellow lentils
3 cups water or stock
4 canned tomatoes, drained and crushed
1 green chili, sliced lengthways and seeded
2 tbsps natural yogurt or soured cream
1 tbsp butter
1 medium onion, chopped, or sliced into rings
Salt and pepper
1-2 sprigs fresh coriander leaves, chopped

Step 1 Wash the lentils thoroughly in cold water, rinsing and draining them 4 or 5 times.

1. Wash the lentils in 4-5 changes of water. Drain them well and put them into a large pan with water or stock.
2. Cover the pan and bring the lentils to the boil over a moderate heat. Reduce the heat and simmer for about 10-15 minutes. or until the lentils are soft. You may need to add extra water.
3. Using a balloon whisk, beat the lentils until they are smooth.
4. Add the tomatoes and chili and simmer for

2 minutes, then stir in the yogurt or soured cream. Reheat, but do not boil.

5. Melt the butter in a small pan and fry the onion gently, until it is soft, but not colored.

Step 3 Using a balloon whisk, beat the lentils until they are smooth.

Step 4 Add the tomatoes and chili and simmer for 2 minutes. Stir in the yogurt or soured cream.

6. Pour the soup into serving bowls and sprinkle over the chopped coriander leaves and the fried onion. Discard the green chilies before eating the soup.

Cook's Notes

 TIME: Preparation takes 15-20 minutes, and cooking takes about 15 minutes.

 PREPARATION: The cooked lentils can be puréed in a food processor or liquidizer.

 SERVING IDEAS: Serve with buttered brown bread or crisp rolls.

CHILI WITH THREE BEANS

SERVES 6

Although called a soup, this dish is so hearty that it is really a complete meal in itself.

3 tbsps vegetable oil
2 medium onions, roughly chopped
1 clove garlic, crushed
1 tbsp ground cumin
2 tsps paprika pepper
1 red or green chili, seeded and chopped
1½lbs ground beef
1¾lbs canned tomatoes
3oz tomato paste
1 tsp oregano
1 bay leaf
½ cup beer
Salt and pepper
¼ cup each of canned and drained red kidney beans, white kidney beans, pinto beans and chickpeas.

Step 3 Lightly brown the meat in the frying pan, breaking up any large lumps with a fork.

Step 5 Add the drained beans and chickpeas to the simmering tomato and beef soup, stirring well, to mix thoroughly.

Step 2 Add the garlic, cumin, paprika and chili to the cooked onions.

1. Heat the oil in a large pan. Add the onions and cook gently, until soft but not browned.

2. Add the garlic, cumin, paprika and chili. Cook for 1 minute, before stirring in the beef.

3. Cook the meat until it is lightly browned, breaking it up with a fork to prevent large lumps forming.

4. Stir in the tomatoes and their juice, the tomato paste, oregano, bay leaf and beer. Season to taste, then cover and simmer for 50 minutes, checking the level of liquid several times during cooking and adding a little water, if necessary.

5. Fifteen minutes before the end of the cooking time, stir in the drained beans and chickpeas.

Cook's Notes

TIME: Preparation takes 30 minutes, and cooking takes about 1 hour.

FREEZING: This soup can be frozen for up to three months.

PREPARATION: This soup can be prepared in advance and reheated.

SERVING IDEAS: Serve the soup with corn or tortilla chips and a garnish of sour cream, grated cheese, diced avocado, or chopped green onions.

CHILLED FISH CURRY

SERVES 4-8

*This sophisticated, mild curry will serve four as a refreshing summer
lunch, or eight as an elegant appetizer.*

8oz fresh salmon fillet
12oz whitefish fillet
Chicken stock
Salt and pepper
½ cup mayonnaise
2 cups natural yogurt
2 tsps curry powder
Juice and grated rind of ½ lemon
¾ cup peeled shrimp
Garnish
Kiwi fruit, peeled and sliced
Sprigs fresh mint
Flaked coconut

1. Put the salmon and whitefish fillets into a shallow
pan and add just enough chicken stock to cover.

2. Season to taste and simmer gently, until the fish
is just tender.

3. Remove the fish carefully from the cooking
liquor and leave to cool slightly.

4. In a medium-sized bowl, mix together the
mayonnaise and the yogurt. Blend in the curry
powder and the lemon juice and rind.

5. Flake the cooked fish, removing any bones and
skin. Mix the flaked fish into the curry sauce,
together with the shrimp.

6. Arrange the fish curry on serving plates and
garnish with slices of kiwi fruit, sprigs of fresh mint
and coconut flakes.

Step 4 Blend the
curry powder and the
lemon juice and rind
thoroughly into the
mayonnaise and
yogurt mixture.

Step 1 Put the salmon
and whitefish fillets
into a shallow pan
and pour over just
enough chicken stock
to cover.

Step 5 Flake the
cooked fish, making
sure that all skin and
bones are removed.

Cook's Notes

 TIME: Preparation takes about
20 minutes, and cooking takes
about 6 minutes.

 VARIATION: If you prefer, use
slices of peeled cucumber
instead of the kiwi fruit.

 SERVING IDEAS: Serve with
boiled new potatoes or rice and
a crisp mixed salad.

SEVICHE
SERVES 4

Do not be put off by the thought of eating raw fish, as the cod will "cook" in the spicy marinade and the result is absolutely delicious.

1lb cod fillets
Juice and grated rind of 2 limes
1 shallot, chopped
1 green chili pepper, seeded and finely chopped
1 tsp ground coriander
1 small green pepper, seeded and sliced
1 small red pepper, seeded and sliced
1 tbsp chopped fresh parsley
1 tbsp chopped fresh coriander leaves
4 green onions, chopped
2 tbsps olive oil
Salt and pepper
1 small lettuce

Step 2 Stir the lime juice and rind, together with the shallot and spices, into the strips of cod, mixing thoroughly to coat them evenly with the spice mixture.

Step 4 Stir the peppers, herbs, onion and oil into the drained fish.

Step 1 Cut the skinned cod fillets into thin strips across the grain, removing any bones you may find.

1. Skin the cod fillets and cut them into thin strips across the grain.

2. Put the cod strips into a bowl, pour over the lime juice and rind. Add the shallot, chili pepper and coriander, and stir well to coat the fish completely.

3. Cover the bowl and refrigerate for 24 hours, stirring occasionally.

4. When ready to serve, drain the fish and stir in the peppers, parsley, coriander leaves, onions and oil. Season to taste and serve on a bed of lettuce.

Cook's Notes

 TIME: Preparation takes about 20 minutes, plus 24 hours refrigeration.

 VARIATION: Substitute haddock or monkfish fillets for the cod.

 SERVING IDEAS: Serve with crusty French bread or tortilla chips.

SAMOSAS

SERVES 6

These crispy vegetable-stuffed triangles can be eaten either hot or cold.

Dough
2½ cups all-purpose flour
¼ tsp salt
¼ tsp baking powder
Water, to mix

Filling
3 tbsps oil
1 medium onion, chopped
1lb potatoes, scrubbed and cut into small dice
2 carrots, grated
¼ cup green peas, shelled
¼ cup green beans, chopped
1 tsp chili powder
1 tsp salt
1 tsp garam masala
½ tsp ground turmeric
1 tbsp lemon juice
Oil for deep frying

1. Make the dough by sifting the flour, salt and baking powder into a bowl and adding enough water, a little at a time, to mix to a soft, pliable dough. Cover and leave to stand for 30 minutes.

2. Heat the 3 tbsps oil and fry the onion gently, until it is just soft. Stir in the potatoes and carrots and cook for 3-4 minutes.

3. Add the peas and beans to the potato mixture, cook for a further 2 minutes, then stir in the spices and lemon juice. Cover and simmer until the potatoes are tender. Remove from the heat and allow to cool.

4. Divide the dough into 12 equal-sized balls. Roll each piece out on a floured board, to a thin circle about 6 inches in diameter.

5. Cut each circle in half. Dampen the straight edges of each semicircle and bring them together, overlapping slightly to make a cone.

6. Fill each cone as it is made with a little of the filling, then dampen the open edge and seal by pressing together firmly. For extra firmness you may want to dampen and fold this edge over.

7. Heat the oil for frying. Fry the samosas, a few at a time, until they are golden brown on both sides. Drain on paper towels.

Step 5 Dampen the straight edges of each semicircle and bring them together, overlapping slightly to form a cone, and fill with a little of the vegetable mixture.

Step 7 Fry the samosas, a few at a time, in just enough hot oil to cover.

Cook's Notes

 TIME: Preparation takes about 40 minutes, and cooking takes about 25 minutes.

 WATCHPOINT: Be careful when using chili powder, not to get it into the eyes or mouth. If this happens, rinse thoroughly with plenty of cold water.

 SERVING IDEAS: Serve hot or cold with salad and an Indian chutney.

PENNE WITH SPICY CHILI SAUCE

SERVES 4-6

Penne are hollow pasta tubes which can be bought at most supermarkets. Macaroni can be used equally as well.

1lb canned plum tomatoes
1 tbsp olive oil
2 cloves garlic, crushed
1 onion, chopped
4 strips bacon, chopped
2 red chili peppers, seeded and chopped
2 green onions, chopped
½ cup Pecorino or Parmesan cheese, grated
1lb penne or macaroni
Salt and pepper

1. Chop the tomatoes and sieve them to remove the pips.

2. Heat the oil in a frying pan and fry the garlic, onion and bacon gently for 6-8 minutes.

3. Add the sieved tomatoes, the chili peppers, chopped green onions and half of the cheese. Simmer gently for 20 minutes.

4. Cook the penne or macaroni in boiling water for 10-15 minutes, or until tender. Rinse under hot water and drain well.

5. Put the cooked penne into a warm serving dish and toss them in half of the sauce. Pour the remaining sauce over the top and sprinkle with the remaining cheese.

Step 3 Stir the sieved tomatoes, chili peppers, spring onions and half the cheese into the onion mixture.

Step 5 Toss the cooked penne in half of the sauce, mixing together well to coat evenly.

Cook's Notes

 TIME: Preparation takes about 15 minutes, and cooking takes about 40 minutes.

 VARIATION: Substitute ½ cup chopped button mushrooms for the bacon.

SERVING IDEAS: Garnish the serving dish with green onion flowers and serve with a mixed green salad.

 FREEZING: The sauce for this recipe will freeze for up to 2 months.

SPICED CHICKPEAS

SERVES 6

This very fragrant curry is delicious either on its own, or as part of a larger Indian meal.

1lb chickpeas, soaked overnight in cold water
3 tbsps oil
1 large onion, chopped
2 bay leaves
2 green chilies, sliced in half lengthways
1 inch piece cinnamon stick
1 inch piece fresh root ginger, grated
4 cloves garlic, crushed
1½ tsps ground coriander
4 cloves, ground
1 tsp cumin seeds, ground
Seeds of 4 large black cardamoms, ground
Seeds of 4 small cardamoms, ground
10 oz canned tomatoes, chopped
½ tsp black pepper
½ tsp salt
6 sprigs fresh coriander leaves, chopped

1. Cook the chickpeas in their soaking water, until they are soft. Drain and reserve 1 cup of the cooking liquid.

2. Heat the oil in a frying pan and fry the onions gently, until they are soft, but not colored. Add the bay leaves, chilies, cinnamon, ginger and garlic and fry for a further 1 minute.

3. Stir in the ground spices, the tomatoes and the salt and pepper.

4. Add the reserved chickpea cooking liquid and the drained chickpeas. Mix well. Sprinkle with the chopped coriander leaves, cover and simmer for 10 minutes, adding a little extra liquid, if necessary.

Step 1 Cook the chickpeas in their soaking water.

Step 2 Fry the bay leaves, cinnamon, ginger and garlic with the onion for 1 minute.

Step 4 Mix the chickpeas thoroughly into the spicy sauce.

Cook's Notes

 TIME: Preparation takes about 15 minutes, plus overnight soaking. Cooking takes about 45-50 minutes.

 PREPARATION: Add 1 tsp of baking powder to the chickpeas when soaking overnight, to make them really tender. The chickpeas can be cooked in a pressure cooker for 10-15 minutes.

WATCHPOINT: Take great care not to get the juice from the chilies into the eyes or mouth. If this happens, rinse thoroughly with cold water.

RED BEAN CURRY

SERVES 4

This colorful curry is very easy to make. The beans must be cooked thoroughly before use.

½ cup dried red kidney beans, soaked overnight
3 tbsps oil
2 medium onions, chopped
1 bay leaf
1 inch piece cinnamon stick
6 cloves
Seeds of 6 green cardamoms
2 green chilies, quartered
3 cloves garlic, crushed
1 inch piece fresh root ginger, grated
½ tsp chili powder
¼ tsp ground turmeric
1½ tsps ground coriander
1 tsp ground cumin
1 tsp garam masala
15oz canned tomatoes, chopped
½ tsp salt
2-3 sprigs fresh coriander leaves, chopped

1. Cook the kidney beans, boiling them rapidly for 10 minutes and then simmering for at least 30 minutes, until they are soft. Remove from the heat and allow them to cool in the cooking liquid.

2. Heat the oil in a large saucepan and cook the onions, until they are soft. Add the bay leaf, cinnamon, cloves and cardamoms and fry for 1 minute.

3. Add the green chilies, garlic and ginger, and fry for about 30 seconds, before mixing in the ground spices and cooking for a further 30 seconds, stirring continuously, to prevent them burning.

4. Add the tomatoes and season with the salt.

5. Drain the beans and reserve the cooking liquid. Add the beans to the tomatoes and mix well, bring to the boil, then stir in 1 cup of the bean liquid.

6. Simmer for 10 minutes, then stir in the chopped coriander.

Step 2 Fry the bay leaf, cinnamon, cloves and cardamoms for 1 minute in the hot oil.

Step 3 Stir the ground spices whilst frying, to prevent them burning, as this would taint the flavor of the sauce.

Cook's Notes

 TIME: Preparation takes about 15 minutes, plus overnight soaking. Cooking takes about 45 minutes.

PREPARATION: If you have a pressure cooker, you can cook the beans in it for about 10 minutes.

 VARIATION: Use any of the different types of dried beans, instead of the red kidney beans.

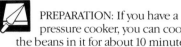 COOK'S TIP: This curry is a hot one. If you like a milder curry, remove the seeds from the green chilies before cooking.

TAMARIND CHICKEN SATAY
SERVES 4

Traditionally satay is served as only a part of a meal, but this version is so good that it needs only a tomato sambal as an accompaniment.

4 chicken breasts, skinned, boned and cut into
    ½ inch cubes
Marinade
1 tbsp oil
2 inch piece tamarind, soaked in ½ cup hot water
    or lemon juice
2 cloves garlic, crushed
1 tsp ground cardamom
½ tsp ground nutmeg
Salt and pepper
1 tsp kecap manis (sweet soy sauce)
Tomato and Chili Sambal
2 red chili peppers
1 small piece fresh ginger, grated
1 clove garlic, crushed.
1lb fresh tomatoes, peeled and seeded
4 tbsps oil
1 tbsp lemon or lime juice
1 tbsp dark brown sugar
Salt and pepper

Step 1 Put the chicken and marinade into a large bowl and stir to coat thoroughly.

Step 6 Cook the chicken skewers under a preheated broiler. Use a brush to baste them with the remaining marinade as they cook.

1. Put the chicken in a large bowl. Mix together the marinade ingredients and pour them over the chicken. Stir well and refrigerate for at least 30 minutes.

2. Grind together the chilies, ginger and garlic in a food processor, or using a pestle and mortar. Chop the tomatoes coarsely and blend them into the chili mixture.

3. Heat the oil in a wok or large frying pan and fry the tomato mixture for about 5-6 minutes, stirring occasionally to prevent it sticking. Add the lemon juice and a spoonful of water if the sauce becomes too thick.

4. Stir in the sugar and seasoning to taste.

5. Thread the marinated chicken cubes onto thin wooden skewers.

6. Cook the chicken under a preheated broiler, turning frequently, until golden brown, about 5-8 minutes. Brush the chicken with the remaining marinade during cooking.

Cook's Notes

TIME: Preparation takes about 30 minutes, and cooking takes 10-15 minutes.

SERVING IDEAS: Serve the satay on a bed of rice with the tomato and chili sambal.

PREPARATION: The chicken satay can be cooked very successfully on an outdoor barbecue grill.

COOK'S TIP: If you cannot obtain tamarind use the juice of 2 lemons instead. The kecap manis may be hard to find and can be replaced by ½ tsp dark brown sugar and 1 tsp dark soy sauce.

CARIBBEAN SHRIMP AND SWEET POTATOES IN COCONUT SAUCE

SERVES 6

Sweet potatoes are now widely available in most supermarkets and this recipe makes delicious use of them.

1lb sweet potatoes, peeled and diced
1 large onion, chopped
1 clove garlic, crushed
1-inch piece of fresh ginger, grated
1 red or green chili pepper, seeded and chopped
¼ tsp ground cumin
¼ tsp ground coriander
¼ tsp ground allspice
2 tbsps coconut cream, OR
½oz creamed coconut, dissolved in 2 tbsps boiling water
2 cups water
¾ cup peeled shrimp
4oz chicory, shredded
8oz Chinese cabbage, shredded
1 tbsp dark brown sugar
2 tbsps lime juice
Salt
Shredded coconut, to sprinkle

1. In a large saucepan, mix together the sweet potatoes, onion, garlic, ginger, chili pepper, spices, coconut cream and water.

2. Bring to the boil and simmer until the potato is almost tender.

3. Add the shrimp, chicory and Chinese cabbage.

Step 1 Mix together the sweet potatoes and the onion, garlic, ginger, chili pepper, spices, coconut cream and water in a large pan.

Step 3 Simmer the chicory and Chinese cabbage with the shrimp and potatoes, until they are hot but still crisp.

Simmer for 4-5 minutes, until the ingredients are warmed through, but the leaves are still crisp.

4. Add the sugar and lime juice and season to taste.

5. Serve sprinkled with the shredded coconut.

Cook's Notes

 TIME: Preparation takes about 20 minutes, and cooking takes 20-30 minutes.

 SERVING IDEAS: Serve with boiled rice, mixed with cooked peas and corn.

 VARIATION: Yams are a white version of sweet potato and can be used in this recipe equally well.

 WATCHPOINT: Great care must be taken when using fresh chilies. Do not get the juice into the eyes or mouth. If this should happen, rinse with lots of cold water.

PORK WITH LIME AND CHILI
SERVES 4

Creamy coconut and fragrant spices blend together to complement the pork beautifully.

1 clove garlic, crushed
1 tsp brown sugar
1 tsp oil
1 tsp lime juice
1 tsp cornstarch
1lb lean pork, cut into 1 inch cubes
½ cup oil, for deep-frying
1 green chili, seeded and thinly sliced
1 red chili, seeded and thinly sliced
8 green onions, trimmed and sliced diagonally
1 tsp ground turmeric
1 tsp ground coriander
1 tsp ground cumin
1 tsp ground nutmeg
Pinch ground cloves
4 tbsps soy sauce
Juice and rind of 1 lime
½ cup coconut milk
Salt and pepper

1. Combine the garlic, sugar, oil, lime juice and cornstarch in a large bowl. Stir in the pork and coat thoroughly with the garlic and lime juice mixture. Allow to stand in the refrigerator for at least 1 hour.

2. Heat the oil for frying in a wok and add the pork cubes. Cook, stirring frequently, for about 10 minutes until golden brown and cooked through. Drain and set aside.

3. Remove all except about 1 tbsp of the oil. Reheat and add the chilies and onions. Stir-fry for about 2 minutes.

4. Add the ground spices and fry for a further 30 seconds. Stir in the remaining ingredients and bring to the boil.

5. Add the fried pork to the sauce and heat through. Adjust the seasoning and serve.

Step 1 Put the pork into the garlic and lime juice mixture in the bowl and stir to coat thoroughly

Step 3. Stir-fry the onions and chilies in about 1 tbsp of the oil for about 2 minutes.

Cook's Notes

TIME: Preparation takes about 20 minutes, plus at least 1 hour marinating. Cooking takes about 20 minutes.

COOK'S TIP: If you have no fresh coconut milk, dissolve 1oz creamed coconut in ½ cup hot water and use that instead.

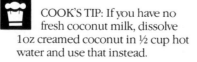

VARIATION: Use chicken instead of the pork.

 SERVING IDEAS: Serve on a bed of rice, garnished with slices of lime.

VEGETABLE KEDGEREE

SERVES 4-6

A rich combination of spices makes this rice extremely appetizing and colorful.

Generous cup long grain rice
1 cup red lentils
2½ cups tepid water
½ cup butter, or 4 tbsps vegetable oil
1 medium onion, chopped
½ tsp grated fresh root ginger
½ tsp finely chopped garlic
1 inch piece cinnamon stick
6 cloves
1 bay leaf
1 tsp ground coriander
¼ tsp ground turmeric
½ tsp salt
2 green chilies, sliced in half lengthways

1. Wash the rice and lentils in 4-5 changes of cold water. Soak them in the tepid water for 30 minutes.

2. Heat the butter or oil in a large saucepan. Add the onion and fry for 2-3 minutes.

3. Add the ginger, garlic, cinnamon, cloves and bay leaf and fry for a further minute.

4. Drain the rice and lentils, reserving the water. Add the rice and lentils to the fried onions, together with the coriander, turmeric, salt and chilies.

5. Fry, stirring constantly, for 2-3 minutes, until the rice is thoroughly coated with the oil.

6. Pour over the reserved water and stir well. Bring the liquid to the boil, then stir once and cover the pan with a tight-fitting lid.

7. Reduce the heat and simmer for 8-10 minutes, without stirring, until the water has been absorbed and the rice and lentils are tender.

Step 1 Wash the rice and lentils in a colander, running 4-5 changes of water through them.

Step 2 Heat the butter or oil in a large saucepan. Add the onion and fry for 2-3 minutes.

Step 5 Fry the rice and lentils with the onion for 2-3 minutes, stirring constantly, to coat the rice evenly with the oil.

Cook's Notes

 TIME: Preparation takes about 15 minutes, and cooking takes about 30 minutes.

 PREPARATION: If the lid of your saucepan does not fit tightly, lay a sheet of aluminum foil over the pan and press the lid carefully onto this to form a seal.

SERVING IDEAS: Serve with vegetable curry, or sliced hard-cooked eggs.

CHICKEN TIKKA

SERVES 4-6

Red food coloring gives this dish its traditional appearance, but the taste will not be affected if you prefer not to use it.

½ cup natural yogurt
1 tsp chili powder
2 tsps ginger paste
2 tsps garlic paste
2 tsps garam masala
½ tsp salt
¼ tsp red food coloring
Juice of 1 lemon
3lb roasting chicken, cut into 8-10 pieces
Oil for brushing

Step 2 Add the chicken pieces to the yogurt mixture, stirring well, to make sure they are evenly coated.

Step 1 In a large bowl, mix together the yogurt, chili powder, ginger and garlic pastes, garam masala, salt, coloring and lemon juice.

Step 3 Line a broiler with aluminum foil and arrange the chicken pieces on this.

1. In a large bowl, mix together the yogurt, chili powder, ginger and garlic pastes, garam masala, salt, coloring and lemon juice.

2. Add the chicken pieces to the yogurt mixture and mix in well to ensure they are evenly coated.

3. Line a broiler with aluminum foil and arrange the chicken pieces on this, together with the yogurt sauce. Preheat the broiler to moderate and broil the chicken pieces for about 5-6 minutes on each side, brushing with a little oil if necessary, to prevent them burning.

Cook's Notes

 TIME: Preparation takes about 10 minutes, and cooking takes about 30 minutes.

 PREPARATION: On request, most butchers will cut the chicken into pieces for you.

VARIATION: Use chicken drumsticks instead of a whole cut chicken.

 SERVING IDEAS: Serve with wedges of lemon and a crisp lettuce and tomato salad.

SPICED SALMON STEAKS

SERVES 4

A blend of spices and sugar makes this easy-to-prepare salmon dish very out of the ordinary.

½ cup soft light brown sugar
1 tbsp ground allspice
1 tbsp mustard powder
1 tbsp grated fresh ginger
4 salmon steaks, 1 inch thick
1 cucumber
1 bunch green onions
2 tbsps butter
1 tbsp lemon juice
2 tsps chopped fresh dill weed
1 tbsp chopped fresh parsley
Salt and pepper

1. Mix the sugar and spices together and rub the mixture into the surface of both sides of the salmon steaks. Allow the salmon steaks to stand for at least 1 hour in the refrigerator.

2. Meanwhile prepare the vegetables. Peel the cucumber and cut into quarters lengthways. Remove the seeds and cut each quarter into 1 inch pieces.

3. Trim the roots from the green onions and cut down some, but not all, of the green part.

4. Put the cucumber and green onions into a saucepan, along with the butter, lemon juice, dill, parsley and seasoning. Cook over a moderate heat for about 10 minutes, or until the cucumber is tender and turning translucent.

5. Put the salmon steaks under a preheated moderate broiler and cook for about 5-6 minutes on each side.

6. Serve with the cucumber and green onion accompaniment.

Step 1 Rub the sugar and spice mixture into both surfaces of each salmon steak.

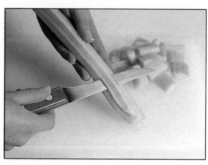

Step 2 Cut the peeled cucumber into quarters lengthways. Remove the seeds and cut each strip into 1-inch lengths.

Step 4 Cook the cucumber and onions with the herbs, flavorings, and butter, until the cucumber is beginning to soften and become translucent.

Cook's Notes

 TIME: Preparation takes about 15 minutes, plus standing time of 1 hour, and cooking takes 12-15 minutes.

 PREPARATION: The salmon steaks are ideal for cooking on an outdoor barbeque.

 VARIATION: Substitute cod or haddock steaks for the salmon.

BEEF AND LEEK SKEWERS

SERVES 4

An unusual combination, these kebabs are nutritious, as well as being very tasty.

4 tbsps castor sugar
2 tbsps tamarind extract
1 tbsp grated fresh ginger
½ cup light soy sauce
Black pepper
1lb rump steak
4 leeks
3 tbsps vegetable oil

Step 4 Thread the beef and leeks alternately onto thin wooden kebab skewers.

Step 2 Cut the beef into 1-inch cubes and the trimmed leeks into 1-inch pieces.

Step 6 Pour the marinade mixture over the cooked kebabs and cook quickly to reduce it to a syrupy sauce.

1. In a large bowl, mix together the sugar, tamarind extract, ginger, soy sauce and pepper.

2. Cut the steak into 1-inch cubes. Trim the leeks to leave only the white and pale green parts and cut these into 1-inch pieces.

3. Put the beef and leeks into the marinade mixture and mix together thoroughly to coat evenly. Allow to stand for 30 minutes.

4. Thread the beef and leeks alternately onto thin wooden kebab skewers.

5. Heat the oil in a large shallow frying pan. Cook the kebabs in the oil, turning frequently to prevent them burning.

6. Add the marinade mixture to the pan and cook quickly, until it has reduced to a thick syrup.

7. Coat the kebabs with the marinade syrup before serving.

Cook's Notes

TIME: Preparation takes about 15 minutes, plus standing time of 30 minutes. Cooking takes about 10 minutes.

PREPARATION: If tamarind extract is not available, use 2 tbsps lemon juice.

VARIATION: Substitute cubes of skinned chicken breast for the beef.

SERVING IDEAS: Serve with boiled rice and a mixed salad.

CHICKEN MOGHLAI WITH CORIANDER CHUTNEY

SERVES 4-6

The creamy spiciness of the chicken is a good contrast to the hotness of the chutney.

4 tbsps oil
3lbs chicken pieces, skinned
1 tsp ground cardamom
½ tsp ground cinnamon
1 bay leaf
4 cloves
2 onions, finely chopped
1-inch piece fresh ginger, grated
4 cloves garlic, crushed
¼ cup ground almonds
2 tsps cumin seeds
Pinch cayenne pepper
1 cup light cream
6 tbsps natural yogurt
2 tbsps roasted cashew nuts
2 tbsps golden raisins
Salt

Chutney
3oz fresh coriander leaves
1 green chili pepper, chopped and seeded
1 tbsp lemon juice
Salt and pepper
Pinch sugar
1 tbsp oil
½ tsp ground coriander

Step 7 Stir the yogurt, cashews and golden raisins into the chicken. Heat through gently to plump up the golden raisins, but do not allow the mixture to boil.

1. To prepare the chicken, heat the oil in a large frying pan. Fry the chicken pieces on each side until golden brown.

2. Remove the chicken and set aside. Put the cardamom, cinnamon, bay leaf and cloves into the hot oil and meat juices and fry for 30 seconds. Stir in the onions and fry until soft but not brown.

3. Stir the ginger, garlic, almonds, cumin and cayenne pepper into the onions. Cook gently for 2-3 minutes, then stir in the cream.

4. Return the chicken pieces to the pan, along with any juices. Cover and simmer gently for 30-40 minutes, or until the chicken is cooked and tender.

5. Whilst the chicken is cooking, prepare the chutney. Put the coriander leaves, chili, lemon, seasoning and sugar into a blender or food processor and work to a paste.

6. Heat the oil and cook the ground coriander for 1 minute. Add this mixutre to the processed coriander leaves and blend in thoroughly.

7. Just before serving, stir the yogurt, cashews and golden raisins into the chicken. Heat through just enough to plump up the golden raisins, but do not allow the mixture to boil.

8. Serve at once with the coriander chutney.

Cook's Notes

 TIME: Preparation takes about 25 minutes, and cooking takes 30-40 minutes.

 PREPARATION: The coriander chutney can be prepared using a pestle and mortar, if a blender or food processor is not available.

 SERVING IDEAS: Serve with boiled rice and a cucumber and tomato salad.

LAMB KORMA

SERVES 4

*One of the best known Indian curries, a korma is rich, spicy and
a traditional favorite.*

3 tbsps vegetable oil
1 medium onion, sliced
1-inch piece cinnamon stick
6 cloves
Seeds of 6 small cardamoms
1 bay leaf
1 tsp black cumin seeds
2 tsps ginger paste, or grated fresh ginger
1 tsp garlic paste, or 2 cloves garlic, crushed
1lb shoulder of lamb, cubed
1 tsp chili powder
1 tsp ground coriander
2 tsps ground cumin.
¼ tsp ground turmeric
½ cup natural yogurt
½ cup water
Salt to taste
1 tbsp ground almonds
2 green chilies, halved and seeded
2 sprigs fresh coriander leaves, chopped

Step 3 Stir the yoghurt into the lamb korma, and mix well, to blend thoroughly.

Step 5 Add a little extra water, if necessary, together with the almonds, chilies and coriander leaves, to produce a medium-thick gravy.

Step 1 Fry the whole spices with the onion for 1 minute.

1. Fry the onion in the oil until golden brown. Add the cinnamon, cloves, cardamoms, bay leaf and the cumin seeds. Fry for 1 minute.

2. Add the ginger and garlic pastes and the cubed lamb. Sprinkle over the chili powder, ground coriander, cumin and turmeric and mix together well.

3. Stir in the yogurt, cover the pan and cook over a moderate heat for 10-15 minutes, stirring occasionally.

4. Add the water and salt to taste, re-cover and simmer gently for 30-40 minutes, or until the meat is tender.

5. Just before serving, add the almonds, chilies and coriander leaves. Stir in a little more water if necessary, to produce a medium-thick gravy.

Cook's Notes

 TIME: Preparation takes about 15 minutes, and cooking takes about 40-50 minutes.

 SERVING IDEAS: Serve with boiled rice, or chapatis.

 FREEZING: Korma freezes well for up to 3 months, but do not add the chilies before freezing, as the process intensifies their hotness.

SPICED BEEF

SERVES 4

Fragrant and spicy, this delicious Chinese dish is quick and easy to make.

1lb fillet of beef
1 tsp soft brown sugar
2-3 star anise, ground
½ tsp ground fennel
1 tbsp dark soy sauce
1-inch piece fresh root ginger, grated
½ tsp salt
2 tbsps vegetable oil
6 green onions, sliced
1 tbsp light soy sauce
½ tsp freshly ground black pepper

Step 3 Put the sliced beef, ginger and salt into the marinade and stir well to coat evenly.

Step 5 Stir-fry the beef with the green onions for 4 minutes.

Step 1 Cut the beef into thin strips 1 inch long.

1. Cut the beef into thin strips 1 inch long.

2. In a bowl, mix together the sugar, spices and dark soy sauce.

3. Put the beef, ginger and salt into the soy sauce mixture and stir well to coat evenly. Cover and allow to stand for 20 minutes.

4. Heat the oil in a wok or large frying pan and stir-fry the onions quickly for 1 minute.

5. Add the beef and fry, stirring constantly, for 4 minutes, or until the meat is well browned.

6. Stir in the soy sauce and black pepper and cook gently for a further 1 minute.

Cook's Notes

 TIME: Preparation takes about 30 minutes, and cooking takes 5-6 minutes.

 VARIATION: Add 1 cup sliced button mushrooms and 8oz cooked Chinese egg noodles.

 SERVING IDEAS: Serve the beef with a spicy dip.

280

CHICKEN TOMATO

SERVES 4-6

Made with a very fragrant selection of spices, this dish is sure to become a firm favorite.

1 onion, peeled and chopped
3 tbsps oil
1-inch piece cinnamon stick
1 bay leaf
6 cloves
Seeds of 6 small cardamoms
1-inch piece fresh ginger, grated
4 cloves garlic, crushed
3lb roasting chicken, cut into 8-10 pieces
1 tsp chili powder
1 tsp ground cumin
1 tsp ground coriander
14oz canned tomatoes, chopped
1 tsp salt
2 sprigs fresh coriander leaves, chopped
2 green chilies, halved and seeded

1. In a large saucepan, fry the onion in the oil, until it has softened. Add the cinnamon, bay leaf, cloves, cardamom seeds, ginger and garlic. Fry for 1 minute.

2. Add the chicken pieces to the saucepan. Sprinkle the chili powder, ground cumin and coriander over the chicken in the pan. Fry for a further 2 minutes, stirring continuously, to ensure the spices do not burn.

Step 2 Fry the chicken and spices together, stirring continuously, to prevent the spices burning.

Step 3 Mix the canned tomatoes and remaining seasonings into the chicken, stirring thoroughly to blend the spices evenly.

3. Stir in the remaining ingredients, mixing well to blend the spices evenly. Cover the pan and simmer for 40-45 minutes, or until the chicken is tender.

Cook's Notes

 TIME: Preparation takes about 30 minutes, and cooking takes about 40-50 minutes.

 PREPARATION: If you ask your butcher, he will joint the chicken for you.

 SERVING IDEAS: Serve with boiled rice.

SPICED FRUIT SALAD

SERVES 6

Sweet and spicy, this fruit salad is certainly out of the ordinary.

1 mango, peeled and cubed
1 small pineapple, skinned, cored and cubed
2 bananas, peeled and sliced
12 litchis, peeled and stone removed
2 kiwi fruit, peeled and sliced
1 small melon, peeled and cubed
2 oranges, peeled and segmented
½ cup palm sugar, or light brown sugar
1 tsp tamarind extract
2 tbsps water
Juice of 1 lime
1-inch piece fresh ginger, grated
½ tsp ground nutmeg
¼ tsp ground cinnamon
¼ tsp ground coriander

1. Prepare all the fruit over a bowl, to catch the juice. Arrange the prepared fruit in a serving bowl.

Step 1 Prepare the fruit over a bowl, so that the juice can be caught and used in the fruit salad.

Step 2 Combine the spices with the liquids, mixing them together well to blend thoroughly.

Step 2 Stir the spicy juice mixture thoroughly into the prepared fruit.

2. In a small bowl, combine the sugar with the tamarind, water, lime juice and spices. Stir this into the prepared fruit, together with any fruit juice, mixing well to blend thoroughly.

3. Chill the fruit salad for at least 1 hour before serving, stirring it again before you do.

Cook's Notes

TIME: Preparation takes about 30 minutes, plus chilling time of at least 1 hour.

COOK'S TIP: If tamarind extract is unobtainable, substitute the juice of ½ lemon and omit the water as well.

VARIATION: Ring the changes by using other combinations of exotic and more common types of fruit.

RHUBARB TART

SERVES 8

An ideal dessert to make when rhubarb is plentiful. The juice which is left over makes a refreshing drink when diluted with chilled soda water.

2lbs rhubarb, cut into 1-inch pieces
2½ cups superfine sugar
½ cup butter
3 eggs
2 tbsps white wine
2¼ cups all-purpose flour
2 tsps baking powder
½ cup soured cream
1 tsp ground cinnamon
½ cup ground almonds
Powdered sugar, to dredge

1. Put the rhubarb into a bowl and sprinkle with 1¾ cups of the sugar. Cover and allow to stand for 1-2 hours.

2. Cream the butter with ½ cup of the remaining sugar, until it is light and fluffy.

3. Beat one of the eggs and add this and the wine to the creamed butter and sugar. Sift in the flour and baking powder and mix together well.

4. Knead the base mixture together until it forms a smooth dough. Wrap the dough in wax paper and chill for 30 minutes in the refrigerator.

5. Roll out the dough on a lightly floured board and use it to line a well-greased, loose-based, or spring-clip, 10 inch round pie pan, pressing the dough well into the base and up the sides of the pan.

6. Strain the rhubarb and arrange the pieces in the dough case. Bake in a preheated oven, 350°F for 30 minutes.

7. Beat together the cream and the remaining eggs and sugar. Stir in the cinnamon and ground almonds, mixing well to ensure they are thoroughly blended.

8. Remove the flan from the oven and pour the cream topping over the rhubarb. Return the flan to the oven and cook at the same temperature for a further 20-25 minutes, or until the topping is golden brown.

9. Ease the flan out of the pan and cool completely before dredging with powdered sugar and serving.

Step 5 Roll out the pastry and carefully line a 10 inch flan ring, pressing the pastry well down onto the bottom and against the sides.

Step 6 Strain off the juice which has been drawn out of the rhubarb and put the rhubarb into the lined flan.

Cook's Notes

 TIME: Preparation takes about 30 minutes, plus 1-2 hours standing time for the rhubarb. Cooking takes 30 minutes for the base, followed by 20-25 minutes for the topping.

 VARIATION: Use 2lbs stoned and quartered red plums instead of the rhubarb.

 SERVING IDEAS: Serve with whipped heavy cream.

 FREEZING: This tart will freeze well if "open frozen" initially, and then wrapped in freezer wrap and stored. It will keep for 6-8 weeks.

APPLE NUT TART

SERVES 6

*The sweet, spicy flavor of cinnamon blends perfectly with the apples
and nuts in this traditional dessert.*

2¼ cups all-purpose flour
Generous ½ cup superfine sugar
½ cup butter, cut into pieces
1 egg
1lb dessert apples, peeled, cored and sliced
½ cup hazelnuts, coarsely ground
1 tsp ground cinnamon
Juice of 1 lemon
3 tbsps apricot brandy (optional)
¼ cup apricot jam
½ cup chopped hazelnuts

Step 6 Melt the apricot jam in a small saucepan over a low heat and pour it over the layers of apples and hazelnuts.

Step 2 Make a well in the center of the flour and butter mixture and drop in the egg. Using a knife, gradually mix the flour into the egg.

Step 5 Layer the apples and ground hazelnuts in the pastry case.

1. Sieve together the flour and 8 tbsps of the sugar into a bowl. Rub in the butter, until the mixture resembles fine breadcrumbs.

2. Make a well in the center of the flour mixture and drop in the egg. Gradually incorporate the flour into the egg using a knife or, as the mixture becomes firmer, your fingers. Continue kneading the mixture together, until it forms a smooth dough.

3. Wrap the dough in wax paper and chill for at least 30 minutes in the refrigerator.

4. Roll out the dough and use it to line an 8 inch greased pie pan.

5. Layer the apple slices and the ground hazelnuts in the pastry case. Sprinkle over the cinnamon, remaining sugar, lemon juice and apricot brandy, if using.

6. Put the apricot jam into a small saucepan and heat through gently until it has melted. Pour the melted jam over the layers of apple and hazelnut.

7. Sprinkle with the chopped hazelnuts and bake in a preheated oven, 425°F, for 35-40 minutes, or until the fruit is soft and the tart is golden brown.

Cook's Notes

 TIME: Preparation takes about 20 minutes, and cooking takes about 40 minutes.

 SERVING IDEAS: Serve with clotted cream.

 FREEZING: The tart can be frozen for 6-8 weeks.

CARROT HALVA

SERVES 6

An unusual and fragrant dessert which is very sweet and spicy.

2lbs carrots, grated
1¾ cups evaporated milk
½ cup sugar
1-inch piece cinnamon stick
2 bay leaves
½ cup blanched almonds, chopped
½ cup unsalted butter
8 green cardamoms, seeds removed and crushed
¼ cup pistachio nuts, chopped

Step 2 Stirring constantly, continue cooking the carrot mixture until it changes color from orange to a deep red or brown.

Step 1 Simmer the carrots in a saucepan with the milk, sugar and spices, until the liquid has almost completely evaporated.

Step 3 Spread the halva mixture onto a flat serving dish, and level the top with a palette knife.

1. Put the carrots, milk and sugar into a heavy-based saucepan, along with the cinnamon stick and bay leaves. Cook over a low heat, until the liquid has almost completely evaporated.

2. Stir in the almonds, butter and cardamom seeds. Continue cooking over the low heat, stirring continuously, until the mixture in the pan changes

color from orange to a deep red or brown. This may take up to 40-45 minutes.

3. Drain off any oil which may appear, and spread the halva mixture onto a flat dish.

4. Serve hot, or cold, sprinkled with the pistachio nuts.

Cook's Notes

 TIME: Preparation takes 15 minutes, and cooking takes about 1 hour.

VARIATION: Use chopped walnuts instead of almonds.

 SERVING IDEAS: Carrot halva is traditionally served as part of a festive meal, decorated with thin strips of gold leaf, which can be bought from delicatessens.

SPICED CRÈME BRÛLÉE

SERVES 4

A delicious variation on a classic dessert.

1 cup milk
1 cup heavy cream
1 stick cinnamon
2 tsps coriander seeds, lightly crushed
1 vanilla bean
4 egg yolks
1½ tsps cornstarch
6 tbsps superfine sugar
Demerara, or soft light brown sugar

Step 4 Stirring constantly, cook the custard over a gentle heat, until it is thick enough to coat the back of a spoon.

Step 2 Beat the egg yolks, cornstarch and sugar together until pale in color and creamy-textured.

Step 7 Sprinkle each of the set custards, which are standing in the ice, with a thin layer of sugar.

1. Pour the milk and cream into a heavy-based saucepan. Add the spices and vanilla bean and heat gently until almost, but not quite, boiling. Allow to cool slightly.

2. Beat the egg yolks, cornstarch and sugar together until light in color.

3. Strain the milk and cream mixture gradually onto the egg yolks, beating between additions.

4. Pour the egg and cream mixture back into the pan and place over a gentle heat. Bring the mixture to just below boiling point very slowly, stirring constantly, to prevent curdling. Continue stirring,

until the mixture has thickened enough to coat the back of a spoon.

5. Remove the custard from the heat and strain it into four custard cups. Chill until set.

6. When set, put the custards into a roasting pan and surround them with ice. Preheat a broiler to the highest temperature.

7. Sprinkle a thin layer of sugar over the top of each custard and place under a broiler, until the sugar melts and caramelizes.

8. Before serving, chill the custards in the refrigerator, until the sugar layer is crisp.

Cook's Notes

 TIME: Preparation takes about 15 minutes, and cooking takes 20-30 minutes.

 COOK'S TIP: If the egg mixture curdles, stand the saucepan in a bowl of cold water and whisk it rapidly with a balloon or electric whisk.

 SERVING IDEAS: Serve with crisp crackers and/or fresh fruit.

CHOCOLATE SPICE CAKE

MAKES 1 8-INCH CAKE

*What a difference! The addition of spices sets this cake apart from
ordinary chocolate cakes.*

5 eggs, separated
¾ cup superfine sugar
3oz bitter chocolate, melted
¾ cup all-purpose flour ⎫
½ tsp ground nutmeg ⎪
½ tsp ground cinnamon ⎬ sifted together
½ tsp ground cloves ⎭

Topping
1 tbsp confectioners' sugar
1 tsp ground cinnamon

1. Grease and line an 8-inch spring-form cake pan
with wax paper.

2. Brush the paper with melted butter and dust
with a little extra flour.

3. Put the egg yolks and sugar into a mixing bowl
and whisk them hard, until the mixture is thick
and creamy.

4. Stir in the melted chocolate and fold in the flour
and spices.

5. Whisk the egg whites until they are stiff and
form soft peaks. Fold these carefully into the
chocolate mixture.

6. Pour the cake mixture into the prepared pan and
bake in a preheated oven, 350°F, for 40-45 minutes,
or until a skewer inserted into the middle of the
cake comes out clean.

7. Leave the cake to cool in the tin for 10 minutes,
then turn out onto a wire rack and leave to cool
completely.

8. Mix together the confectioners' sugar and
cinnamon. Sieve this over the top of the cake,
before serving.

Step 1 Line the cake
pan with wax paper.
Fit a circle of paper
in the bottom and
carefully lay a strip of
paper around the
sides, clipping the
bottom edge, so that
it sits in neatly. Lay
another circle of
paper over the clipped
edge on the base.

Step 3 Beat the egg
yolks and sugar
together vigorously,
until they are as thick
and creamy as softly
whipped heavy
cream.

Step 8 Mix together
the confectioners'
sugar and cinnamon
and sieve this over
the cake.

Cook's Notes

 TIME: Preparation takes
30 minutes, and cooking takes
about 40-45 minutes.

PREPARATION: Whisking the
egg yolks and sugar to the
required consistency is easier if
done over a pan of gently simmering
water.

 VARIATION: Decorate the
cooked cake with whipped
cream and serve with fresh
strawberries.

SPICED COOKIES

MAKES ABOUT 15 COOKIES

Crunchy and wholesome, these spicy cookies are a tea-time treat.

1 cup whole-wheat flour
½ tsp bicarbonate of soda
1 tsp ground cinnamon
1 tsp ground mixed spice
½ cup rolled oats
6 tbsps soft brown sugar
6 tbsps butter
1 tbsp corn syrup
1 tbsp milk

Step 3 Pour the melted mixture into the dry ingredients and mix thoroughly to form a soft, pliable dough.

1. Put the flour, bicarbonate of soda, cinnamon, mixed spice, oats and sugar into a bowl and stir well to blend thoroughly. Make a well in the middle.

2. In a small saucepan, melt the butter with the syrup and milk over a gentle heat.

3. Pour the melted mixture into the dry ingredients and beat well, until the mixture forms a smooth, pliable dough.

4. Divide the mixture into about 15 small balls. Place these onto lightly greased cookie sheets, keeping them well spaced, to allow the mixture to spread.

5. Flatten each ball slightly with the back of a

Step 5 Place the balls of cookie dough a little apart on the baking sheets, to allow for spreading. Flatten each ball slightly with the back of a wetted spoon.

Step 6 Allow the cookies to cool before removing them from the baking tray.

wetted spoon, and bake in a preheated oven, 350°F, for about 15 minutes, or until golden brown.

6. Allow the cookies to cool on the sheet before removing them.

Cook's Notes

 TIME: Preparation takes about 20 minutes, and cooking takes about 15 minutes.

 VARIATION: Substitute ground ginger for the cinnamon and mixed spice.

 PREPARATION: If you are worried that the cookies may stick to the baking sheet, line it with lightly-greased silicone paper.

 COOK'S TIP: Heat a metal tablespoon, and use this to measure out the corn syrup, to avoid a sticky mess.

SPICY FRESH MANGO JUICE
SERVES 4

*Golden and exotic, this drink is ideal for serving as
a non-alcoholic cocktail.*

1 cup tinned mango pulp
Juice 1 lemon
1 tbsp clear honey
¼ tsp ground ginger
¼ tsp ground nutmeg
½ cup unsweetened orange juice
½ cup water
1 small piece of fresh root ginger (optional)
Orange slices to decorate

1. Put the mango pulp, lemon juice, honey, spices, orange juice and water into a blender or food processor and blend until smooth.

2. Put 2 or 3 ice cubes each into 4 glasses and divide the mango juice equally between them.

3. If using the fresh ginger, put this into a garlic crusher and squeeze a few drops of ginger into each glass.

4. Decorate with a slice of orange on the rim of each glass and serve.

Step 1 In a liquidizer or food processor, blend together the mango pulp, lemon juice, honey, spices, orange juice and water.

Step 3 Crush the root ginger in a garlic crusher, adding just a few drops to each glass.

Cook's Notes

 TIME: Preparation takes 15 minutes.

PREPARATION: If you cannot buy a can of mango pulp, either peel, stone and purée the flesh of 2 very ripe mangoes in a liquidizer or food processor, or use a can of whole mangoes and purée them.

 VARIATION: Add ⅓ cup of white rum at the blending stage, to give an added kick.

SPICED TEA

SERVES 6

An unusual and interesting way of serving tea, which is refreshing whether served hot or cold.

3½ cups water
1½ cups milk
½-inch piece cinnamon stick
4 cloves
Seeds of 4 small cardamoms, crushed
6 tea bags, or 2 tbsps tea leaves
Sugar to taste

Step 2 Add the tea bags or tea leaves and allow to infuse for 2 minutes.

Step 1 Simmer the spices with the water and milk for 1 minute.

Step 4 Strain the tea into cups, or a jug, through a muslin-lined sieve.

1. Put the water, milk, cinnamon, cloves and cardamom seeds into a saucepan, bring to the boil and simmer for 1 minute.

2. Add the tea bags or tea leaves. Remove the pan from the heat and cover. Allow to stand for 2 minutes.

3. Stir well and add sugar to taste.

4. Strain into cups through a muslin-lined sieve and serve hot, or strain into a jug and refrigerate until cold. Serve in tall glasses.

Cook's Notes

 TIME: Preparation takes 5 minutes plus chilling time, if desired. Cooking takes about 1-2 minutes.

 VARIATION: Omit the milk and replace it with water, if black tea is preferred.

 SERVING IDEAS: If you serve the tea cold, put 2 ice cubes into each glass and decorate the glass with a strip of orange peel.

Microwave Hot`n´Spicy

Hot and spicy food is popular the world over. Spices stimulate and excite the appetite and, surprisingly, are also said to aid digestion! Microwave ovens are perfect for cooking spicy foods because they bring out the flavor of the food so well. Spices also give excellent color to microwaved food, which may otherwise look bland.

As you might imagine, the range of hot and spicy foods is enormous, so we've gathered together a selection of thirty recipes from around the world: Indian, Chinese, Spanish and Mexican cuisines are well represented, together with recipes from the American Southwest and Bayou country.

Besides their aromatic spiciness, these recipes have one other thing in common: they are all designed to be cooked, quick as a flash, in your microwave oven.

CALAMARES ESPAÑA

SERVES 4

The sweet, rich taste of squid blends perfectly with zesty orange,
tomato and chili in this Spanish-style appetizer.

2 medium-sized squid
1 bay leaf
1 small onion, finely chopped
2 tbsps olive oil
1 clove garlic, finely chopped
2 tbsps flour
8oz canned plum tomatoes
1 chili pepper, seeded and finely chopped
Grated rind and juice of ½ orange
½ cup white wine
1 tbsp tomato paste
1 tsp oregano
1 tsp basil
Salt and pepper
Fresh coriander leaves to garnish

3. Peel the purplish membrane off the tail portion of the squid. Split the tail in half, lengthwise, and wash it well. Cut the tail into pieces about 2 inches wide.

4. Score each section in a lattice pattern at ¼-inch intervals. Separate the tentacles.

5. Put the squid, bay leaf and onion into a casserole with hot water. Cover loosely and cook for 1 minute on HIGH.

6. Heat the olive oil for 30 seconds on HIGH in a medium-sized bowl. Add the garlic and cook for a further 1 minute on HIGH.

7. Stir in the flour. Mix in the cooking liquid from the squid together with the tomatoes and remaining

Step 1 Separate the head and tail of each squid and remove the ink sac and quill.

Step 5 Cook the squid, bay leaf and onion in water until squid is tender and begins to curl.

1. Separate heads of the squid from the tails. Remove the ink sac and reserve for the sauce if desired. Remove the quill and discard.

2. Cut the tentacles above the eyes, and reserve. Discard the eyes and head.

sauce ingredients. If using the ink, break the ink sac into the sauce ingredients.

8. Cook the sauce, uncovered, for 5 minutes on HIGH. Mix with the squid and serve garnished with fresh coriander leaves.

Cook's Notes

TIME: Preparation takes about 20 minutes, and cooking takes about 8 minutes.

SERVING IDEAS: This can be served either hot or cold, as a starter for 4 or a main course for 2 people, with pasta or rice.

WATCHPOINT: When cooking seafood of any kind in a microwave oven, watch it carefully to be sure it does not overcook and become tough. Squid cook especially fast and will begin to pop if overcooked.

TACOS VERACRUZ

SERVES 4

The seafood "cousin" of the beef taco is every bit as spicy and every bit as much fun to put together and to eat.

Topping
1 ripe avocado, peeled and mashed
2 tomatoes, seeded and chopped
1 small clove garlic, crushed
1 tbsp lime or lemon juice

Filling
1 tbsp oil
1 shallot, finely chopped
½ green pepper, chopped
1 tsp ground cumin
½ red or green chili pepper, seeded and finely
   chopped
4 tbsps tomato paste
6 tbsps water
Salt and pepper
¾ cup cooked, peeled shrimp, roughly chopped

4 taco shells

1. First mix the topping ingredients together, cover and set aside.

2. Heat the oil in a small, deep bowl for 30 seconds on HIGH. Add the shallot, green pepper, cumin and chili pepper and cook for 2-3 minutes to soften slightly. Stir once or twice during cooking.

3. Add the tomato paste and water. If the sauce is too thick add an additional spoonful of water.

4. Add the salt and pepper and stir in the shrimp. Cook for 2-3 minutes on MEDIUM to heat the shrimp through.

5. Spoon into the taco shells and top with the avocado mixture.

Step 1 Mix the topping ingredients together, mashing the avocado into small pieces. The mixture should not be smooth.

Step 2 Soften the shallot and green pepper in the oil before adding the remaining sauce ingredients.

Step 5 Spoon the filling and topping into open taco shells.

Cook's Notes

TIME: Preparation takes about 15 minutes, and cooking takes about 6 minutes.

COOK'S TIP: When heating taco shells in a microwave oven, stand them on their open ends. This keeps them from closing up.

VARIATION: Use crabmeat in place of the shrimp.

CHILI SHRIMP

SERVES 4

_For a spicy, spirited start to an oriental feast, these shrimp are quick
and easy and full of flavor._

1lb large shrimp
2 tbsps oil
2 cloves garlic, crushed
2 tbsps chili sauce (hot or sweet)
1 tbsp rice wine
1 tbsp lemon juice
Salt

1. Remove the heads and shells of the shrimp, but

leave on the very ends of the tails. Wash, devein and pat dry.

2. Put the oil and garlic into a bowl and cover with plastic wrap. Cook on HIGH for 1 minute.

3. Stir in the chili sauce, wine, lemon juice and salt. Cook for 30 seconds on HIGH.

4. Add the shrimp and cook for 3-4 minutes on MEDIUM.

Step 1 Shell the shrimp, removing their heads but leaving the tails intact.

Step 4 Add the shrimp to the oil and garlic and stir well before cooking further.

Cook's Notes

 TIME: Preparation takes about 10-15 minutes, and cooking takes 4-5 minutes.

 VARIATION: If uncooked shrimp are not available, use cooked shrimp and cut the cooking time by half.

 SERVING IDEAS: As an appetizer these may be served hot or cold. Chili pepper flowers make an attractive garnish, but are not to be eaten. To make them, cut chili pepper in thin strips from the pointed end to the stem end, but not completely through the stem. Rinse out the seeds and leave pepper in iced water for several hours. The strips will open up like petals.

PORK SATAY WITH PEANUT SAUCE

SERVES 4

*Fragrant spices and hot chilies are characteristic ingredients in
Indonesian food such as this delicious appetizer.*

Juice of 2 limes
Salt and pepper
1½lbs pork tenderloin, cut into 1-inch cubes
1 large red pepper, cut into 1-inch pieces
2 tbsps oil
1 shallot, finely chopped
1 small green chili pepper, seeded and finely
    chopped
½ cup chicken or vegetable stock
1 tsp cornstarch
½ cup crunchy peanut butter
1 clove garlic, crushed
1 tsp ground cumin
1 tsp ground coriander
1 bunch fresh coriander leaves, to garnish

Step 3 Add the stock, peanut butter and other sauce ingredients and cook to thicken.

Step 4 Thread the pork and red pepper onto wooden skewers. Do not pack together too tightly.

Step 2 In a small bowl, cook the shallot in the oil before adding the chili pepper.

1. Mix the lime juice, salt and pepper together and mix in the pork and the pepper pieces. Leave in a cool place for 1 hour.

2. Heat 1 tbsp oil in a small bowl and add the shallot. Cook for 2 minutes on HIGH, add the chili pepper and cook for 1 minute more on HIGH.

3. Mix the stock with the cornstarch, and add the peanut butter, spices and seasoning. Cook for 1 minute on HIGH. Set aside.

4. Thread the meat and red pepper onto 12 small, wooden skewers. Heat a browning tray for 5 minutes on HIGH. Add the remaining 1 tbsp oil and brown the satay for 3 minutes on HIGH, turning frequently.

5. Transfer to a roasting rack, and cook for 6 minutes on MEDIUM.

6. Arrange sprigs of coriander leaves on serving plates and put the satay on top. Spoon over some of the peanut sauce and serve the rest separately.

Cook's Notes

 TIME: Preparation takes about 10 minutes, plus 1 hour marinating time. Cooking takes about 13 minutes.

 PREPARATION: The sauce may be served at room temperature or cooked just before serving. It does not reheat well.

SERVING IDEAS: This appetizer can also be a main course if served with rice.

INDIAN OMELET

MAKES 1

Omelets aren't necessarily French. This recipe shows an Indian influence using sunny tomatoes, pungent coriander and hot chili to add interest to eggs.

1 tbsp butter or margarine
½ onion, finely chopped
1 small tomato, peeled, seeded and chopped
½ green chili, seeded and chopped
1 sprig coriander, chopped
2 eggs, separated
1 tsp water
Salt and pepper

Step 3 Fold the stiffly beaten egg whites gently but thoroughly into the yolks.

Step 1 Cook the onion in the butter and add the tomato, chili and coriander.

Step 4 Spoon the egg mixture into the pie dish and smooth the top.

1. Melt the butter in a shallow pie pan for 30 seconds on HIGH. Cook the onion for 1-2 minutes to soften and add the tomato, chili and coriander.

2. Beat the egg yolks with the water.

3. Beat the egg whites until stiff but not dry and fold into the yolks.

4. Spoon the egg mixture into the pie dish, smoothing the top. Cook for 4 minutes on MEDIUM or until set.

5. Fold over to serve, or turn out of the dish and cut into wedges.

Cook's Notes

 TIME: Preparation takes about 10 minutes, and cooking takes 5-6 minutes.

 PREPARATION: Microwave omelettes are lighter and fluffier than those cooked conventionally, but they can overcook very quickly, so careful attention is needed.

VARIATION: A spicier omelet can be created by adding cumin or curry powder to the dish while softening the tomato and chili.

SPICY CHICKEN KEBABS WITH AVOCADO SAUCE

SERVES 4

Curry powder makes microwaved chicken more interesting. Avocado sauce provides a wonderful contrast of taste, texture and color.

3 chicken breasts, skinned and boned

Marinade
2 tbsps vegetable oil
1 clove garlic, crushed
1 tbsp curry powder
¼ tsp cayenne pepper
1 tbsp chopped coriander leaves
Juice and grated rind of 1 lime
Salt and pepper

Sauce
1 tbsp vegetable oil
½ tsp finely chopped onion
1 tsp mango chutney
1 large avocado, peeled and stone removed
½ cup plain yogurt
2 tsps lime juice to taste

1. Cut chicken into strips 1 inch wide. Combine ingredients for the marinade and mix in the chicken to coat each piece. Leave to marinate for 1 hour.

2. Thread the meat onto wooden skewers and put onto a roasting rack. Cook for 5 minutes on HIGH.

3. Turn kebabs while cooking. Leave to stand, covered in plastic wrap, for 1 minute.

4. Put the oil and onion for the sauce into a small bowl. Cook for 1 minute on HIGH, and stir in the chutney.

5. Put avocado flesh into a food processor with the seasoning, yogurt and lime juice. Add onion and chutney, and process until smooth. Serve with the chicken kebabs.

Step 1 Cut chicken into strips and marinate in the spice mixture.

Step 2 Thread the meat onto skewers and place on a microwave roasting rack.

Step 3 Turn kebabs and baste frequently with the remaining marinade.

Cook's Notes

 TIME: Preparation time takes about 10 minutes, plus 1 hour marinating time, and cooking takes about 6 minutes.

 PREPARATION: Depending on your oven, you may want to cook the chicken on a medium setting to prevent the flesh splitting which can occur on high settings.

COOK'S TIP: When preparing sauces with avocado, leave the stone in the mixture until ready to serve. This will help keep the mixture green.

KUNG-PAO LAMB

SERVES 4

*This memorable dish, with its unusual blend of flavors, is named
after a governor of Szechuan, whose official title was "Kung Pao".*

1lb lamb fillet or meat from the leg, thinly sliced
2 tbsps oil
1 clove garlic, finely chopped
1 small piece fresh ginger root, grated
½ red chili pepper, seeded and finely chopped
4 tbsps soy sauce
½ cup stock
2 tbsps white wine
1 tsp vinegar
1 tsp sugar
1 tbsp cornstarch
1 small red pepper, cut in small dice
1 small green pepper, cut in small dice
Dash sesame oil
4 green onions, sliced
½ cup roasted peanuts

Step 3 Blend the soy sauce, stock, wine, vinegar, sugar and cornstarch and mix into the browned meat.

Step 5 Stir in the sesame oil, peanuts and onions for the last 30 seconds of cooking.

Step 1 In a preheated browning dish, cook the lamb in the oil, pressing the meat against the dish to promote browning.

1. Heat a browning dish for 5 minutes on HIGH. Combine the lamb and oil and add to the dish. Cook for about 2 minutes, turning often. Cook in two batches if necessary.

2. Add the garlic, ginger and chili pepper and cook for a further 2 minutes on HIGH.

3. Mix the soy sauce, stock, wine, vinegar, sugar and cornstarch together and add to the meat.

4. Cover the browning dish or transfer the ingredients to a covered casserole dish. Cook on MEDIUM for a further 4-6 minutes or until the lamb is tender.

5. Add the diced peppers and cook for a further 1 minute on HIGH. Stir in the sesame oil, the green onions and peanuts. Heat for 30 seconds on HIGH.

Cook's Notes

 TIME: Preparation takes about 20 minutes, and cooking takes 10-11 minutes.

 VARIATION: Other nuts such as cashews or almonds may be used instead of peanuts.

 SERVING IDEAS: Serve with plain boiled rice or fried rice.

SZECHUAN BEEF

SERVES 4

Szechuan food is the spiciest of all Chinese cuisine. When cooked in a microwave oven, this meal is even faster than a takeout.

1lb rump steak, thinly sliced
2 tbsps oil
½ dried chili pepper, seeded and crushed
4 tbsps soy sauce
½ cup stock
2 tbsps cornstarch
3 sticks celery, finely shredded
1 sweet red pepper, finely shredded

Step 4 Add the celery and red pepper and mix with the meat and sauce.

Step 1 Mix the meat and oil together well before adding to the hot browning dish.

Step 5 Cook for a further 1 minute or until the sauce has thickened and cleared.

1. Heat a browning dish according to the manufacturer's instructions, on HIGH. Combine meat and oil and add to the dish.

2. Cook for 2 minutes on HIGH in 2 or 3 batches. Reheat browning dish for 2 minutes after each batch.

3. Add the crushed chili pepper. Mix the soy sauce

and stock and gradually stir into the cornstarch. Pour over the steak and cook for 2-3 minutes.

4. Add the celery and red pepper and mix together with the meat and sauce.

5. Cook for a further 1 minute on HIGH until the sauce has thickened but the vegetables are still crisp.

Cook's Notes

 TIME: Preparation takes about 20 minutes, and cooking takes 7-10 minutes.

 VARIATION: If dried chili peppers are unavailable, substitute fresh chilies to taste.

 WATCHPOINT: When removing a browning dish from the microwave oven, always use oven gloves to protect hands. Also, always place hot browning dish on a heatproof mat to protect work surfaces.

VINDALOO

SERVES 4-6

A vindaloo is one of the hottest curries and not for the faint-hearted!
Beef or lamb can also be cooked the same way.

1 tbsp oil
3 cloves garlic, crushed
¼ tsp each of ground cumin, coriander, cinnamon,
   cloves, black pepper, ginger
1½ tsps turmeric
1 tsp mustard seed
1lb pork tenderloin, cut into cubes
3 bay leaves
4 tbsps tamarind extract
2 tsps tomato paste
2 tsps sugar
3 tbsps vinegar
Water or stock to moisten
1-2 green chilies, seeded and chopped
Salt
1 tbsp cornstarch mixed with 3 tbsps water or stock
   (optional)

Step 1 Add the crushed garlic, spices and mustard seed to the oil and cook for 1 minute.

1. Heat the oil and add the garlic, spices and mustard seed. Cook for 1 minute on HIGH.

2. Allow to cool and pour over the pork cubes in a shallow dish. Stir to coat and add the bay leaves. Leave to marinate overnight in the refrigerator,

stirring occasionally.

3. Mix the tamarind, tomato paste, sugar and vinegar and pour over the meat.

4. Add water or stock to come a quarter of the way up the meat, and sprinkle over the chilies. Cover

Step 3 Mix together the tamarind extract, tomato paste, vinegar and sugar and pour this over the meat.

Step 4 Add water or stock to come a quarter of the way up the meat.

the dish and cook for 20 minutes on MEDIUM, adding more water or stock if drying out.

5. When the meat is tender, leave the vindaloo to stand for 5 minutes before serving. If desired, the sauce may be thickened with the cornstarch and water or stock. Cook for 2-3 minutes or until clear.

Cook's Notes

 TIME: Preparation takes about 20 minutes, but meat should marinate overnight for full flavor. Cooking takes 23-24 minutes.

 COOK'S TIP: Most meats benefit from the medium range of settings in microwave ovens which means slower cooking but gives a tender result. The meat will still cook in about half the time of conventional cooking.

 BUYING GUIDE: Tamarind extract is available from Indian groceries and also from delicatessens. Substitute 2 tbsps mango chutney mixed with 2 tbsps lemon juice, if it is unobtainable.

PEPPERCORN LAMB

SERVES 4

A special dish for a special dinner, this can be made hotter with the addition of more green peppercorns.

4 tbsps butter or margarine
1½ lbs lamb fillet or meat from the leg cut into
    ¼-inch slices
2 shallots, finely chopped
3 tbsps flour
1 clove garlic, finely minced
1 tsp ground allspice
1 cup beef stock
1 tsp tomato paste
1 tbsp canned green peppercorns, rinsed and
    drained
2 pimentos cut into thin strips
¼ cup heavy cream
Salt and pepper

3. Cook the shallots and flour to brown slightly.

4. Add the garlic, allspice, stock and tomato paste. Season with salt and pepper and cook for 2-3 minutes on HIGH, until starting to thicken.

5. Add the lamb, cover and cook for 10 minutes on MEDIUM, or until the lamb is tender.

6. Add the peppercorns, pimento and cream and cook for 2 minutes on HIGH. Adjust the seasoning and leave to stand for 2 minutes, covered.

Step 4 Add the garlic, allspice, stock, tomato paste and seasonings and cook until beginning to thicken.

Step 3 Cook the shallots and flour in the browning dish until slightly colored.

Step 6 When lamb is cooked, add the peppercorns, pimento and cream to the sauce.

1. Heat a browning dish according to the manufacturer's instructions on HIGH. Melt the butter for 1 minute on HIGH and add the slices of lamb.
2. Cook for 2 minutes on HIGH, in 2 or 3 batches. Remove the meat and set aside.

Cook's Notes

 TIME: Preparation takes about 13 minutes, and cooking takes 21-22 minutes. Allow 2 minutes standing time.

PREPARATION: When using a browning dish, press the meat firmly against the hot surface of the dish for best results.

$ BUYING GUIDE: Green peppercorns are available bottled in brine or canned. If bottled in brine, peppercorns need to be rinsed.

TACOS

SERVES 4

Enjoy a taste of Mexico in this easily prepared snack. With various colorful toppings to choose from, you can vary the taste to suit yourself.

½lb ground beef
1 small onion, chopped
1 tbsp raisins
1 tbsp pine nuts
1 tbsp corn
2 tsps chili powder
4oz canned tomatoes
Salt and pepper
8 taco shells

Toppings
1 cup grated cheese
½ cup sour cream
4 tomatoes, chopped
½ head lettuce, shredded
1 chopped avocado

Step 3 Spoon off any excess fat from the meat before adding the other ingredients.

Step 4 Spoon the meat mixture into the taco shells and reheat if necessary.

Step 2 Cook the meat in a covered dish, stirring occasionally to break meat into small pieces.

1. Put the beef and onion into a 1 quart casserole. Break the meat up well with a fork.

2. Cover and cook for 4 minutes on HIGH, stirring occasionally to break into small pieces.

3. Drain any fat from the meat and add the raisins, nuts, sweetcorn, chili powder and tomatoes.

4. Cover and cook on MEDIUM for 8 minutes. Adjust seasoning. Spoon into the taco shells and serve with the various toppings.

Cook's Notes

 TIME: Preparation takes about 15 minutes, and cooking takes about 12 minutes.

 BUYING GUIDE: Taco shells are now readily available in supermarkets and delicatessens.

 PREPARATION: Reheat unfilled taco shells by standing them on paper towels on their open ends. This stops shells from closing up.

 VARIATION: Pine nuts, which are expensive, can be replaced with walnuts or almonds or the nuts may be omitted altogether.

MEXICAN PORK CASSEROLE

SERVES 4

All the favorite flavors of Mexican cooking—chickpeas, beans, peppers, chilies and spices—combine with pork in one easy-to-cook casserole.

2 tsps oil
1lb pork tenderloin, cut into 1-inch cubes
¼ tsp ground cumin
¼ tsp ground coriander
1 small onion, chopped
1 clove garlic, crushed
2 tbsps flour
1 tbsp instant coffee
1½ cups stock
½ red pepper, diced
½ green pepper, diced
1 small chili pepper, seeded and chopped
2½ cups canned red kidney beans, rinsed
2½ cups canned chickpeas, rinsed
Tortilla chips to garnish

Step 3 Add the coffee and stock to the casserole, stirring constantly to blend well.

Step 5 Add the beans and chickpeas to the casserole and heat through.

Step 2 Cook the cumin, coriander, garlic, onion and flour for 1-2 minutes.

1. Heat a browning dish for 5 minutes on HIGH. Put in the oil and add the pork cubes. Cook for 4 minutes on HIGH, stirring frequently, until slightly browned.

2. Add the cumin, coriander, garlic, onion and flour, and cook for 1-2 minutes on HIGH.

3. Dissolve the instant coffee in the stock and add to the casserole, stirring well.

4. Add the peppers, cover, and cook on MEDIUM for 30 minutes.

5. Add the beans and chickpeas and heat for 4 minutes on MEDIUM. Serve with tortilla chips.

Cook's Notes

 TIME: Preparation takes 15 minutes, and cooking takes about 38 minutes.

 COOK'S TIP: The addition of coffee will make the sauce richer and browner, but the overall taste will not be of coffee.

 VARIATION: Rice may be served instead of the tortilla chips as an accompaniment.

JAMBALAYA

SERVES 4

This classic dish comes from New Orleans in Bayou country.
Whilst the ingredients list looks complicated, the preparation couldn't
be easier.

8oz spicy sausage, such as Pepperoni or Merguez,
    skinned and diced
8oz cooked ham, cubed
1 green pepper, seeded and cut into 1-inch pieces
1 medium onion, roughly chopped
1 clove garlic, finely chopped
1 red or green chili, seeded and finely chopped
2 tbsps olive oil
10oz canned tomatoes
1 tbsp tomato paste
2 tbsps white wine or lemon juice
1 tsp chopped marjoram
1 bay leaf
¼ tsp grated fresh nutmeg
Salt and pepper
4oz peeled, cooked shrimp
2 tomatoes, peeled, seeded and cut into large
    pieces
1½ cups cooked long grain rice

Step 2 Cook the sausage, ham, pepper, onion, garlic and chili until the vegetables are nearly tender.

1. Place the sausage, ham, green pepper, onion, garlic, chili and olive oil in a large casserole or deep bowl. Stir to coat all the ingredients in oil and cover the bowl loosely.

2. Cook for 6-7 minutes or until the onion and pepper are almost tender.

3. Mix the canned tomatoes, tomato paste and white wine or lemon juice and add to the bowl.

Step 3 Mix all the remaining ingredients except the tomatoes, rice and shrimp together. Cover the bowl with cling film, piercing it or folding back a corner to allow the steam to escape.

Add the marjoram, bay leaf, grated nutmeg, salt and pepper and loosely cover the bowl.

4. Cook for 2-3 minutes on HIGH, and add the shrimp, tomatoes and rice. Re-cover the bowl and cook for a further 4 minutes, or until all the ingredients are hot. Remove the bay leaf before serving.

Cook's Notes

 TIME: Preparation takes about 20 minutes, and cooking takes 14-17 minutes.

 COOK'S TIP: Rice can be cooked successfully in the microwave oven for 12-15 minutes on HIGH in liquid. Leave to stand for 5 minutes covered, stirring occasionally.

 VARIATION: Chicken can be used instead of the ham; cut it into 1-inch pieces and cook with the onion and pepper. Salami or garlic sausage can be substituted for the Pepperoni or Merguez.

SHRIMP AND TAMARIND

SERVES 4

Tamarind has an exotic sweet-sour taste that goes very well with shrimp and combines perfectly with the spices and chilies in this sauce.

2lbs large shrimp
2 tbsps butter or margarine
4 shallots, finely chopped
1 tbsp ground coriander
4 crushed cardamoms
2 tsps turmeric
Pinch nutmeg
1 green chili, seeded and shredded
1 pimento, shredded
Juice of 1 lime
1 tbsp sugar
1 tbsp tamarind extract
¾ cup natural yogurt
Salt and pepper

Step 1 Peel the shrimp and use a toothpick or skewer to remove the black veins.

1. Peel and devein the shrimp and set aside.

2. Heat a browning dish according to the manufacturer's directions. Add the butter or margarine and shallots and cook for 2 minutes on HIGH.

3. Add the spices and shrimp and cook for 1-2 minutes on HIGH.
4. Pour into a casserole and add the chili, pimento,

Step 3 Combine the spices and shrimp in a browning dish and cook briefly.

Step 5 Stir the yogurt into the sauce before leaving it to stand.

lime juice, sugar and tamarind. Stir well and cook for 2 minutes on HIGH.

5. Stir in the yogurt and salt and pepper and leave to stand for 3 minutes before serving.

Cook's Notes

TIME: Preparation takes about 20 minutes, and cooking takes 5-6 minutes plus 3 minutes standing time.

VARIATION: If using uncooked shrimp, add 1-2 minutes to the cooking time.

SERVING IDEAS: Serve with rice and with an accompaniment of cucumber and yogurt with chopped mint.

MALABARI FISH

SERVES 4

Fish curries are unusual, at least to Western palates, and this one is rather special. It has a spicy-rich coconut flavored sauce with the addition of pineapple, raisins and almonds.

4 tbsps shredded coconut
½ cup water
4 tbsps oil
1 onion, finely chopped
½ tsp each ground cinnamon, nutmeg, cumin,
    coriander, turmeric and chili powder
Pinch ground cloves
6 cardamoms
1 bay leaf
1 tsp grated fresh ginger
1 clove garlic, crushed
1lb whitefish, skinned, boned and cut into
    2-inch pieces
8oz canned pineapple chunks and juice
1 tbsp chopped coriander leaves
1-2 green chilies, seeded and finely chopped
Pinch salt and pepper
1 tbsp cornstarch
1 tbsp blanched almonds
1 tbsp raisins
½ cup natural yogurt

Step 5 Strain the infused coconut, mix the liquid with the cornstarch and stir it into the fish.

Step 6 Add the pineapple, almonds, raisins and yogurt and mix together well. Leave to stand.

1. Place the coconut and water in a dish and heat for 30 seconds on HIGH. Leave to infuse.

2. Place the oil in a casserole and add the onion. Cover and cook for 2 minutes on HIGH.

3. Add all the spices, the bay leaf, ginger and garlic and heat for 2 minutes on HIGH.

4. Add the fish and strained juice from the pineapple. Add the coriander, chilies, salt and pepper. Cover and cook for 6 minutes on HIGH.

5. Remove the fish and keep it warm. Strain the coconut and mix the liquid with the cornstarch. Stir into the sauce and cook for a further 2-3 minutes on HIGH, stirring carefully, or until it thickens and clears.

6. Return the fish to the sauce and add the pineapple, almonds, raisins and yogurt. Cover and leave to stand for 3-5 minutes before serving. Remove the bay leaf.

Cook's Notes

 TIME: Preparation takes about 25 minutes, and cooking takes 12-13 minutes.

 PREPARATION: Even though microwave ovens reheat food well, fish dishes are best prepared just before serving.

 COOK'S TIP: Whenever infused liquid is called for in a recipe, use the microwave oven to speed up the process.

SHRIMP AND ZUCCHINI

SERVES 4

Indian cuisine often combines aromatic spices with fiery chilies to set the taste buds tingling.

1lb large shrimp
2 tbsps oil
1 tsp paprika
½ tsp turmeric
1½ tsps ground cumin
Grated fresh ginger
1 clove garlic, crushed
1 red chili, seeded and shredded
2 zucchini, cut in matchsticks
7oz canned tomatoes, crushed
1 bay leaf
2-3 tsps cornstarch mixed with 3 tbsps lemon juice
Salt and pepper

Step 4 Add the shrimp and cook briefly. Cover the bowl tightly and set aside to finish cooking.

Step 3 Combine the vegetables, bay leaf, cornstarch with lemon juice and seasoning. Cook for 5 minutes or until the sauce thickens.

1. Shell and devein the shrimp.

2. Pour the oil into a casserole and add the spices, ginger, garlic and chili. Cook for 2 minutes on HIGH.

3. Add the zucchini, tomatoes, bay leaf, the cornstarch mixed with lemon juice and salt and pepper. Cook on HIGH for 5 minutes.

4. Add the shrimp and cook for 2 minutes on HIGH then leave to stand for 5 minutes to finish cooking. Remove the bay leaf.

Cook's Notes

TIME: Preparation takes about 25 minutes, and cooking takes 9 minutes, plus 5 minutes standing time.

SERVING IDEAS: Serve with plain boiled rice or rice pilaff. Accompany with mango chutney and yogurt.

PREPARATION: During standing time, the food continues to cook in its own heat. Ingredients that only need reheating can be added at this time.

WATCHPOINT: When cooking seafood in a microwave oven, be careful not to overcook as it quickly toughens.

LIME AND CHILI CHICKEN
SERVES 4

*Branding with hot skewers gives microwaved chicken a "barbecued"
look. Chilies and limes give it a distinctive taste.*

4 boneless chicken breasts
2 limes
1 green chili pepper
Pinch sugar
Salt and pepper
6 tbsps heavy cream

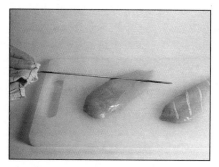

Step 2 Skin the chicken breasts and brand with hot skewers to make a pattern.

Step 4 Place the chicken in a casserole with sugar, chili, salt, pepper and lime juice.

Step 6 Stir the cream into the juices in the casserole.

1. Heat 2 metal skewers in a gas flame or on an electric burner.

2. Skin the chicken breasts and make a pattern on the flesh with the hot skewers.

3. Squeeze 1 lime for juice. Peel and slice the other lime thinly. Remove the seeds from the chili pepper and slice it very thinly.

4. Put the chicken into a casserole. Sprinkle over a pinch of sugar, the sliced chili pepper, salt, pepper and lime juice.

5. Cover and cook for 10 minutes on MEDIUM. Remove the chicken and keep warm.

6. Stir the cream into the juices in the casserole. Cook for 2 minutes on HIGH, stirring frequently. Pour over the chicken and garnish with the sliced lime.

Cook's Notes

TIME: Preparation takes about 20 minutes, and cooking takes about 12 minutes.

PREPARATION: The skewers take about 15 minutes to become hot enough to sear the chicken. Aluminum skewers will melt in the heat, so use stainless steel. Do not put skewers into the microwave oven.

WATCHPOINT: Use oven gloves to handle the skewers, which will heat through to the ends.

SPICY TOMATO CHICKEN

SERVES 4

Worcestershire sauce provides the hotness in this barbecue-type tomato sauce. It's a perfect way to spice up chicken.

4 chicken breasts, skinned and boned
¼ cup chicken stock or water
1lb canned tomatoes
2 tbsps Worcestershire sauce
1 clove garlic, crushed
2 tbsps tomato paste
2 tbsps cider vinegar
2 tbsps light brown sugar or honey
1 small onion, finely chopped
1 bay leaf
Pinch allspice
Salt and pepper
4 tomatoes, skinned, seeded and cut into thin strips
   to garnish

Step 3 Cook the sauce uncovered to reduce it.

Step 4 In a food processor, blend the sauce until smooth.

Step 1 Place the chicken in one layer in a large casserole, cover and cook until white and opaque.

1. Place the chicken in one layer in a large casserole with the stock or water. Cover tightly and cook on MEDIUM for 10 minutes. Leave to stand, covered, for at least 5 minutes while preparing the sauce.

2. Combine all the sauce ingredients with the cooking liquid from the chicken in a deep bowl.

3. Cook, uncovered, for 7 minutes on HIGH, until the sauce reduces and thickens.

4. Remove the bay leaf and blend the sauce in a food processor until smooth.

5. Arrange the chicken breasts on a serving plate and coat with the sauce. Add the tomato strips and reheat for 30 seconds on HIGH before serving.

Cook's Notes

TIME: Preparation takes about 15 minutes, and cooking takes about 17 minutes plus 5 minutes standing time.

VARIATION: This spicy hot barbecue-type sauce is equally good with pork tenderloin or even fish and shellfish.

SERVING IDEAS: Rice or pasta are good accompaniments together with a green salad. Corn on the cob makes another good accompaniment.

TANDOORI GUINEA FOWL

SERVES 4

This marinade gives color and flavor to the guinea fowl and turns your microwave into an Indian "tandoor," or oven.

4 Guinea fowl

Marinade
1 small onion, chopped
1 small piece fresh ginger, grated
2 tsps ground coriander
2 tsps ground cumin
2 tsps paprika
1 tsp turmeric
1 tsp chili powder
1 cup plain yogurt
Juice of 1 lime
2 green chili peppers, seeded and chopped
2 tbsps chopped fresh chives
Salt and pepper

To Serve
1 head of lettuce, broken into leaves
4 tomatoes, cut in wedges
1 lemon, cut in wedges

1. Combine all the marinade ingredients together. Skin the fowl and cut them in half. Prick the flesh and rub in the marinade. Leave for 1 hour.

2. Cook on HIGH for 20 minutes or until juices run clear, basting frequently with the marinade.

3. Leave to stand, loosely covered, for 5 minutes before serving.

4. Heat any remaining marinade on MEDIUM for 1 minute, but do not allow to boil.

5. Pour over the chicken and serve on a bed of lettuce with tomato and lemon wedges.

Step 1 Prick the skin of the fowl and rub in the marinade.

Step 2 Baste or brush frequently with the marinade while cooking.

Cook's Notes

TIME: Preparation takes about 20 minutes plus 1 hour to marinate the fowl. Cooking takes about 15 minutes.

COOK'S TIP: A spicy, colorful coating such as this gives microwave-cooked chicken a more appetizing appearance.

 BUYING GUIDE: Guinea fowl are available from butchers and supermarkets. Chicken portions may be substituted, if necessary.

LEMON CHICKEN

SERVES 4

*This Oriental dish has a fresh-tasting lemony sauce with red pepper
flakes providing just the right amount of hotness.*

4 chicken breasts, skinned, boned and cut into thin
strips

Marinade
4 tbsps soy sauce
2 tsps dry sherry or shao-hsing wine
Salt and pepper

Sauce
3 tbsps salted black beans
2 tbsps water
6 tbsps lemon juice
1 cup chicken stock
4 tbsps sugar
1 tsp sesame oil
3 tbsps cornstarch
2 cloves garlic, finely chopped
¼ tsp red pepper flakes

Lemon slices to garnish

1. Mix chicken with the marinade ingredients,
cover and refrigerate for 30 minutes.

2. Crush the black beans, combine with the water
and leave to stand until ready to use.

3. Combine remaining sauce ingredients in a
shallow dish. Add the chicken, marinade and black
beans, cover and cook on HIGH for 7-9 minutes,

Step 2 Crush the
black beans into the
water and leave to
soak.

Step 3 Combine all
the sauce ingredients
with the chicken,
marinade and black
beans.

stirring halfway through the cooking time.

4. Once the cornstarch has cleared, leave the
chicken to stand, covered, for 2 minutes before
serving. Garnish with lemon slices.

Cook's Notes

TIME: Preparation takes about
30 minutes. Cooking takes
7-9 minutes plus 2 minutes standing
time.

SERVING IDEAS: Serve with
either plain boiled rice or fried
rice.

WATCHPOINT: Because the
seeds are included in dried red
peppers and because the drying
process intensifies flavor, red pepper
flakes are hotter than fresh chilies.

BUYING GUIDE: Salted beans
are available in delicatessens
and Chinese grocers. Bottled black
bean sauce is available in
supermarkets and can be substituted.

DICED CHICKEN AND PEPPERS

SERVES 4

Chinese cooking is quick and so is microwave cooking, so why not combine them in a spicy and colorful chicken dish.

2 tbsps oil
1 clove garlic, minced
1lb chicken meat, skinned, boned and diced
1 small red chili pepper, seeded and diced
1 tsp cornstarch
2 tbsps white wine
2 tbsps soy sauce
4 tbsps chicken stock
2 green peppers, diced
Pinch sugar (optional)
Salt
½ small can bamboo shoots, diced

and stock. Stir well and cover the dish.

4. Cook for 7-9 minutes on HIGH, stirring halfway through the cooking time. Add the green pepper, sugar, if using, and salt if needed.

5. Cook for 30 seconds on HIGH, add bamboo shoots and leave to stand, covered, for 2 minutes before serving.

Step 4 Stir halfway through cooking and add the green pepper and sugar, if using.

Step 2 Cook the garlic in the oil, add the chicken and stir to coat.

Step 5 Add the bamboo shoots, cover and leave to stand.

1. Heat the oil for 30 seconds on HIGH in a large casserole dish.

2. Add the garlic and cook for 30 seconds on HIGH. Add the chicken and stir to coat with oil.

3. Add the chili pepper, cornstarch, wine, soy sauce

Cook's Notes

TIME: Preparation takes about 20 minutes, and cooking takes 8½-10½ minutes plus 2 minutes standing time.

 PREPARATION: Chinese cooking, whether done in a wok or in a microwave oven is very quick. It helps to have all the ingredients prepared before beginning to cook.

SERVING IDEAS: Accompany the dish with plain boiled rice, fried rice or Chinese noodles.

EGGPLANT SLICES IN YOGURT

SERVES 4-6

The Indian influence in this dish is obvious. Methi is a traditional Indian herb, but coriander is easier to find.

2 large eggplants, cut into ¼-inch-thick rounds
Salt
3 tbsps oil
1 tsp chili powder
¼ tsp turmeric
1 tsp garam masala
1 green chili, seeded and thinly sliced
½ cup natural yogurt
1 sprig methi or corinader leaves, chopped
Paprika

Step 2 Preheat the oil and then cook the rinsed and dried eggplant slices.

Step 1 Score the eggplant slices and sprinkle them with salt.

1. Lightly score the eggplants on both sides and sprinkle with salt. Leave to stand for 30 minutes, drain and pat dry.

2. Heat the oil in a casserole for 30 seconds on HIGH and stir in the chili powder, turmeric, garam masala, chili and eggplant slices.

3. Cover the dish and cook on HIGH for 2-3 minutes. Pour over the yogurt and leave to stand for 3-5 minutes.

4. Sprinkle over the methi or coriander leaves and the paprika and serve hot or cold.

Cook's Notes

 TIME: Preparation takes about 10 minutes, and cooking takes 2-4 minutes.

PREPARATION: Eggplants can taste bitter. To remedy this, sprinkle with salt and stand for 30 minutes to draw out the juices. Be sure to rinse well and then pat dry.

 SERVING IDEAS: This makes a good starter or side dish.

DAHL

SERVES 4

Nutritious lentils are a perfect foil for spices. A microwave oven makes cooking pulses faster and easier.

1 cup lentils, brown or green
4 tbsps butter or margarine
1 large onion, finely chopped
1 clove garlic, crushed
1 red or green chili pepper, seeded and finely
   chopped
1 tsp each ground cumin, coriander and turmeric
½ tsp each ground cinnamon and nutmeg
3 cups vegetable stock
Salt and pepper
1 bay leaf
Chopped fresh coriander leaves

1. Cover the lentils with water and soak overnight.

Step 1 Place the lentils in a bowl and cover them with water. Cover the bowl and microwave to boil the water.

Alternatively, microwave for 10 minutes on HIGH to bring to the boil and then allow the lentils to boil for 2 minutes. Leave to stand, covered, for 1 hour.

2. Melt the butter or margarine for 1 minute on HIGH in a large casserole. Add the onion, garlic, chili pepper and spices. Cook for 4 minutes on MEDIUM.

3. Drain the lentils and add to the casserole with the vegetable stock, salt, pepper and bay leaf. Cover and cook on HIGH for 45 minutes, or until the lentils are soft and tender.

4. Allow to stand, covered, for 5-10 minutes before serving. Remove the bay leaf and add the chopped coriander. If preferred, the dahl can be puréed before serving.

Step 3 Drain the precooked lentils and add them to the other ingedients.

Cook's Notes

 TIME: Preparation takes about 25 minutes plus soaking time, which will vary according to method used. Cooking takes about 45 minutes plus 5-10 minutes standing time.

! WATCHPOINT: Incompletely cooked pulses can be dangerous to eat. Make sure lentils are soft and properly cooked, according to instructions.

SPICY CUCUMBERS

SERVES 4

*This unusual side dish is Chinese in origin. Brief microwave cooking
helps intensify the flavors.*

1 large cucumber
Salt
3 tbsps light soy sauce
Pinch five-spice powder
¼ tsp red pepper flakes
2 tsps sesame oil
1 tbsp rice vinegar
3 tbsps coriander leaves

1. Peel thin strips off the cucumber for a green and white striped effect.

2. Cut in half lengthwise, or in quarters if the cucumber is thick.

3. Cut each length into 2-inch pieces. Sprinkle with salt and leave to stand for 30 minutes. Wash and dry well.

Step 1 Peel thin strips of skin from the cucumber to make stripes.

4. Combine the cucumber with all the remaining ingredients except the coriander in a deep bowl. Partially cover and cook for 2 minutes on HIGH.

5. Add the coriander and leave in the bowl to cool. When cold, refrigerate. Serve on the same day.

Step 3 Sprinkle the cucumber with salt and leave it in a colander to drain either in the sink or on paper towels.

Step 5 Add the coriander to the warm cucumber and leave to cool in the bowl.

Cook's Notes

 TIME: Preparation takes about 30 minutes since the cucumbers must be salted and left to stand. Cooking takes 2 minutes.

 COOK'S TIP: Salting cucumbers helps to draw out excess moisture and keeps the dressing from becoming watery. It also makes cucumbers more digestible.

 SERVING IDEAS: Serve as a starter to a Chinese meal or as an accompaniment to cold or barbecued meat or poultry.

CURRIED VEGETABLES

SERVES 6-8

The vegetables in this delicious golden sauce can be varied according to season. Even frozen vegetables get a lift from this combination of spices.

1 tbsp oil
1 onion, finely chopped
1 green chili pepper, seeded and finely chopped
1 small piece fresh ginger, grated
2 cloves garlic, crushed
½ tsp ground coriander
½ tsp ground cumin
1 tsp ground turmeric
2 potatoes, peeled and diced
1 eggplant, cut into small cubes
14oz canned tomatoes, drained
1 small cauliflower, cut into flowerets
½ cup vegetable or chicken stock
8oz okra, trimmed and washed
1 cup roasted, unsalted cashews
4 tbsps shredded coconut
4 tbsps natural yogurt

1 minute on HIGH.

3. Add the potatoes, eggplant and tomatoes. Cover loosely and cook on HIGH for 8-10 minutes or until the potatoes and eggplant are almost tende

4. Add the cauliflower, stock and okra. Cover

Step 3 Add the potatoes, eggplant and tomatoes.

Step 2 Stir the spices into the onion, chili, ginger and garlic.

Step 4 Finally add the cauliflower and okra, which need less cooking.

1. Heat the oil in a large bowl or casserole dish for 1 minute on HIGH. Add the onion, chili pepper, ginger and garlic. Cook on HIGH for 1 minute further.

2. Add the spices and cook for an additional

loosely and cook on HIGH for 3-4 minutes, or until the vegetables are almost tender.

5. Add the cashews and the shredded coconut. Add salt and pepper to taste and serve hot, topped with natural yogurt.

Cook's Notes

 TIME: Preparation takes about 25 minutes, and cooking takes 13-16 minutes.

COOK'S TIP: If the spices are cooked for a minute before adding any liquid, they will lose their harsh raw taste and develop a fuller flavor.

 SERVING IDEAS: Serve as a side dish to a full Indian meal or with grilled meat or poultry. For a vegetarian meal add rice and use vegetable stock.

SWEET-SOUR CABBAGE

SERVES 4

*Crisp cabbage gets a sweet and sour taste with the zip of chili pepper
in this oriental relish.*

1 medium head white cabbage, about 2lbs
1 small red chili pepper (use less if desired)
½ cup light brown sugar
6 tbsps rice vinegar
2 tbsps light soy sauce
Salt
3 tbsps oil

1. Cut the cabbage into ½-inch slices, discarding the core.

2. Cut the chili pepper into short, thin strips, discarding the seeds.

3. Mix all the ingredients together except the oil.

4. Pour the oil into a large bowl and heat for 2 minutes on HIGH. Add the cabbage mixture and cover the bowl with pierced plastic wrap.

5. Cook on HIGH for 9-11 minutes. Allow to cool in the bowl, stirring frequently. When cold, refrigerate.

Step 1 Cut the cabbage into slices, discarding the core.

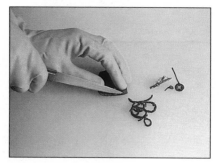

Step 2 Cut the chili into thin strips, discarding the seeds. Wear rubber gloves to handle hot chilies.

Cook's Notes

 TIME: Preparation takes about 20 minutes, and cooking takes 11-13 minutes.

 COOK'S TIP: The cabbage will keep for several days if stored in its liquid in the refrigerator.

 SERVING IDEAS: Serve as a Chinese starter or as a side dish.

ZUCCHINI CURRY

SERVES 4-6

Zucchini are delicious in a spicy tomato sauce. They are especially good cooked in a microwave oven because they keep their color and texture.

1 tbsp oil
1 tsp cumin seed
1 tsp mustard seed
½ tsp chili powder
¼ tsp ground turmeric
8oz canned tomatoes and juice
1 green chili, seeded and finely chopped
8oz zucchini, cut into ¼-inch slices
Salt
1 tbsp cornstarch mixed with 3 tbsps water (optional)

1. Heat the oil for 30 seconds on HIGH and add the cumin seed, mustard seed, chili powder and turmeric. Cook for 1-2 minutes on HIGH.

2. Add the tomatoes and juice, chili pepper and zucchini. Cover and cook on HIGH for 3 minutes.

3. Add salt to taste and leave to stand for 1 minute before serving.

4. If desired, thicken the sauce with the cornstarch and water. Cook for a further 1-2 minutes on HIGH.

Step 1 Add the whole and ground spices to the oil and cook briefly.

Step 2 Add the tomatoes and their juice to the spices together with the chili and zucchini.

Cook's Notes

 TIME: Preparation takes about 20 minutes, and cooking takes 4-7 minutes.

 PREPARATION: Cooking the cumin seed before adding the other ingredients will develop its flavor and soften the seeds.

 SERVING IDEAS: This can be served as a main course for an Indian vegetarian meal or as a side dish with meat or poultry.

CHICKPEAS WITH SPICES

SERVES 4-6

A sunny, spicy dish that is as good cold as it is hot. Serve it on a bed of rice for a vegetarian main course.

2 tbsps oil
1 small onion, finely chopped
1 clove garlic, minced
1 small piece fresh ginger, grated
1 tsp ground coriander
1 tsp chili powder
¼ tsp ground turmeric
4oz canned tomatoes, roughly chopped, plus juice
1 green chili, seeded and chopped
Salt
2 sprigs fresh coriander, chopped
1 bay leaf
15oz canned chickpeas
4 cardamoms
Juice of 1 lemon

1. Put the oil in a casserole and add the onion garlic, ginger and ground spices. Cook for 1 minute on HIGH.

Peel the ginger and use the fine side of a grater to produce a purée. Discard any stringy pieces.

Step 2 Make sure the cardamom pods are sufficiently well crushed to release the seeds within.

Step 2 Add the chickpeas with half of their can liquid to the other ingredients.

2. Add the tomatoes and juice, chili, salt, coriander and bay leaf. Add the chickpeas and half of their liquid, salt, cardamoms and lemon juice and cover the casserole.

3. Cook on HIGH for 4-6 minutes or until completely heated through. Remove the bay leaf before serving.

Cook's Notes

 TIME: Preparation takes 15 minutes, and cooking takes 5-6 minutes.

VARIATION: Fresh tomatoes may be used instead of canned ones. Use about 8oz peeled and seeded tomatoes, roughly chopped. Water or stock may be necessary if using fresh tomatoes.

 SERVING IDEAS: Serve as a side dish with other curries or with chicken dishes.

Healthy Eating

"Healthy eating" is a much used and abused phrase. Recent headlines about which foods we should or should not eat have created the idea that healthy eating is faddy and boring. How wrong this is.

To understand properly the meaning of healthy eating we really must return to basics. All it means is eating a healthy balance of a whole range of foods in moderation. How can this be considered faddy or boring?

This chapter contains a range of delicious recipes, some of which are new ideas, while others are well-known family favorites. All of them, however, include natural, fresh and unrefined ingredients. Some of the recipes are cooked in a different way, others use the ingredients in an unusual way, but all of them present the food in an appetizing, inventive and above all healthy way.

We hope that by trying these recipes, you will discover that healthy eating is not just for those who can afford the time and money, but is for everyone who cares enough to change just a few basic shopping and cooking routines in order that their health and vitality may be improved.

TOMATO SOUP
SERVES 6

This healthy version of a firm family favorite is high in fiber, low in fat and hearty enough to be a complete meal in itself.

4oz whole-wheat macaroni
1 tbsp polyunsaturated sunflower oil
1 small onion, peeled and chopped
1 small green pepper, seeded and chopped
2 tbsps whole-wheat flour
4 cups vegetable stock
1lb fresh tomatoes, cored and finely chopped
2 tbsps tomato paste
1 tbsp grated horseradish
Freshly milled sea salt and black pepper

Step 3 Add the stock to the onion, pepper and flour mixture gradually, beating well between additions to ensure that the soup is smooth.

Step 2 Stir the onion and pepper into the hot oil, mixing well to coat them evenly.

Step 5 Pour the tomato mixture into a liquidizer or food processor and blend for about 30 seconds, or until the tomatoes have been completely broken down.

1. Cook the macaroni in enough boiling salted water to cover for about 15 minutes, or until it is just soft. Drain and rinse the macaroni in cold water, then set aside until required.

2. In a large saucepan heat the oil until it is hot. Stir in the onion and the pepper, cover the pan and cook for 3-4 minutes over a moderate heat.

3. Stir the flour into the onion mixture and add the stock gradually, stirring well between additions.

4. Add the tomatoes, the tomato paste and the horseradish, and simmer for 15 minutes.

5. Put the tomato mixture into a liquidizer or food processor and process for about 30 seconds, or until smooth. Return the soup to the saucepan and season with salt and pepper to taste.

6. Add the macaroni to the soup and simmer for 10 minutes before serving.

Cook's Notes

TIME: Preparation takes about 15 minutes, and cooking takes about 45 minutes.

PREPARATION: If you do not have a liquidizer or food processor, you can push the tomato soup through a wire sieve, using a metal spoon. However, this does have the disadvantage of removing the tomato skins and pips, which are an excellent source of fiber.

SERVING IDEAS: Serve the soup topped with 1 dessertspoon of 1% fat fromage frais, or natural yogurt and a sprinkling of chopped fresh parsley or basil.

CREAMY SPINACH SOUP

SERVES 4

*High in fiber and low in calories, this soup is ideal for those who want
a hearty meal, but not a hearty waistline.*

1¾lbs fresh spinach
1 tbsp polyunsaturated sunflower oil
1 large onion, chopped
¼ cup whole-wheat flour
3 cups skim milk
Freshly ground sea salt and black pepper
Pinch ground nutmeg
½ cup 1% fat fromage frais, or natural yogurt

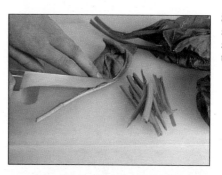

Step 1 Wash the spinach thoroughly and trim away any tough stalks.

1. Wash the spinach thoroughly and trim away any tough stalks. Shred the spinach finely.

2. Heat the oil in a large frying pan and fry the chopped onion gently, until transparent, but not colored.

3. Stir the flour into the onion, and add the milk gradually, stirring between additions, until the mixture has thickened.

4. Stir the spinach into the onion and milk mixture and cook for 5 minutes over a gentle heat, adding a little water or milk, if the mixture becomes too thick.

Step 4 Stir the spinach into the onion and milk sauce. Cover and simmer the spinach for about 5 minutes.

5. Season with salt, pepper and nutmeg to taste.

6. Put the soup into a liquidizer or food processor and blend for about 30 seconds, until the spinach has been roughly chopped.

7. Return the soup to the saucepan, cover and cook for a further 5 minutes.

8. Stir all but 2 tbsps of the fromage frais or yogurt into the soup and reheat gently, without boiling.

9. Pour the soup into individual bowls and garnish with a swirl of the remaining fromage frais or yogurt.

Step 6 Blend the soup in a liquidizer or food processor, until the spinach is roughly chopped.

Cook's Notes

 TIME: Preparation takes about 10 minutes, and cooking takes about 30 minutes.

 VARIATION: If you cannot get fresh spinach, you can substitute a 11oz pack frozen chopped spinach in its place.

 FREEZING: This soup will freeze well for up to 6 weeks.

MINESTRONE SOUP

SERVES 4-6

This famous vegetable and pasta soup from Italy can be made in many different ways. The recipe below is a simple but delicious one, which can be varied to suit individual tastes.

3 tbsps olive oil
1 medium onion, chopped
2 cloves garlic, crushed
2 medium potatoes, scrubbed and diced
3 carrots, diced
2 sticks celery, roughly chopped
6oz cabbage, shredded
4-5 fresh or canned tomatoes, chopped
3 cups water, or vegetable stock
1 bouquet garni
1 cup fresh or frozen peas, shelled
¼ cup cooked red kidney beans
4oz macaroni, or any pasta shape
Freshly ground sea salt and black pepper, to taste
½ cup fresh Parmesan cheese, grated

1. Heat the olive oil in a saucepan and fry the onion and garlic gently for about 2-3 minutes, until the onion is soft but not colored.

2. Stir in the potatoes, carrots and celery and fry for a further 3 minutes.

3. Stir in the cabbage and tomatoes, and cook for a further 5-6 minutes.

4. Add the water, or stock, to the vegetables in the saucepan, and drop in the bouquet garni.

5. Add the peas, kidney beans and pasta, cover the pan and simmer gently for 10-15 minutes, or until the pasta is just tender.

6. Remove the bouquet garni, season with the salt and pepper, and ladle into individual serving bowls. Sprinkle generously with the grated Parmesan cheese.

Step 1 Gently fry the chopped onion and the crushed garlic in the olive oil, until they are soft, but not colored.

Step 2 Stir the potatoes, carrots and celery into the onion and garlic mixture, and fry gently for about 3 minutes, until the vegetables have softened.

Cook's Notes

TIME: Preparation takes about 20 minutes, and cooking takes about 30 minutes.

PREPARATION: If you like a thicker soup, stir 2 tbsps tomato purée into the soup 5 minutes before serving.

VARIATION: Substitute any vegetable of your choice for the carrots, celery, potatoes or cabbage in this recipe. It is traditional for minestrone soup to have peas and beans in it, so do not change these.

SERVING IDEAS: Serve minestrone soup with crusty whole-wheat rolls.

SALMON PÂTÉ

SERVES 4

This highly nutritious, elegant pâté is low in fat and very quick to prepare.

8oz canned red or pink salmon, drained
½ cup low fat curd cheese
Few drops lemon juice
Pinch ground mace, or ground nutmeg
¼ tsp tabasco sauce
Freshly ground sea salt and black pepper
2 tbsps 1% fat fromage frais, or low fat natural yogurt
4 small pickles

1. Remove any bones and skin from the salmon. In a bowl, work the fish into a smooth paste with the back of a spoon.

Step 1 Put the salmon into a small bowl and work it with the back of a spoon, until it becomes a smooth paste.

2. Beat the curd cheese until it is smooth.

3. Add the salmon, lemon juice, seasonings, and fromage frais or natural yogurt to the curd cheese and mix well, until thoroughly incorporated.

4. Divide the mixture equally between 4 individual custard cups. Smooth the surfaces carefully.

5. Slice each pickle lengthways, 4 or 5 times, making sure that you do not cut completely through the gherkin at the narrow end. Splay the cut ends into a fan, and use these to decorate the tops of the pâtés in the custard cups.

Step 5 Slice each pickle lengthways, 4 or 5 times, taking great care not to cut right through the pickle at the narrow end. Spread each of the cut ends out carefully into a fan shape. Use these to garnish the tops of the pâtés.

Cook's Notes

 TIME: Preparation takes about 15 minutes.

 PREPARATION: If you have a food processor or liquidizer, you can work the curd cheese and salmon together in this, instead of beating them in a bowl.

 VARIATION: Use canned tuna fish in place of the salmon, and stir in 1 tsp horseradish sauce, instead of the tabasco sauce.

SERVING IDEAS: Serve with toast, or crispy whole-wheat rolls.

GIANFOTTERE SALAD

SERVES 4

This interesting Italian-style salad makes the most of delicious summer vegetables.

1 small eggplant
2 tomatoes
1 large zucchini
1 red pepper
1 green pepper
1 medium onion
1 clove garlic, peeled
4 tbsps olive oil
Freshly ground sea salt and black pepper
1lb whole-wheat pasta spirals, or bows

1. Cut the eggplant into ½-inch slices. Sprinkle with salt and leave for 30 minutes.

2. Chop the tomatoes roughly and remove the woody cores.

3. Cut the zucchini into ½-inch slices.

4. Core and seed the peppers, and chop them roughly.

5. Peel and chop the onion. Crush the garlic.

Step 1 Cut the eggplant into ½-inch slices. Lay the slices in a shallow dish and sprinkle with plenty of salt. Leave the eggplant for about 30 minutes to degorge.

6. Heat 3 tbsps olive oil in a frying pan, and fry the onion gently, until it is transparent but not colored.

7. Rinse the salt from the eggplant thoroughly and pat dry with paper towels. Chop the eggplant roughly.

8. Stir the eggplant, zucchini, peppers, tomatoes and garlic into the onion, and fry gently for 20 minutes. Season with salt and pepper to taste, and allow to cool completely.

Step 8 Add the eggplant, zucchini, peppers, tomatoes and garlic to the onion in the frying pan, and cook gently for about 20 minutes, stirring occasionally, to ensure that all the vegetables cook evenly.

9. Cook the pasta spirals in plenty of boiling salted water for 10-15 minutes, or until tender.

10. Rinse the pasta spirals in cold water and drain well.

11. Put the pasta spirals into a large mixing bowl, and stir in the remaining 1 tbsp olive oil.

12. Stir the vegetables into the pasta spirals, mixing well to make sure that they are all evenly distributed.

Cook's Notes

 TIME: Preparation takes about 30 minutes, and cooking takes about 30 minutes.

PREPARATION: Degorging is the process of removing moisture from a vegetable by sprinkling it with salt and allowing the salt to draw out the water.

VARIATION: If you cannot obtain eggplant, substitute sliced mushrooms. Do not degorge these.

 SERVING IDEAS: Serve this salad with fish, or eggs.

RICE AND NUT SALAD

SERVES 4

This refreshing salad is high in protein from the rice, nuts and beans, and very low in saturated fats.

2 tbsps olive oil
2 tbsps lemon juice
Freshly ground sea salt and black pepper
¾ cup golden raisins
⅓ cup currants
1¼ cups cooked brown rice, well drained
¾ cup blanched almonds, chopped
½ cup cashew nuts, chopped
½ cup shelled walnuts, chopped
15oz canned peach slices in natural juice,
   drained and chopped
¼ cucumber, cubed
¼ cup cooked red kidney beans
1 tbsp pitted black olives

1. Put the olive oil, lemon juice and salt and pepper into a screw top jar. Shake vigorously, until the mixture has thickened.

Step 1 Put the olive oil, lemon juice and salt and pepper into a screw top jar. Shake vigorously, until the mixture has thickened.

2. Put the golden raisins and the currants into a small bowl, and cover with boiling water. Allow to stand for 10 minutes, before draining the fruit.

Step 2 Put the golden raisins and currants into a small bowl, and pour on enough boiling water to just cover. Allow the fruit to stand in the water for 10 minutes to plump up, before draining and discarding the water.

3. Mix together the rice, nuts, soaked fruit, peaches, cucumber, kidney beans and olives in a large mixing bowl.

4. Pour the dressing over the salad, and mix together thoroughly, to ensure all the ingredients are evenly coated.

Step 4 Pour the salad dressing over the rice and nut mixture. Stir thoroughly to coat all the salad ingredients completely.

Cook's Notes

 TIME: Preparation will take about 15 minutes.

 PREPARATION: If you would like to create a more subtle flavor, soak the golden raisins and currants in hot jasmine tea, instead of water.

 VARIATION: Use a 15oz can apricot halves in natural juice, in place of the can of peaches.

 SERVING IDEAS: Serve the salad on a bed of crisp lettuce, or endive, chopped.

ONION, EGG AND TOMATO BAKE

SERVES 2-4

_This versatile dish can be served either as a lunch or supper dish
for 2 or, in individual dishes, as an appetizer for 4._

2 tbsps olive oil
2 medium onions, sliced
¼ cup whole-wheat flour
½ cup skim milk
Freshly milled sea salt and black pepper, to taste
4 eggs, hard-cooked
2 tomatoes, thinly sliced
3 tbsps fresh whole-wheat breadcrumbs
1 tbsp freshly grated Parmesan cheese

Step 2 Stir the milk into the flour and oil mixture gradually, beating well and returning the pan to the heat between additions, until the sauce is smooth.

1. Heat the oil in a pan and fry the onions gently until they are softened, but not colored. Remove from the pan with a slotted spoon and set aside.

2. Stir the flour into the oil in the pan, and cook for 1 minute. Add the milk gradually, beating well between additions. Simmer gently for 2-3 minutes, stirring continuously.

3. Add the onions to the sauce and season well to taste.

4. Cut the eggs in half and remove the yolks. Push the yolks through a metal sieve and set the sieved yolks to one side.

5. Rinse and chop the egg whites and place them in the bottom of a medium-sized ovenproof dish, or 4 individual custard cups.

6. Cover the chopped egg whites with the onion mixture and then top this with a layer of sliced tomatoes.

7. Put the breadcrumbs and Parmesan cheese into a mixing bowl, and stir in the sieved egg yolks, mixing well, until all the ingredients are thoroughly incorporated. Sprinkle this over the layer of tomatoes.

8. Bake in a preheated oven, 400°F, for 15-20 minutes, or until golden brown.

Step 4 Push the egg yolks through a metal sieve, using the back of a wooden spoon.

Cook's Notes

 TIME: Preparation takes about 15 minutes, and cooking takes 20-25 minutes.

PREPARATION: If there is not enough oil left in the frying pan after the onions have been removed, heat a further 1 tbsp of olive oil . before adding the flour.

 SERVING IDEAS: Serve with a crisp green salad.

SHRIMP RISOTTO

SERVES 4

*High in fiber and in flavor, shrimp risotto is a delicious
way to stay healthy.*

1lb unpeeled shrimp
1 glass white wine
4 fresh tomatoes
3 cloves garlic
1 large onion
3 tbsps olive oil
2 tbsps chopped fresh parsley
1 cup brown rice
1 tsp tomato paste
Freshly ground sea salt and black pepper
2 tbsps grated Parmesan cheese

1. Peel the shrimp, leaving 4 unpeeled for a garnish. Put the shrimp shells and the wine into a saucepan and bring to the boil. Remove the pan from the heat and allow to cool completely before straining out the shrimp shells, and reserving the liquid.

Step 1 Put the wine and the shrimp shells into a small saucepan and bring to the boil. Immediately they have boiled, remove the pan from the heat and allow to cool completely.

2. Chop the tomatoes roughly, and remove the woody cores. Peel and chop the garlic and onion.

3. Heat the olive oil in a large frying pan, or saucepan. Cook the onion and garlic gently in the oil, without browning them. Stir in the parsley and cook for about 30 seconds.

4. Add the rice to the fried onion, and stir well to coat the grains with the oil.

Step 4 Add the rice to the onion mixture, and stir well to coat each rice grain with the oil.

5. Add the wine, tomato paste, tomatoes and just enough cold water to cover the rice.

Step 5 Add the tomato paste to the rice and enough water to barely cover, before simmering for about 20 minutes, until the rice is just tender.

6. Season the rice with salt and pepper, and cook for about 20 minutes, until all the water is absorbed and the rice is tender.

7. When the rice is cooked, stir in the peeled shrimp and the cheese. Heat through gently, before piling into a serving dish, and topping with the unpeeled shrimp as a garnish.

Cook's Notes

TIME: Preparation takes about 15 minutes, and cooking takes about 25 minutes.

SERVING IDEAS: Serve the risotto with a fresh mixed salad.

PREPARATION: If all the water is absorbed before the rice is cooked, add a little more, but take care not to add too much, or the rice will become stodgy.

EGGPLANT BAKE

SERVES 6

This substantial eggplant main course has an unusual flavor which is sure to keep your family, or guests, guessing as to the "secret" ingredient.

3 large eggplants
2 tsps freshly ground sea salt
Malt vinegar
2 tbsps sunflower oil
2 large onions, sliced
2 fresh green chilies, seeded and chopped
15oz can peeled tomatoes, chopped
½ tsp chili powder
1 tsp crushed garlic
½ tsp ground turmeric
Vegetable oil, for deep-frying
4 tbsps natural yogurt, or 1% fat fromage frais
1 tsp freshly ground black pepper
4 tomatoes, thinly sliced
1½ cups Edam cheese, finely grated

1. Cut the eggplants into ¼-inch-thick slices. Lay the slices in a shallow dish, and sprinkle with 1 tsp of the salt and enough malt vinegar to cover.

2. Allow the eggplants to marinate for 20-30 minutes. Drain thoroughly.

3. Heat the sunflower oil in a frying pan, and fry the onions gently, until they are golden brown. Add the chilies, chopped tomatoes, chili powder, garlic, turmeric and the remaining salt. Mix well, and simmer for 5-7 minutes.

4. Remove the pan from the heat and leave the tomato mixture to cool.

5. Put the tomato mixture into a food processor, or liquidizer, and blend until smooth. Set aside.

Step 9 Cover the eggplant slices in the dish with half the tomato sauce and half the yogurt, or fromage frais. Sprinkle with the black pepper.

6. Heat the vegetable oil for deep-frying, and deep-fry the drained, marinaded eggplants, until they are golden brown, approximately 2-3 minutes.

7. Drain the fried eggplant slices on paper towels.

8. Grease a large, deep baking dish and arrange half the fried eggplant slices, closely together, in the bottom of the dish.

9. Cover the eggplant slices in the dish with half the tomato sauce and half the yogurt, or fromage frais. Sprinkle with the black pepper.

10. Place the remaining eggplant slices over the yogurt and top with the remaining sauce and the remaining yogurt.

11. Arrange the tomato slices on top and sprinkle with the grated cheese. Bake in a preheated oven, 350°F, for 10-15 minutes, or until the cheese has melted and turned golden brown.

Cook's Notes

TIME: Preparation takes about 30 minutes, and cooking takes about 30-40 minutes.

PREPARATION: If you do not have a liquidizer or food processor, the sauce can be puréed, by pushing it through a wire sieve using the back of a wooden spoon. This does, however, remove a lot of the valuable fiber.

SERVING IDEAS: Serve hot, as a main course, with whole-wheat bread, or pitta bread.

FISH, ZUCCHINI AND LEMON KEBABS

SERVES 4

*Ask your fishmonger to fillet and skin the sole for you, if you feel that
you cannot do it yourself.*

16 small, thin sole fillets, or 8 larger ones, skinned
   and cut in half lengthways
4 tbsps olive oil
1 clove garlic, crushed
Juice ½ lemon
Finely grated rind ½ lemon
Freshly ground sea salt and black pepper, to taste
3 drops tabasco sauce
2 medium-sized zucchini, cut into ¼-inch slices
1 green pepper, halved, seeded and cut into 1-inch
   pieces

1. Roll up each sole fillet like a jelly roll and
secure with a wooden pick.

2. Place the fish rolls in a shallow dish. Mix
together the olive oil, garlic, lemon juice, lemon
rind, salt and pepper and tabasco sauce.

3. Spoon the olive oil mixture evenly over the fish
rolls, and chill for about 2 hours.

4. Remove the wooden picks, and carefully thread
the rolled fish fillets onto kebab skewers alternately
with the zucchini slices and pieces of green pepper.

5. Brush each threaded kebab with a little of the
lemon and oil marinade.

6. Arrange the kebab skewers on a broiler pan and
cook under a moderately hot broiler for about 8
minutes, carefully turning the kebabs once or twice
during cooking and brushing them with a little of
the remaining marinade, if required.

Step 1 Roll up each sole fillet like a jelly roll, from the narrow end, and secure each roll with a wooden pick.

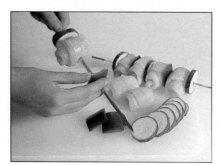

Step 4 Thread the rolled fish fillets onto kebab skewers alternately with the zucchini slices and pieces of green pepper.

Cook's Notes

 TIME: Preparation takes about 30 minutes, plus 2 hours chilling time, and cooking takes about 8 minutes.

 COOK'S TIP: The marinade ingredients are delicious used with other types of fish.

 VARIATION: If sole is not in season, substitute small dab or plaice.

 SERVING IDEAS: Serve the kebabs on a bed of brown rice, sprinked with chopped parsley.

BAKED STUFFED MACKEREL

SERVES 4

Mackerel should be eaten the day it is caught, so this is a recipe for people living near the sea. It is also very useful for people on self-catering holidays at the seaside, because it is so easy to prepare.

¼ cup polyunsaturated margarine
1 small onion, finely chopped
1 tbsp medium oatmeal
⅓ cup fresh whole-wheat breadcrumbs
1½ tsps chopped fresh lemon thyme
1½ tsps chopped fresh parsley
Freshly ground sea salt and black pepper
2-3 tbsps hot water, if required
4 mackerel, cleaned and washed thoroughly

---

1. In a large frying pan, melt the margarine. Fry the chopped onion in the margarine until it is soft, but not colored.

Step 1 Fry the chopped onion, until it is soft but not colored.

2. Add the oatmeal, breadcrumbs, herbs and seasoning to the fried onion, and mix well to form a firm stuffing, adding a little hot water to bind, if necessary.

Step 2 Add the oatmeal, bread-crumbs, herbs and seasoning to the fried onion, and mix well to form a firm stuffing, binding with a little of the hot water, if necessary.

Step 3 Fill the cavities of each fish with equal amounts of the onion and oatmeal stuffing. Push the stuffing well into the back of the fish to preserve its shape.

3. Fill the cavities of the fish with the stuffing and wrap each one separately in well-greased aluminum foil.

4. Place each fish parcel in a roasting pan, or on a cookie sheet, and cook in a preheated oven, 375°F, for half an hour.

Cook's Notes

 TIME: Preparation takes about 15 minutes, and cooking takes about 30 minutes.

 VARIATION: The stuffing in this recipe is also delicious with herrings, or whiting.

 SERVING IDEAS: Serve this dish garnished with fresh watercress and new potatoes.

TARRAGON CHICKEN PANCAKES

SERVES 4

These attractive pancakes look sophisticated enough for a dinner party, but are so easy to make, you can indulge yourself at any time.

1 cup all-purpose whole-wheat flour
1 egg
1 cup skim milk
Polyunsaturated vegetable oil, for frying
6 tbsps all-purpose unbleached flour
1 cup skim milk
Freshly ground sea salt and black pepper, to taste
8oz cooked chicken, chopped
1 avocado pear, peeled, halved, stoned and chopped
2 tsps lemon juice
1 tbsp chopped fresh tarragon

1. Put the whole-wheat flour into a large bowl, and make a slight well in the center. Break the egg into the well and begin to beat the egg carefully into the flour, incorporating only a little flour at a time.

2. Add the first cup of milk gradually to the egg and flour mixture, beating well between additions, until all the milk is incorporated and the batter is smooth.

3. Heat a little oil in a small frying pan, or crêpe pan, and cook about 2 tbsps of the batter at a time, tipping and rotating the pan, so that the batter spreads evenly over the base to form a pancake. Flip the pancake over, to cook the second side.

4. Repeat this process until all the batter has been used up. Keep the pancakes warm, until required.

5. Blend the plain flour with a little of the skim milk, and gradually add the rest of the milk, until it is all incorporated.

6. Pour the flour and milk mixture into a small pan, and cook over a moderate heat, stirring continuously,

until the sauce has thickened. Season to taste.

7. Stir the chopped chicken, avocado, lemon juice and tarragon into the sauce.

8. Fold each pancake in half, and then in half again, to form a triangle.

9. Carefully open part of the triangle out to form an envelope, and fill this with the chicken and avocado mixture.

Step 1 Put the flour into a bowl and make a slight well in the center. Break the egg into this well, and beat gently, incorporating a little of the flour at a time.

Step 3 Using a small frying pan, or crêpe pan, heat a little hot oil and fry 2 tbsps of the batter at a time. Tip and rotate the pan whilst cooking, to distribute the batter evenly over the base, and make a nice thin pancake.

Cook's Notes

 TIME: Preparation takes about 25 minutes, and cooking takes about 25 minutes.

 PREPARATION: Use 1 cup 1% fat fromage frais, instead of the skim milk, for a luxurious change to this recipe.

 SERVING IDEAS: Serve piping hot, garnished with watercress and a crisp green salad.

PIQUANT PORK CHOPS
SERVES 4

The spicy sauce in this recipe completely transforms the humble pork chop.

4 lean pork chops, trimmed of fat and rind
1 tbsp polyunsaturated vegetable oil
1 small onion, chopped
1 tbsp unrefined brown sugar
1 tbsp dry mustard, any flavor
2 tsps tomato paste
1 beef stock cube
1 cup water
1 tbsp Worcestershire sauce
2 tbsps fresh lemon juice

1. Broil the pork chops under a preheated hot broiler for 6-7 minutes on each side.

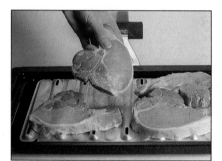

Step 1 Arrange the trimmed pork chops on a rack in a broiler pan, to allow the fat to drain away as they cook.

2. Heat the oil in a large frying pan, and fry the onion gently, until it is lightly browned.

3. Stir the sugar, mustard powder, tomato paste and beef stock cube into the cooked onion. Mix the ingredients together well, then add the water and bring to the boil, stirring continuously.

4. Stir the Worcestershire sauce and the lemon juice into the onion and spice mixture, then check the seasoning, adding freshly ground sea salt and black pepper to taste.

5. Put the pork chops into an ovenproof baking dish, or shallow casserole, and pour the sauce over them.

6. Cook in a preheated oven, 350°F, for about 40-45 minutes, or until the meat is tender.

Step 3 Stir the sugar, mustard powder, tomato paste and beef stock cube into the cooked onion. Mix the ingredients together well, then add the water and bring to the boil, stirring continuously.

Step 5 Pour the piquant sauce over the broiled pork chops in the ovenproof baking dish.

Cook's Notes

 TIME: Preparation takes about 30 minutes, and cooking takes about 1 hour.

 FREEZING: This dish freezes well, and can be kept for up to 2 months. Freezing should take place before the final cooking period.

 SERVING IDEAS: Serve with creamed potatoes and green vegetables.

STIR-FRIED CALVES' LIVER WITH PEPPERS AND CARROTS

SERVES 4

Calves' liver is a little more expensive than other types of liver, but is so delicious and so nutritious, that it should be used more frequently.

2 tbsps olive oil
1 onion, thinly sliced
1 clove garlic, cut into very thin strips
1¼ lbs calves' liver, cut into thin strips
2 tbsps seasoned whole-wheat flour
4 tbsps dry sherry
½ cup water, or vegetable stock
1 green pepper, seeded and cut into thin strips
3 large carrots, cut into strips
Freshly ground sea salt and black pepper, to taste
2 cups bean sprouts

1. Heat the olive oil in a large pan, or wok. Add the onion and garlic, and stir-fry for 3 minutes.

2. Roll the strips of liver in the seasoned flour and add them to the wok, along with the onion. Stir-fry quickly, until the liver is sealed on the outside, but is still pink in the center.

3. Stir the sherry into the liver, and bring to a rapid boil. Add the water, or stock, to the liver, along with the green pepper, carrots and seasoning to taste.

4. Stir-fry the liver in the sauce for 3 minutes, over a high heat.

5. Add the bean sprouts to the wok and stir-fry for 1 minute, or just long enough to heat the bean sprouts through, without cooking them.

Step 2 Roll the strips of calves' liver in the seasoned flour, until they are evenly coated on all sides.

Step 5 Stir the bean sprouts into the liver mixture and heat through for about 1 minute, until they are warm, but still crunchy.

Cook's Notes

 TIME: Preparation takes 15-20 minutes, and cooking takes 10-12 minutes.

 VARIATION: Use lambs' or pigs' liver for a stronger flavor.

 SERVING IDEAS: Serve with a bowl of brown rice and a tasty tomato salad.

CHICKEN ESCALOPES

SERVES 4

Chicken is an excellent meat for those wishing to keep a check on the amount of saturated fat in their diet. This simple recipe makes the most of tender chicken breasts.

4 chicken breasts, boned and skinned
2 tbsps seasoned whole-wheat flour
8 tbsps fresh whole-wheat breadcrumbs
1 tbsp chopped fresh sage
1 egg, beaten
2 tbsps polyunsaturated margarine
1 tbsp olive oil
¼ cup low calorie mayonnaise
½ cup low fat natural yogurt or 1% fat fromage frais
1 tsp grated fresh horseradish
2 tbsps chopped shelled walnuts

1. Dust the chicken breasts lightly in the seasoned flour.

2. Mix together the whole-wheat breadcrumbs and the fresh sage, on a plate.

3. Dip the floured chicken breasts first into the beaten egg, and then into the sage and breadcrumb mixture, pressing the crumbs onto the chicken breasts, to make sure they are coated thoroughly.

4. Chill the chicken breasts for 30 minutes in the refrigerator.

5. Heat the margarine and oil in a large, shallow frying pan. Add the prepared chicken breasts and fry them gently on each side for 5 minutes, or until they are golden and the meat is tender and cooked.

6. Mix together the mayonnaise, yogurt, horseradish and chopped walnuts.

7. Arrange the cooked escalopes on a serving plate and pour a little of the yogurt and walnut sauce over them before serving.

Step 1 Dust the chicken breasts lightly in the seasoned flour.

Step 3 Dip the floured chicken breasts firstly into the beaten egg and then into the breadcrumb and sage mixture, making sure that they are completely covered with the breadcrumbs.

Step 5 Fry each chicken breast gently in the hot margarine and oil for about 5 minutes on each side, until they are lightly golden and the meat is tender and cooked.

Cook's Notes

 TIME: Preparation takes about 20 minutes, and cooking takes about 10-15 minutes.

 VARIATION: Use chopped fresh tarragon leaves, instead of the sage.

 SERVING IDEAS: Serve with new potatoes and cooked green beans.

SOUTH SEAS MEATBALLS

SERVES 4

An unusual way of serving a favorite family meal.

1lb extra lean ground beef
1 egg, beaten
Freshly ground sea salt and black pepper
1 tbsp sunflower oil
3 small shallots, chopped
2 tbsps whole-wheat flour
1lb canned pineapple chunks in natural juice
1 tbsp soy sauce
1 tsp wine vinegar
½ green pepper, seeded and finely chopped
¼ cup blanched slivered almonds

1. Put the beef into a large bowl and mix in the egg and the seasoning.

2. Divide the beef mixture into 8, and roll into balls. Dust your hands lightly with flour, and flatten each ball slightly.

3. Brush the meat balls with a little of the oil, and grill under a hot broiler for 10-15 minutes, turning them once during cooking, to cook each side.

4. Heat the tablespoon of oil in a frying pan and fry the shallots gently for 3 minutes, until they are transparent, but not brown.

5. Stir the flour into the onions, and cook for about 1 minute.

6. Add the juices from the canned pineapple gradually to the flour mixture, stirring well between additions, until all the juice is incorporated and the sauce is smooth.

Step 2 Divide the beef mixture into 8, and shape into 8 balls. Flatten the balls slightly with lightly floured hands.

Step 3 Brush the meatballs with a little oil, and arrange them on a lined broiler pan, before broiling.

7. Add the soy sauce and vinegar, and season with salt and pepper.

8. Stir the pineapple chunks, green pepper and almonds into the sauce.

9. Add the cooked meatballs to the sauce and heat gently for about 10-15 minutes until they are warmed right through.

Cook's Notes

 TIME: Preparation takes about 20 minutes, and cooking will take about 20-25 minutes.

 VARIATION: Use 1lb ground chicken for an interesting variation.

 SERVING IDEAS: Serve the meatballs in the sauce, surrounded by a bed of rice.

ROAST HERBED LEG OF LAMB

SERVES 6

The next time you cook a leg of lamb for the Sunday roast, try this recipe for an interesting and delicious change.

3½lb leg of lamb
2-3 cloves garlic
2 bay leaves
½ cup polyunsaturated margarine
1½ cups breadcrumbs
1 tsp chopped fresh thyme
1 tsp chopped fresh rosemary
1 tbsp chopped fresh parsley
Juice of 2 lemons
Freshly ground sea salt and black pepper

Step 3 Spread the margarine, breadcrumb and herb mixture over the upper surface of the meat using a palette knife.

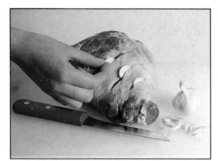

Step 2 Make small slits in the underside of the leg of lamb, and insert thin slices of garlic into these.

Step 5 30 minutes before the end of the cooking time, roll back the foil and baste the joint with the meat juices.

1. Prepare a sheet of foil large enough to wrap around the meat completely.

2. Peel and slice 1 or 2 of the garlic cloves. Make small cuts in the underside of the meat and insert the slices of garlic into this. Put the meat onto the foil with the bay leaves underneath.

3. In a small bowl, mix the margarine thoroughly with the remaining ingredients. Spread this mixture over the upper surface of the meat, using a wetted palette knife.

4. Loosely wrap the foil around the joint of meat, place in a roasting pan and roast in a preheated oven, 400°F, for about 1¾ hours.

5. Unwrap the foil and baste the meat with the melted fat that has collected in the base of the pan.

6. Continue roasting, uncovered, for a further 30 minutes, until the crust is brown and crisp.

Cook's Notes

 TIME: Preparation takes about 15 minutes, and cooking takes about 30 minutes per 1lb, plus 30 minutes. This may be reduced to 25 minutes per 1lb, plus 25 minutes extra cooking, if you like slightly rarer meat.

COOK'S TIP: The breadcrumb mixture in this recipe is also delicious when used to coat a joint of gammon.

 SERVING IDEAS: Serve with buttered new potatoes and seasonal vegetables.

LIVER AND BACON KEBABS

SERVES 4

*These economical and delicious kebabs are exceptionally nutritious
and are also very quick and easy to prepare.*

12oz lambs' liver, trimmed
6oz lean back bacon
1 cup small button mushrooms
2 tbsps polyunsaturated vegetable oil
½ cup very fine whole-wheat breadcrumbs
½ tsp paprika pepper
Freshly ground sea salt

1. Wipe the liver and cut away any coarse tubes.

2. Cut the liver into 1-inch cubes.

3. De-rind the bacon and cut each strip in half lengthways. Roll each bacon strip into small bacon rolls.

Step 3 De-rind the strips of bacon and cut them in half lengthways. Roll up the bacon strips like a jelly roll, starting from the narrow end.

4. Wipe and trim the mushrooms.

5. Preheat the broiler to a moderate heat. Line the broiler pan with foil.

6. Thread the bacon rolls, liver and mushrooms alternately onto 4 skewers. Brush the meat and vegetables with a little of the oil.

Step 6 Thread the bacon rolls, liver and mushrooms alternately onto 4 skewers. Brush with a little of the oil.

7. On a plate, mix together the breadcrumbs, paprika and salt.

8. Turn the kebabs in the breadcrumbs until they are evenly coated.

9. Arrange the kebabs on the broiler pan and broil for 5-10 minutes, turning the kebabs frequently, and brushing them with any of the oil that remains, to prevent them burning.

Step 8 Turn the kebabs in the breadcrumb mixture on the plate, until they are evenly coated, pressing the breadcrumbs onto the kebabs, if necessary.

Cook's Notes

 TIME: Preparation will take about 20 minutes, and cooking takes about 5-10 minutes.

 VARIATION: Use zucchini, or peppers, instead of the mushrooms if liked.

 SERVING IDEAS: Serve the kebabs on a bed of rice, mixed with the vegetables of your choice.

PORK BURGERS

SERVES 4

For healthier burgers, make sure that the mince is very lean and broil the burgers rather than fry them.

1lb extra lean, raw ground pork
1 small onion, finely chopped
¾ cup fresh whole-wheat breadcrumbs
1 stock cube, crumbled
1 tsp chopped fresh parsley
Freshly ground sea salt and black pepper, to taste
1 tbsp tomato paste
1 tsp made mustard
1 egg, beaten

To Serve
4 whole-wheat rolls
Crisp lettuce leaves and tomato and cucumber slices

1. In a large bowl, mix together the ground pork, onion and breadcrumbs.

2. Stir in all the remaining burger ingredients and mix together thoroughly before dividing into quarters, and forming each quarter into a hamburger shape with lightly floured hands.

3. Arrange the burgers on a broiler pan and cook under a preheated hot broiler for 6-7 minutes on each side, turning the burgers, to prevent them burning.

4. Split the baps in half, and lay a lettuce leaf on the bottom half of each bap.

Step 2 Add the remaining burger ingredients to the mince and onion mixture. Mix them together thoroughly, to ensure that the seasonings are fully incorporated.

Step 3 Arrange burgers on a broiler pan and cook under a preheated hot broiler for 6-7 minutes on each side.

5. Put the cooked burger on top of the lettuce leaf and arrange cucumber and tomato slices over it. Top with the remaining half of the roll and serve.

Cook's Notes

 TIME: Preparation takes about 20 minutes, and cooking takes about 15 minutes.

 COOK'S TIP: These burgers are especially suitable for children's parties.

 SERVING IDEAS: Serve with tasty home-made pickles or relishes, and lots of salad.

FREEZING: You can freeze these burgers raw for up to 3 months, providing that the meat used in their preparation has not been frozen before.

HONEY PLUM COBBLER

SERVES 6-8

*This pudding derives its name from the "cobbles" that the scones
arranged around the edge of the pudding are supposed to represent.*

2lbs ripe plums, halved and pitted
4-6 tbsps clear honey, to taste
2 cups whole-wheat self-rising flour
2 tbsps unrefined soft brown sugar
1 tbsp polyunsaturated margarine
½ cup low fat natural yogurt, or 1% fat fromage frais
A little skim milk, for glazing

1. Put the plums into an ovenproof dish with the
honey. Cover the dish with a sheet of aluminum
foil and cook in a preheated oven, 400°F for
15 minutes.

2. Put the flour and sugar into a large mixing bowl
and rub in the margarine with your fingertips.

3. Using a round-bladed knife, stir the yogurt into
the flour mixture, until it forms a soft, but firm,
dough.

Step 3 Using a round-
bladed knife, stir the
yogurt into the flour
mixture, until it forms
a soft but firm dough.

4. Lightly flour a pastry board, or work surface,
and knead the dough until it is smooth.

Step 5 Cut 2-inch
circles out of the
dough with a cookie
cutter, to form the
cobbles.

Step 7 Arrange the
scone cobbles around
the edge of the dish,
overlapping them
slightly and brushing
them with a little milk
to glaze.

5. Roll the dough out until it is approximately
¾ inch thick. Cut out rounds of dough using a
2 inch cutter, to form the cobbles.

6. Remove the plums from the oven and leave to
cool.

7. Arrange the cobbles around the edge of the
dish, overlapping them slightly. Brush the top of
each cobble with a little milk.

8. Return the dish to the oven and cook until the
cobbles are well risen and brown.

Cook's Notes

TIME: Preparation takes about
30 minutes, and cooking takes
about 45 minutes.

VARIATION: Use any fruit
suitable for stewing, in place of
the plums.

SERVING IDEAS: Serve piping
hot with spoonfuls of 1% fat
fromage frais and a sprinkling of
cinnamon or mixed spice.

LEMON AND GINGER CHEESECAKE

SERVES 6-8

This fresh, creamy-tasting cheesecake is full of wholesome ingredients.

3 tbsps polyunsaturated margarine, melted
2 tbsps soft unrefined brown sugar
1 cup whole-wheat cookies, crushed
¾ cup low fat curd cheese
2 eggs, separated
Finely grated rind 1 lemon
2 tbsps soft unrefined brown sugar
½ cup natural yogurt, or 1% fat fromage frais
½oz powdered gelatin
3 tbsps hot water
Juice ½ lemon
3 pieces preserved stem ginger, rinsed in warm
    water and chopped
4 tbsps thick natural yogurt, or 1% fat fromage frais
Fine matchstick strips lemon peel, or twists of
    lemon, to decorate

1. Lightly grease a 7-inch pie pan.

2. Mix the melted butter with the soft brown sugar and the crushed cookies. Press the crumb mixture evenly over the base of the dish.

3. Chill the base, for at least 1 hour, in the refrigerator.

4. Beat the curd cheese with the egg yolks, lemon rind and sugar. Stir in the yogurt.

5. Dissolve the gelatin in the water, and add this to the cheese mixture, stirring thoroughly, to incorporate evenly.

6. Stir in the lemon juice, and put the cheese mixture to one side, until it is on the point of setting.

7. Whisk the egg whites, until they are stiff, but not dry, and fold these lightly, but thoroughly, into the cheese mixture together with the chopped stem ginger.

8. Spoon this mixture into the prepared pie pan, smoothing the surface level.

9. Chill the cheesecake for 3-4 hours, until the filling has set completely. Swirl the natural yogurt over the top of the cheesecake, and decorate with the strips of lemon peel, or lemon twists.

Step 2 Spread the butter and cookie crumb mixture evenly over the base of the prepared flan dish, drawing it slightly up the sides of the dish, and making sure it is pressed down firmly.

Step 5 Mix the dissolved gelatin thoroughly into the cheese and egg mixture, along with the lemon juice. Stir the mixture well, to ensure that the gelatin is evenly blended.

Cook's Notes

 TIME: Preparation takes about 30 minutes, plus chilling time.

 COOK'S TIP: The gelatin will dissove more quickly, if you sprinkle it onto the hot water in a small bowl, and stand this bowl in a larger bowl of hot water. Stir the gelatin, to ensure that no grainy bits remain.

VARIATION: Use an orange, instead of the lemon, and 3 tsps of chopped candied peel, instead of the ginger. Decorate with strips of orange peel, or halved orange slices.

PRUNE, APRICOT AND NUT TORTE

SERVES 6-8

This spectacular shortcake is ideal as the centerpiece for a cold buffet table, or as a sumptuous cake for tea.

¾ cup dried apricots
¾ cup dried prunes
1 cup red wine, or dry cider
1 cup whole-wheat flour
½ cup polyunsaturated margarine
½ cup unrefined soft brown sugar
½ cup hazelnuts, freshly ground
3 tbsps finely chopped walnuts
2 tbsps clear honey, warmed
1 tbsp pine nuts
1 tbsp hazelnuts

1. Put the apricots and prunes into a large mixing bowl. Warm the wine, or cider, pour this over the dried fruits and leave them to stand for 4 hours, or until they are moist and plump.

2. Put the flour into a large bowl, and rub in the margarine with your fingertips, until the mixture resembles soft breadcrumbs.

3. Add the brown sugar, ground hazelnuts and the finely chopped walnuts to the flour mixture, and knead the mixture, until it forms a soft dough.

4. Grease the base of an 8-inch fluted, loose-bottomed pie pan, and press the nut dough evenly into the pan.

5. Bake the dough in a preset oven, 375°F, for approximately 15 minutes.

6. Drain the prunes and apricots, and dry them thoroughly on paper towels.

7. Remove the shortcake from the oven, and arrange the soaked fruits in an attractive pattern over the top.

8. Cover with a piece of foil, and return the whole shortcake to the oven for a further 10 minutes.

9. Remove the shortcake from the oven, and allow it to cool for a few minutes in the pan, before removing it carefully and placing it on a wire rack to cool completely.

10. When the shortcake has cooled, transfer it to a serving plate, and glaze the top of the fruits with the warmed honey.

11. Sprinkle the pine nuts and the whole hazelnuts over the fruit, before serving.

Step 1 Put the apricots and prunes into a large bowl, with the wine, or cider, and leave the fruit to soak for 4 hours, until plump.

Step 4 Press the nut dough evenly over the base of a loose-bottomed flan pan, making sure that it is pressed well into the edges and is of equal thickness all over.

Cook's Notes

TIME: Preparation takes about 30 minutes, plus 4 hours soaking time, and cooking takes about 25 minutes.

VARIATION: For a very subtle flavour, use warm jasmine or orange blossom tea, to soak the fruits in, instead of the wine or cider.

SERVING IDEAS: Serve the shortcake warm from the oven, instead of allowing it to cool.

SCRAP BREAD PUDDING

SERVES 6-8

*This is the real bread pudding that our grandmothers used to make,
and we loved so much. Yet if you look down the list of ingredients,
you will see that it reads like a shopping list from a health farm.*

8oz whole-wheat bread scraps, crusts removed
1 cup skim milk
¼ cup whole-wheat flour
1 tsp baking powder
2oz vegetable suet, chopped
1 tsp grated lemon rind
1 tsp mixed spice
¼ cup each of currants, raisins and golden raisins
2 tbsps mixed cut peel
2 tbsps unrefined soft brown sugar
1 egg, beaten

1. Break the bread into small pieces and put these into a large bowl. Pour the milk over the bread and allow to stand for about half an hour.

2. Put the flour into a small bowl and mix in the baking powder, chopped vegetable suet, lemon rind and spice.

3. Squeeze as much milk as possible out of the bread into a separate bowl. Beat all the lumps out of the bread with a fork, or whisk.

4. Stir the flour and suet mixture into the bread, along with the dried fruit and the sugar.

5. Add the beaten egg and the reserved milk to the bread and fruit mixture.

6. Pour the bread and fruit mixture into a well-greased, ovenproof baking dish, or pan. Stand the dish, or pan, in a roasting pan and pour in enough hot water to come halfway up the sides of the baking dish.

7. Put the bread pudding into a preheated oven, 350°F, and cook for 1-1¼ hours.

8. Allow the pudding to cool slightly, before turning out onto a serving plate, if serving hot, or onto a wire cooling rack to allow to cool, before cutting into squares and serving like a cake.

Step 1 Break the bread into small pieces and put these into a large bowl. Pour the milk over the bread and allow to stand for about half an hour.

Step 3 Beat all the lumps out of the bread with a fork, or whisk.

Cook's Notes

 TIME: Preparation takes about 40 minutes, and cooking takes about 1¼ hours.

 PREPARATION: For a completely authentic taste, the scrap bread pudding should be steamed. To do this, turn the mixture into a well-greased pudding bowl, cover with wax paper and steam, in a steamer for 2½ hours.

SERVING IDEAS: Dust the pudding lightly with unrefined granulated sugar before serving.

 FREEZING: This pudding will freeze for up to 2 months.

COFFEE PECAN PIE

SERVES 6-8

Sumptuous and rich, this traditional American pie is ideal for serving after a celebration meal.

6oz whole-wheat digestive cookies
4 tbsps polyunsaturated margarine, melted
1 cup pecan nut halves
6oz marshmallows
1 cup strong decaffeinated black coffee
½oz gelatin
3 tbsps hot water
1 egg white
½ cup 1% fat fromage frais

1. Crush the cookies into fine crumbs and mix together with the melted butter.

2. Press the crumb mixture onto the base and halfway up the sides of a well-greased 7-inch spring-form cake pan. Chill the cookie crumb base for at least 1 hour.

3. Reserve 8 pecan nut halves for decoration, and chop the remainder finely.

4. In a large saucepan, dissolve the marshmallows in the coffee, by heating gently and stirring frequently.

5. Sprinkle the gelatin onto the hot water and stir, until it is clear and has dissolved completely.

6. Carefully pour the gelatin into the marshmallow mixture, and stir well, to ensure that it is evenly mixed in. Leave the coffee and marshmallow mixture to cool, until it is almost set.

7. Whisk the egg white until it forms soft peaks, and fold this carefully into the fromage frais.

8. Fold the fromage frais into the coffee and marshmallow mixture with a metal spoon,

incorporating as much air as possible, and making sure that the fromage frais is evenly blended.

9. Stir in the chopped nuts and pour the mixture onto the chilled base.

10. Chill the pie in the refrigerator for at least 3 hours, until completely set.

11. Remove the sides of the pan, and slide the pie carefully onto a serving dish. Decorate with the reserved nut halves.

Step 3 Chop the remainder of the pecan nuts.

Step 4 Put the marshmallows and the coffee into a large saucepan, and heat gently, stirring all the time, until the marshmallows have completely dissolved.

Cook's Notes

TIME: Preparation takes about 20 minutes, plus at least 4 hours chilling time.

PREPARATION: The gelatin will dissolve more quickly, if after you sprinkle it onto the hot water, you stand the small bowl in a larger bowl, half filled with boiling water.

COOK'S TIP: To remove the cake from the pan, run a round bladed knife, which has previously been dipped into boiling water, carefully around the edge, to loosen the sides.

SUMMER PUDDING

SERVES 6-8

A classic dessert, which makes good use of nutritious fresh fruits.

1½ lbs mixed, fresh soft fruit
½ cup unrefined granulated sugar
9-10 slices whole-wheat bread, thickly cut and with
  crusts removed

1. Put all the fruit into a saucepan with the sugar and heat gently, until the sugar has dissolved, but the fruit is not completely cooked. Shake the pan whilst heating, so that the fruit will stay as whole as possible.

2. Remove the pan from the heat and leave the fruit to cool.

3. Line the base and sides of a 3 cup pudding basin with 6 or 7 slices of the bread, trying not to leave any gaps between each slice.

4. Put the fruit mixture into the center of the pudding, and cover the top completely with the

Step 3 Line the base and sides of a 3 cup pudding basin with 6 or 7 slices of the bread, making sure that there are no gaps between the slices.

remaining bread slices.

5. Press the top bread slices down firmly, and place a saucer, or small plate, on top of the pudding. Weigh the plate down, with a heavy weight.

6. Chill the pudding in the refrigerator overnight. Turn the pudding out of the bowl carefully, and decorate with fresh soft fruit according to choice.

Cook's Notes

 TIME: Preparation takes about 10-15 minutes, plus overnight chilling time.

 PREPARATION: Do not overcook the fruit for this recipe, or there will be too much juice and the bread will not be able to absorb it.

 COOK'S TIP: If you do not have a heavy weight handy, a bag of sugar, or flour, will do equally well.

 SERVING IDEAS: Serve with a spoonful of 1% fat fromage frais.

 FREEZING: Summer pudding freezes very well for up to 3 months.

GUINNESS CAKE

MAKES 1 CAKE

Dark and moist, this delicious cake is full of fibre and wholesome ingredients.

1 cup polyunsaturated margarine
¾ cup unrefined soft brown sugar
1 cup Guinness, or stout
1 cup raisins
1 cup currants
1 cup golden raisins
½ cup chopped mixed peel
1¼ lbs whole-wheat all-purpose flour
1 tsp mixed spice
1 tsp nutmeg
½ tsp bicarbonate of soda
3 eggs, beaten

1. Grease and line a 9-inch cake pan with wax or silicone paper.

2. Put the margarine, the sugar and the Guinness into a large saucepan and bring the ingredients slowly to the boil, stirring all the time, until the sugar and the margarine have melted.

3. Stir the dried fruit and peel into the Guinness mixture, and bring all the ingredients back to the boil. Simmer for 5 minutes. Remove from the heat and leave, until the mixture is quite cold.

4. Put the flour, spices and bicarbonate of soda into a large mixing bowl.

5. Beat the cooled fruit mixture and the eggs into the flour, mixing well with a wooden spoon, to ensure that the flour is thoroughly incorporated and there are no lumps.

6. Pour the cake mixture into the prepared pan, and bake in the center of a preheated oven, 325°F for 2 hours.

7. Cool the cake in the pan, before turning it out.

Step 1 Line the base and the sides of the greased cake pan with wax or silicone paper, making sure that it fits well into the corners and over the base of the pan.

Step 3 Simmer the dried fruit and peel in the sugar and Guinness mixture for 5 minutes, stirring occasionally, to prevent the mixture from burning.

Cook's Notes

 TIME: Preparation takes about 20 minutes, plus cooling time, and cooking takes about 2 hours.

 COOK'S TIP: To test whether the cake is cooked, push a metal skewer or darning needle into the center of the cake. If it is clean when pulled out, the cake is done.

 SERVING IDEAS: This cake is ideal to be used as a Christmas, or rich birthday cake and can be decorated to suit the occasion with almond paste and icing.

 FREEZING: This cake will freeze very well for up to 6 months.

CARROT CAKE

MAKES 1 LOAF

Do not let the idea of carrots in a cake put you off trying this recipe. Carrots have long been used as a sweet ingredient, and this cake is moist and absolutely delicious.

¾ cup polyunsatured margarine
¾ cup soft unrefined brown sugar
2 eggs, well beaten
2 cups whole-wheat all-purpose flour
1½ tsps bicarbonate of soda
½ tsp baking powder
½ tsp ground cinnamon
¼ tsp cardamom seeds, crushed
8oz peeled carrots, grated
½ cup raisins
½ cup walnuts, chopped
2 tbsps clear honey
Powdered sugar, for dredging

1. Cream the margarine and sugar together, until they are light and fluffy.

Step 1 Cream the margarine and sugar together, until they are light and fluffy.

2. Add the eggs, a little at a time, beating well after each addition, until they are fully incorporated.

3. Mix the flour with the bicarbonate of soda, baking powder, cinnamon and cardamom. Fold these dry ingredients into the egg mixture gently, but thoroughly.

Step 3 Fold the dry ingredients carefully, but thoroughly, into the egg mixture, using a metal spoon and incorporating as much air into the mixture as possible.

Step 4 Stir the carrots, raisins, nuts and honey into the cake mixture, mixing well to blend thoroughly.

4. Stir in the carrots, raisins and nuts, along with the honey. Mix well, to blend thoroughly.

5. Pour the carrot mixture into a well-buttered 10-inch loaf tin. Bake in a preheated oven, 350°F for 45-50 minutes, or until a fine metal skewer comes out clean, when inserted into the center of the cake.

6. Cool the cake in the pan for 10-15 minutes, before turning out carefully onto a wire rack, to cool completely.

7. Drizzle the cake with powdered sugar before serving.

Cook's Notes

 TIME: Preparation takes about 30 minutes, and cooking takes about 45-50 minutes.

 COOK'S TIP: If the mixture begins to curdle when the eggs are added to the butter and sugar, stir in a tablespoon of flour with each addition of egg, and then beat thoroughly.

SERVING IDEAS: Serve the cake as an interesting dessert with a spoonful of 1% fat fromage frais.

APRICOT AND WALNUT TEABREAD

MAKES 1 LOAF

Good news for those with a sweet tooth, cakes and teabreads are an excellent and delicious way of introducing fibre into the diet, and this recipe is no exception.

¾ cup polyunsaturated margarine
½ cup unrefined soft brown sugar, or molasses
3 eggs, beaten
2 cups whole-wheat self-rising flour
2 tbsps skim milk
¾ cup dried apricots, chopped
½ cup shelled walnuts, chopped
2 tsps clear honey, warmed
Few extra chopped dried apricots, to decorate

1. Lightly grease a 2lb loaf pan and line the base with a piece of wax paper.

Step 1 Lightly grease 2lb loaf pan, and base line the pan with a piece of wax or silicone paper.

2. Cream together the margarine and sugar, until light and fluffy.

3. Beat in the eggs, a little at a time, adding a teaspoonful of flour with each addition of egg, if the mixture shows signs of curdling.

4. Fold in the flour carefully and, finally, stir in the milk, apricots and nuts.

Step 4 Fold in the flour carefully and, finally, stir in the milk, apricots and nuts.

Step 7 As soon as the loaf comes out of the oven, brush the top with warmed honey and sprinkle with the extra chopped apricots.

5. Put the mixture into the prepared loaf pan, smoothing the top level.

6. Bake in a preheated oven, 325°F, for 1½ hours, or until a skewer inserted into the center of the loaf comes out clean.

7. As soon as the loaf comes out of the oven, brush the top with the warmed honey and sprinkle with the extra chopped apricots. Leave to cool in the pan for a few minutes, before turning out and leaving to cool completely.

Cook's Notes

 TIME: Preparation takes about 20 minutes, and cooking takes about 1½ hours.

 VARIATION: Substitute any favorite dried fruit and nuts for the fruit and nuts suggested in this recipe.

 FREEZING: This teabread will freeze well for up to 2 months.

GOLDEN RAISIN SODA BREAD

MAKES 1 ROUND LOAF

High in fiber and low in fat, this sweet soda bread is very easy to make.

1lb whole-wheat flour
1 tsp freshly ground sea salt
1 tsp of bicarbonate of soda
1 tsp cream of tartar
1 tbsp unrefined soft brown sugar
½ cup golden raisins
½ cup low fat natural yogurt
Generous ½ cup skim milk

1. Put the flour, salt, bicarbonate of soda and cream of tartar into a mixing bowl.

2. Stir the sugar and the golden raisins into the flour, and make a slight well in the center.

3. In a jug, mix together the yogurt and the milk. Pour this mixture gradually into the well in the flour, and mix with a round-bladed knife, to form a firm but not too stiff dough.

4. Turn the dough onto a floured board and knead it until it is smooth.

5. Form the dough into a round, and slightly flatten it with your hand.

6. Cut a deep cross into the top of the dough and brush with a little extra milk. Put the loaf onto a lightly floured cookie sheet, and bake in the center of a preheated oven, 400°F, for 25 minutes.

7. Turn the loaf upside down on the tray and return it to the oven for a further 5 minutes to cook underneath.

8. Wrap the loaf in a damp cloth and place it on its side to cool.

Step 5 Shape the kneaded dough into a round and cut a deep cross into the top of the dough, using a sharp knife.

Step 3 Add the milk gradually to the flour and fruit mixture, mixing it in well with a round-bladed knife, to form a firm but not too stiff dough.

Step 8 Wrap the loaf in a damp cloth, and place it on its side to cool.

_____ Cook's Notes _____

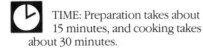 TIME: Preparation takes about 15 minutes, and cooking takes about 30 minutes.

 COOK'S TIP: To test that the loaf is cooked, tap it on the base; when it sounds hollow, the loaf is done.

 FREEZING: This loaf will freeze for up to 2 months.

Microwave Healthy Eating

We are all becoming more health conscious. Even the most traditional among us are beginning to look for healthier ways of eating. This is one of the ways a microwave oven can help out in the kitchen. A microwave oven is of benefit because it turns out healthier meals in double-quick time.

Food cooked in a microwave oven retains all its natural moisture and goodness, so chicken and fish will be tender, juicy and tasty. Vegetables need less water for cooking, so they keep their crisp texture, vibrant color and, most importantly, their vitamins. Cooking by microwaves brings out all the natural flavors of foods, so you'll find you need less salt, which is, of course, another health asset.

While some of the recipes in this chapter use classic health foods such as lentils and other dried pulses, they also use ingredients your family already enjoys; nothing unusual, just good, wholesome foods like fresh vegetables and fruit, protein-rich fish and chicken, and pasta and rice.

GINGERED RUTABAGA

SERVES 4

Rutabaga, sometimes watery when boiled, is light and fluffy when cooked in a microwave oven.

1lb rutabaga, peeled
4 tbsps water
Sea salt
Freshly ground black pepper
1 tbsp low fat spread
2 tbsps fresh ginger, peeled and grated
Fresh ginger, peeled and cut into thin strips, or parsley, to garnish

Step 2 Loosely cover the bowl with plastic wrap, leaving a gap for the steam to escape.

Step 1 Place the small pieces of rutabaga in a bowl with the water and seasoning.

1. Cut the rutabaga into small pieces and place in a bowl with the water, sea salt and freshly ground black pepper.

2. Loosely cover and cook on HIGH for 10-15 minutes or until tender, stirring twice.

3. Drain well and mash thoroughly or purée in a

food processor with the low fat spread. Stir in the ginger.

4. Reheat on HIGH for 1-2 minutes if necessary. Serve hot. Garnish with fresh ginger or parsley.

Step 3 Mash the well-drained rutabaga with the low fat spread until smooth.

Cook's Notes

 TIME: Preparation takes about 10 minutes, and cooking takes 11-17 minutes.

 VARIATION: Combine with parsnips for a slightly different taste. Cook at the same time as the rutabaga.

 SERVING IDEAS: Serve with any roast meat or poultry.

ROSEMARY LYONNAISE POTATOES

SERVES 4

This potato dish cooks in less than half the time it would need in a regular oven.

1lb potatoes
2 tbsps low fat spread
1 tbsp finely chopped rosemary
1 small clove garlic, crushed
1 small onion, finely chopped
2 tbsps skim milk
Sea salt
Freshly ground black pepper

1. Peel and thinly slice the potatoes.

2. Put the low fat spread, rosemary, garlic and onions in an 8-inch, shallow dish and cook on HIGH for 3 minutes until soft.

3. Stir in the skim milk, sea salt and freshly ground black pepper and add the potatoes arranging them

Step 2 Soften the onion, garlic and rosemary in the low fat spread.

neatly in the dish.

4. Cover and cook on MEDIUM for 12-15 minutes until the potatoes are soft. Brown under a broiler if desired.

Step 1 Slice the potatoes thinly and evenly with a food processor or mandoline.

Step 3 Add the potatoes to the other ingredients and arrange them neatly in the dish.

Cook's Notes

 TIME: Preparation takes about 10 minutes, and cooking takes 12-15 minutes.

 VARIATION: Other herbs can be substituted for rosemary. Chopped, cooked ham can be added and the dish served as a light supper or lunch.

SERVING IDEAS: Serve with roast chicken or lamb as a change from roast potatoes. It is also good with gammon or pork.

CABBAGE WITH CARAWAY

SERVES 4

Vegetables cooked in a microwave oven retain all their fresh flavor
and color and their crispy texture too.

1lb green cabbage
4 tbsps water
Sea salt
2 tbsps low fat spread
2 tbsps caraway seeds
Freshly ground black pepper

Step 1 Place the finely shredded cabbage in a roasting bag with the sea salt and water.

Step 2 Use string or a non-metallic tie to secure the bag and place it on an oven turntable.

Step 4 In a bowl, toss the cooked cabbage with the low fat spread and caraway seeds.

1. Finely shred the cabbage and place in a roasting bag with the sea salt and water.

2. Tie loosely and cook on HIGH for 5-6 minutes until cooked but still slightly crisp. Drain well.

3. Place the low fat spread in a large bowl and cook on HIGH for 1 minute or until melted.

4. Add the caraway seeds and pepper and stir well. Add the cooked cabbage and toss. Serve garnished with extra caraway seeds if desired.

Cook's Notes

 TIME: Preparation takes about 5 minutes, and cooking takes 7 minutes.

 SERVING IDEAS: Serve as an accompaniment to roast meats and poultry. This dish is especially good with pork or duck.

 WATCHPOINT: Cabbage cooks very quickly in a microwave oven and may become soggy, so it needs careful watching.

SUCCOTASH

SERVES 4

This colorful dish was named by the American Indians. Updated, it cooks beautifully in a microwave oven.

2¼ cups butter beans
1 medium onion, chopped
1 green pepper, chopped
2 tbsps low fat spread
3 cups frozen corn
½ cup low fat natural yogurt
1 tsp arrowroot

1. To cook the beans in the microwave, pour over boiling water to cover and allow to soak for at least 2 hours, or follow the instructions in the Cook's Tip below for rehydrating pulses.

2. Drain and cover with fresh water. Microwave on HIGH for 10 minutes and then on MEDIUM for 1 hour or until soft.

3. Combine the onions and pepper with the low fat spread, and microwave for 2 minutes on HIGH.

4. Add the cooked beans and the frozen corn and microwave for 4 minutes on HIGH.

5. Mix the arrowroot into 1 tbsp of the yogurt, then add the rest of the yogurt. Stir into the beans and corn before serving.

Step 4 Combine the cooked beans, peppers and onion with the frozen corn and cook until the corn has defrosted and heated through.

Step 1 Soak the beans until they swell in size.

Step 5 Mix the arrowroot with the yogurt and stir it into the vegetables.

Cook's Notes

 TIME: Preparation takes about 1 hour, to rehydrate the beans. Cooking takes about 1 hour.

 SERVING IDEAS: Succotash is often served with bacon, but if you don't eat meat try it with a tomato dish.

 PREPARATION: Although cooking dried pulses in a microwave oven takes almost as long as boiling them, they will have a much better texture with less chance of breaking up.

 COOK'S TIP: To eliminate overnight soaking of dried pulses, cover them with water in a large bowl and heat on HIGH for about 10 minutes or until boiling. Allow to boil for about 2 minutes and then leave to stand for 1 hour.

HEARTY PEA SOUP

SERVES 6

This filling soup is a healthy family favorite. Sausages add extra flavor.

2 cups split peas
6 cups boiling water or stock
2 leeks, sliced
2 medium onions, sliced
1 stalk celery, sliced
2 large carrots, sliced
8oz thickly sliced bacon, diced
1 large smoked sausage, thickly sliced or 8oz
   frankfurters or saveloys, thickly sliced
Sea salt and freshly ground black pepper
Low fat natural yogurt

1. To cook the split peas in the microwave, cover them with boiling water and leave to soak for at least 1 hour.

2. Drain, place them in a large casserole and pour

Step 3 Add the bacon and chopped vegetables to the peas and cook until the vegetables soften.

over half of the boiling water or stock. Microwave for 15 minutes on HIGH, or until the peas are soft.

3. Purée half of the cooked peas and return them to the casserole. Add the chopped vegetables, diced bacon and the rest of the boiling water or stock and microwave for 20 minutes on HIGH, or until the vegetables are soft.

Step 4 Add the sausages to the soup mixture and continue cooking.

4. Add the thickly sliced smoked sausage, frankfurters or saveloys, season to taste with salt and pepper, and microwave for a further 5 minutes on HIGH.

5. Leave to stand for at least 15 minutes before serving. Top each serving with a spoonful of yogurt.

Cook's Notes

TIME: Preparation takes about 20 minutes, plus 1 hour to soak the peas. Cooking takes about 40 minutes.

SERVING IDEAS: Serve this hearty soup with chunks of fresh whole-wheat bread or rolls for a complete, warming winter supper.

FREEZING: Allow the soup to cool completely. Pour into rigid containers, seal, label and freeze for up to 3 months. Reheat using DEFROST or LOW settings and break up the soup as it defrosts.

LENTIL VEGETABLE SOUP

SERVES 4

For convenience this soup can be prepared in advance. It will taste even better reheated as the flavors will have had a chance to develop.

2 cups green or brown lentils
5 cups boiling water or stock
1 bacon or ham bone (optional)
3 medium carrots, sliced
2 leeks, sliced
½ small cabbage, shredded
1 bay leaf
2 cups additional water
½ tsp dried sage
1 tsp sea salt

1. To microwave the lentils, pour over boiling water and allow them to soak for at least 15 minutes.

2. Drain, then cover them with fresh boiling water or stock and microwave on HIGH for 15-20 minutes, or until they are soft.

3. Purée half of the cooked lentils with the cooking liquid. Add the remaining lentils, the bacon or ham bone, if using, the vegetables, herbs, remaining water and salt.

4. Microwave on HIGH for 10-15 minutes, or until all the vegetables are cooked.

Step 3 Transfer half the lentils and their cooking liquid and purée until smooth.

Step 4 Test the vegetables after 10 minutes. If they cut easily, they are sufficiently well cooked.

5. Allow to stand for at least 15 minutes before serving, to allow the flavors to blend.

Cook's Notes

 TIME: Preparation takes about 15 minutes, and cooking takes 25-30 minutes.

 VARIATION: You can vary the vegetables as you wish. Leave out the bacon or ham bone if you wish to make a vegetarian soup.

 SERVING IDEAS: Serve with fresh whole-wheat bread for a complete and satisfying meal.

MACARONI IN TOMATO-YOGURT SAUCE

SERVES 4

For a quick supper dish made from store cupboard ingredients, this dish can't be bettered.

¼ cup dried mushrooms
1 tbsp sunflower oil
1 medium onion, sliced
1 clove garlic, crushed
½ cup tomato juice
1 tsp dried mixed herbs
1½ tsps dried basil
3 cups hot water or vegetable stock
8oz whole-wheat macaroni or whole-wheat pasta
½ cup low fat natural yogurt
Sea salt and freshly ground black pepper to taste

1. Rinse the mushrooms well to remove any grit, then pour boiling water over and leave them to soak while you prepare the sauce.

2. Cook the onion and garlic in the oil for 2 minutes on HIGH.

3. Stir in the tomato juice and herbs, then mix in the water or stock.

4. Drain the mushrooms, remove stalks, slice the

Step 4 Add the uncooked macaroni to the sauce, stirring well to coat it thoroughly.

caps and add to the liquid, then stir in the uncooked macaroni. Partially cover and microwave for 10 minutes.

5. Stir occasionally during the cooking time to prevent the pasta from sticking together.

6. Allow to stand for 5 minutes, covered, to finish cooking. The pasta should be al dente. Just before serving, season to taste and stir in the low fat natural yogurt.

Step 1 Soak the dried mushrooms until they soften and swell in size.

Step 6 Leave to stand for 5 minutes for pasta to finish cooking. Stir in the yogurt.

Cook's Notes

TIME: Preparation takes 15 minutes, and cooking takes about 12 minutes.

PREPARATION: Pasta takes almost as long to microwave as it does to cook conventionally, but it cooks without sticking, and because it finishes cooking during standing time, there is little chance of overcooking.

VARIATION: Use any of the many small pasta shapes available to make this quick and easy vegetarian supper. Green or red pastas are good, too.

SPINACH RISOTTO

SERVES 4

For a quick supper after a busy day, a risotto is the perfect dish and economical, too.

2 tbsps low fat spread
1½ cups brown rice
1 onion, thinly sliced
3 cups hot vegetable stock
½ cup walnuts, roughly chopped
10oz frozen chopped spinach, thawed, or 10oz
    fresh spinach, washed and chopped
½ cup Parmesan cheese, grated
Sea salt and freshly ground black pepper to taste

1. Melt the low fat spread on HIGH for 1 minute, then add the rice and sliced onion.

2. Stir to coat, and microwave for 2 minutes on HIGH.

3. Add the hot stock, partially cover and cook on HIGH for 30-35 minutes, or until the rice is just soft.

Step 1 Stir the rice and onion into the low fat spread before cooking.

Step 3 Add the stock and cook until the rice is just soft.

4. Stir in the walnuts and spinach and microwave for a further 5 minutes on HIGH.

Step 4 Add the walnuts and spinach and cook for a further 5 minutes.

5. Mix in the Parmesan cheese and season to taste just before serving.

Cook's Notes

TIME: Preparation takes 15 minutes, and cooking takes 25-30 minutes.

SERVING IDEAS: Serve as an accompaniment to broiled meat, poultry or fish. For a vegetarian meal, serve with a fresh tomato salad.

BOSTON BAKED BEANS

SERVES 4

An American favorite made quick and easy with the help of canned beans and your microwave oven.

2 tbsps sunflower oil
1 large onion, sliced
1lb pork fat back skinned and diced into 1½-inch
  cubes
2 tbsps tomato ketchup
3 tbsps soft brown sugar
1 tsp mustard powder
1 tbsp malt vinegar
1 tbsp molasses
15oz canned navy beans
1 tbsp cornstarch mixed with a little water
Sea salt and freshly ground black pepper

Step 2 Cook the pork for about 3 minutes or until it loses its pink color.

1. Pour the sunflower oil into a large casserole dish and heat on HIGH for 2 minutes. Add the onion and cook on HIGH for a further 2 minutes.

2. Add the pork and cook on HIGH for 3 minutes.

3. Mix the ketchup, sugar, mustard, vinegar and molasses together.

4. Drain the beans, reserving ½ cup of the liquid. Add the reserved bean liquid and the ketchup mixture to the pork. Stir well. Cover and cook on MEDIUM for 15 minutes.

Step 4 Add the sauce ingredients to the pork, mixing well.

5. Add the beans, cornstarch and water and seasoning. Cook on HIGH for 5 minutes. Leave the casserole for 5-10 minutes before serving.

Step 5 Add the beans and cornstarch and cook until the sauce thickens and clears.

Cook's Notes

 TIME: Preparation takes 15 minutes, and cooking takes about 27 minutes. The casserole should stand for 5-10 minutes before serving to complete cooking.

VARIATION: If desired, the pork may be omitted. Alternatively, bacon or ham may be substituted.

 BUYING GUIDE: Navy beans are usually available in supermarkets, but other varieties such as butter or white kidney beans can be used instead.

RED BEANS AND RICE

SERVES 4

Spicy, without being hot, this combination of beans and rice makes a colorful meal that can be prepared in advance and reheated.

1 cup dried kidney beans
1 medium onion, finely chopped
1 stalk celery, thinly sliced
1 large clove garlic, crushed
½ tsp allspice or mixed spice
1 bay leaf
¾ cup brown rice
1½ cups hot vegetable stock
¼ cup black olives, pitted and sliced
1 cup low fat Cheddar cheese, grated
Sea salt and freshly ground black pepper

1. To cook the beans in the microwave, first pour on boiling water to cover and allow to stand for at least 2 hours. Drain, then cover with fresh boiling water and microwave on HIGH for 35 minutes, or until the beans are tender.

2. Alternatively, the beans may be cooked by any other method.

3. Combine the cooked beans, chopped onion,

Step 3 Combine the beans with the other ingredients in a large casserole and pour over the stock.

celery, garlic, bay leaf and spices with the rice in a casserole.

4. Pour over the boiling stock and microwave on HIGH for 25 minutes, or until the rice is cooked and the liquid is absorbed. Check near the end of the cooking time and add extra liquid if necessary.

5. After the rice is cooked, stir in the olives and the grated cheese and microwave for 1 minute on HIGH to melt the cheese. Season to taste with salt and pepper.

Step 1 Cook the kidney beans until completely soft, but still whole.

Step 5 When the rice has been cooked until soft, stir in the olives and cheese.

Cook's Notes

 TIME: Preparation takes 15 minutes, and cooking takes about 1 hour.

 PREPARATION: If preparing the dish in advance, add the cheese just before reheating to prevent stringiness.

COOK'S TIP: Canned beans may be used instead of dried, but remember that cooked beans are approximately twice the weight and volume of uncooked beans.

PASTA PAPRIKA

SERVES 4

Pasta cooks very well in a microwave oven, without sticking to the pan or steaming up the kitchen!

12oz green or whole-wheat fettucini, fresh or dried
1 tsp sunflower oil
1 large onion, chopped
1 clove garlic, crushed
3 peppers, one green, one red and one yellow, seeded and sliced
1 tbsp olive oil
1lb canned tomatoes, sieved
2 tsps paprika
¼ cup Parmesan cheese, grated

Step 3 Cook the onion, garlic and peppers in a covered bowl until tender.

Step 1 Cook the pasta in a large bowl until just tender.

Step 4 Add the tomatoes and stir the sauce into the pasta.

1. Place the pasta in a large bowl, pour over boiling water to cover and add the sunflower oil. Cook for 5 minutes on HIGH, or until the pasta is just tender. If using fresh pasta, cook for only 2 minutes on HIGH.

2. Allow the pasta to stand in the water while you prepare the sauce.

3. Combine the onion, garlic and sliced peppers with the olive oil and cook for 4 minutes on HIGH.

4. Add the tomatoes and paprika. Stir this sauce into the drained pasta, sprinkle with the Parmesan cheese and cook for 4 minutes on HIGH. Serve immediately.

Cook's Notes

 TIME: Preparation takes 20 minutes, and cooking takes 13 minutes.

 VARIATION: Green peppers may be used in place of the red and yellow peppers although the combination of all three makes an attractive dish.

 SERVING IDEAS: This dish can be served as an accompaniment to broiled chicken or fish, or as a delicious vegetarian main course with a salad and whole-wheat bread.

LASAGNE ROLLS

SERVES 4

Lasagne takes on a new look when the pasta sheets are rolled around a tasty spinach filling.

8oz whole-wheat lasagne
1 tsp sunflower oil
2 cups fresh or frozen spinach, finely chopped
2½ cups low fat cottage cheese
½ cup Parmesan cheese, grated
¼ cup pine nuts
1 egg, beaten
½ tsp sea salt
1 cup tomato paste
¾ cup water
2 tsps mixed herbs

1. Cook the lasagne, two or three sheets at a time, in boiling water to which you have added 1 tsp oil. Place a few sheets in the water, microwave for 1-2 minutes on HIGH, or until they are just soft, but not fully cooked.

Step 1 Cook the sheets of lasagne 2 or 3 at a time in a large bowl.

2. Set aside the cooked sheets separately to prevent them sticking together.

3. Cook the spinach for 5 minutes on HIGH with no additional water, if frozen, or 3 minutes on HIGH with a small amount of water, if fresh.

4. Drain and mix into the cottage cheese. Add the Parmesam cheese, beaten egg, pine nuts and salt and set aside.

5. Prepare a sauce by combining the tomato paste with the water and herbs.

Step 2 To prevent the lasagne sheets sticking together, spread them out on paper towels to drain.

Step 6 Place some of the cottage cheese mixture on each lasagne sheet and roll up.

6. Place a large spoonful of the cottage cheese mixture on each sheet of lasagne and roll them up. Arrange the rolls in a dish, and pour over the sauce.

7. Bake for 10 minutes on HIGH, or until the lasagne is fully cooked and most of the liquid has been absorbed. Check halfway through the cooking time and add more water if the dish seems dry.

Cook's Notes

 TIME: Preparation takes about 35 minutes, and cooking takes about 15 minutes.

VARIATION: Tomato paste is used to make the sauce in this recipe. If desired, substitute a 14oz can of tomatoes and their juice.

 BUYING GUIDE: Pine nuts are available in delicatessens or speciality food stores, but supermarkets often stock them, too. They are expensive, so any other variety of nuts can be used.

SMOKED HADDOCK AND CHIVES AU GRATIN

SERVES 4

Smoked fish combines so well with cheese and chives. Serve this for supper, lunch or even brunch.

12oz smoked haddock, skinned
½ cup white wine
1 bay leaf
¾ cup mushrooms, sliced
2 tbsps low fat spread
2 tbsps whole-wheat flour
½ cup skim milk
Small bunch fresh chives, chopped
½ cup low fat Cheddar cheese, grated
1 tbsp chopped fresh parsley
4 tbsps whole-wheat breadcrumbs

Step 4 Add the cooking liquid and the milk to the sauce. Cook until thickened, whipping frequently.

Step 5 Add the flaked fish to the sauce.

Step 2 Cook the haddock until it flakes easily.

1. Place the haddock in a shallow pan with the wine, bay leaf and mushrooms.

2. Cover and cook on HIGH for 3 minutes, or until the fish is cooked. Set aside.

3. Put the low fat spread in a small bowl and cook on HIGH for 30 seconds. Stir in the flour and cook on HIGH for 30 seconds.

4. Add the cooking liquor from the fish together with the milk and mix well. Cook on HIGH for 2-4 minutes, whipping every minute until thickened.

5. Add the mushrooms, chives and fish, flaking the fish slightly as you do so, and mix well.

6. Divide between four individual gratin dishes. Sprinkle over the cheese, parsley and breadcrumbs and cook on HIGH for 1-2 minutes or brown under the grill.

Cook's Notes

TIME: Preparation takes 10 minutes, and cooking takes 5-8 minutes.

VARIATION: Substitute smoked cod or prepare the dish with unsmoked fish.

SERVING IDEAS: Serve with a salad and whole-wheat or granary bread.

FISHERMAN'S PIE

SERVES 4

Fish is low in fat and calories but high in flavor. For variety, choose a combination of fish and seafood.

1lb fish and shellfish (mixture of whitefish, smoked fish, shrimp and mussels)
1½ lbs potatoes, peeled
2 tbsps low fat spread
4 tbsps hot skim milk
Sea salt and freshly ground black pepper

Sauce
2 tbsps low fat spread
2 tbsps flour
Skim milk
3 tbsps chopped parsley
Dash Tabasco
Sea salt and freshly ground black pepper

Glaze
1 egg, beaten with a pinch of sea salt

1. Skin the fish and remove any bones. Cut into chunks, place in a large bowl and cover with pierced plastic wrap. Cook on HIGH for 4 minutes.

Step 3 Cut the potatoes into even-sized pieces before cooking in a covered bowl with the water.

2. Add the mussels to the bowl and cook for a further 2 minutes on HIGH. Leave to stand, covered, while preparing the potatoes.

3. Place the potatoes in a bowl with 4 tbsps water, cover and cook on HIGH for 10-12 minutes or until tender.

4. Drain well and mash with the low fat spread and hot skim milk until smooth. Season with salt and pepper.

5. Melt the low fat spread for the sauce in a glass measure for 30 seconds on HIGH. Stir in the flour and measure the juices from the fish. Make up to 1 cup with cold skim milk. Stir the skim milk and fish juices into the flour and low fat spread and whisk well.

6. Cook on HIGH for 6 minutes, whisking several times during cooking to prevent lumps forming. Stir in the parsley and add salt and pepper and a dash of Tabasco.

7. Arrange the fish and mussels in a casserole dish and add the shrimp. Pour the sauce over the fish and smooth level.

8. Spoon or pipe the mashed potato on top in a lattice pattern. Glaze the potato with the beaten egg and cook on HIGH for 12-15 minutes, or until heated through. Brown under a preheated broiler before serving.

Step 8 Using a plain piping tip, pipe the mashed potatoes over the fish in a lattice pattern.

Cook's Notes

 TIME: Preparation takes about 15 minutes, and cooking takes about 26-28 minutes.

$ ECONOMY: To cut costs, leave out the shellfish and make up the weight with a more inexpensive fish.

 FREEZING: Allow the pie to cool and then freeze until the potato is firm. Cover the pie well and freeze for up to 2 months.

HADDOCK AND POTATO CURRY

SERVES 4

A taste for curry is quickly satisfied with a microwave oven in the kitchen. It's less expensive than a takeout, too.

8oz potatoes, peeled, if desired, and diced
3 tbsps low fat spread
1 onion, finely chopped
1 fresh green chili, seeded and chopped
1 tsp ground cumin
1 tsp ground coriander
2 cardamom pods
½ tsp tomato paste
Pinch turmeric
Sea salt to taste
½ cup low fat natural yogurt
1lb haddock, skinned, boned and cut into chunks
1 tbsp chopped fresh coriander or parsley
Cucumber twists

1. Place the potatoes in a bowl or roasting bag, add approximately 4 tbsps water and cook, covered, for 4 minutes on HIGH, or until soft. Drain and set aside.

2. In a casserole, melt the low fat spread for 1 minute on HIGH. Stir in the onion and chili and microwave for a further minute on HIGH.

3. Blend in the remaining spices and the tomato paste and cook for 1 more minute on HIGH.

4. Stir in the yogurt, then mix in the cooked potato and the fish, making sure they are well coated with sauce.

Step 1 A roasting bag may be used instead of a covered bowl for microwaving the potatoes.

5. Cover and cook for 5 minutes on HIGH, or until the fish is fully cooked, stirring once during the cooking time. Garnish the curry with the chopped coriander or parsley and the cucumber twists before serving.

Step 3 When the onion and chili are soft, blend in the spices and tomato paste and cook for a further 1 minute.

Cook's Notes

 TIME: Preparation takes 20 minutes, and cooking takes 12 minutes.

 VARIATION: You can use other types of whitefish to make this flavorful curry if you wish.

SERVING IDEAS: Accompany the curry with additional low fat natural yogurt and a selection of chutneys and pickles. Serve with brown rice.

CREAMY FISH CHOWDER

SERVES 4

Soups make economical and healthful meals, whether as lunches, suppers or snacks. Fish, bacon and potatoes are a flavorful combination.

1lb fish trimmings
1 bay leaf
1½ cups water
2 tbsps low fat spread, cut into pieces
3oz rindless bacon, finely chopped
2 medium onions, chopped
1lb potatoes, peeled and diced
1 cup skim milk
1 tsp thyme
½ tsp freshly grated nutmeg
Sea salt and freshly ground black pepper
1lb whitefish fillets, cut into ½-inch chunks
½ cup light cream
Chopped fresh parsley

1. First prepare the stock by combining the fish trimmings, bay leaf and stalks from the parsley with the water.

2. Microwave on HIGH for 5 minutes, or until boiling, then reduce the power and cook for 13 minutes on MEDIUM.

3. Strain the stock and set aside.

4. Place the chopped bacon and onion with the low fat spread in a large 3 quart casserole with a lid and microwave on HIGH for 3 minutes, stirring occasionally.

5. Add the diced potatoes, reserved stock, skim milk, thyme, nutmeg and seasoning. Microwave on HIGH for 20 minutes, or until the potatoes are soft.

6. Liquidize approximately 1½ cups of the soup, then return it to the casserole. Add the chopped fish and cook for a further 5 minutes on HIGH, or until the fish is tender.

7. Stir in the cream and heat through for 1 minute on HIGH. Ladle into bowls to serve and garnish with chopped parsley.

Step 1 Combine the fish bones and trimmings with the other stock ingredients in the largest bowl that will fit in the microwave.

Step 4 Cook the onion and bacon until they are soft but not beginning to color.

Cook's Notes

 TIME: Preparation takes about 30 minutes, and cooking takes about 45 minutes.

 VARIATION: For variety, try substituting smoked haddock for the whitefish or adding ½ cup frozen corn with the fish.

SERVING IDEAS: Serve this hearty supper soup with fresh whole-wheat rolls or croûtons.

STUFFED PEPPERS

SERVES 4

Peppers cook quickly in a microwave oven but retain all their taste and texture, which is very important in healthful eating.

3 large peppers, red, yellow and green
¾lb lean ground beef
1 onion, finely chopped
½ cup cooked brown rice
½ cup raisins
2 tbsps chopped walnuts
1 tbsp Worcestershire sauce
2 tsps brown sugar
2 tsps wine vinegar
Sea salt and freshly ground black pepper

Sauce
1lb canned tomatoes
1 bay leaf
2 tsps chili powder
1 clove garlic, crushed
1 tbsp tomato paste
2 tbsps cornstarch mixed with 2 tbsps water
Salt and pepper

1. Cut the peppers in half and remove the cores and seeds.

2. Place them in 1 layer in a shallow dish with 4 tbsps water. Cover loosely and cook for 4 minutes on HIGH. Leave to stand, covered, while preparing the filling.

3. Cook the beef for 5-6 minutes on MEDIUM in a casserole dish.

Step 4 Cook the beef and onion, breaking it up with a fork as it cooks.

4. Add the onion and increase the setting to HIGH. Cook for another 4-6 minutes breaking the meat up with a fork frequently during cooking.

5. Stir in the rice, raisins, walnuts, Worcestershire sauce, brown sugar, vinegar and seasoning. Drain the peppers and fill with the meat mixture.

6. Combine all the sauce ingredients except the cornstarch and water, in a glass measure. Cook for 12 minutes on HIGH, or until boiling.

7. Stir the cornstarch and water into the sauce. Cook for a further 3 minutes, stirring frequently after 1 minute.

8. Allow to cool slightly, remove the bay leaf and purée the sauce. Strain it if desired and pour over the peppers in a serving dish. Reheat for 1-2 minutes on HIGH.

Cook's Notes

TIME: Preparation takes about 20 minutes, and cooking takes 28-31 minutes.

VARIATION: Many different ingredients can be added to the filling such as corn, olives, mushrooms or low fat cheese. Add to or subtract from the list of ingredients according to preference. Use 3 cups of cooked brown rice instead of the meat for a vegetarian filling and omit the Worcestershire sauce.

FREEZING: Cover well and freeze for up to 3 months. Defrost for 10-15 minutes on LOW or DEFROST and allow to stand for 10 minutes. Cook for 10 minutes on HIGH to reheat and serve immediately.

BRAN AND OAT MEAT LOAF

SERVES 4

*The ever popular meat loaf gets a fiber boost from the addition of oats
and bran. They make a pleasant change texturewise too.*

1lb lean ground beef
1 egg
2 tbsps bran
6 tbsps rolled oats
1 small onion, chopped
1 cup skim milk
1 tsp dried mixed herbs
1 tsp sea salt

Tomato Sauce
1lb canned tomatoes
3 tbsps tomato paste
1 clove garlic, crushed
1 onion, roughly chopped
1 green pepper, diced
1 tbsp cornstarch
2 tbsps cold water
Sea salt and freshly ground black pepper
Raw cane sugar (optional)

1. Mix together all the ingredients for the meat loaf and place the mixture in a loaf pan.

2. Smooth the top and cook for 15 minutes on HIGH. Leave to stand for 10 minutes before turning out.

3. To prepare the sauce, combine the tomatoes and their juice, the paste and garlic. Cook, uncovered, on HIGH for 8 minutes or until boiling.

4. Add the onion and green pepper and cook for 5 minutes on HIGH.

Step 2 When the meat loaf is cooked, it will shrink from the edge of the dish. Leave to stand and pour off any fat.

5. Combine cornstarch with the water and stir into the sauce. Cook for 3-4 minutes on HIGH, or until thickened. Season with salt and pepper and add a pinch of sugar, if desired.

6. Pour the sauce over the meat loaf and reheat, if necessary, for 2 minutes on HIGH.

Step 1 Mix the meat loaf ingredients together and press firmly into a loaf dish.

Step 6 Turn the meat out onto a serving plate or board covered with aluminum foil.

Cook's Notes

 TIME: Preparation takes 20 minutes, and cooking takes about 31-32 minutes.

SERVING IDEAS: Serve with chutney instead of tomato sauce, if desired. Meat loaf is particularly good served with mashed potatoes. It also makes delicious sandwiches.

LAMB COUSCOUS
SERVES 6

Couscous, a form of grain popular in North African cooking, can make meat go further and provide a lot of flavor interest.

1lb lamb fillet, cut into chunks
2 onions, cut into chunks
1 clove garlic, crushed
1 green pepper, sliced
1 large potato, diced
4 carrots, sliced
2 small turnips, diced
1 cup dried apricots, chopped
1 tsp ground coriander
1 tsp ground cumin
1 tsp ground turmeric
1 tsp chili powder
1 cup chickpeas
14oz canned tomatoes, roughly chopped
1lb couscous
3 cups water
1 tsp sea salt

1. To cook the chickpeas in the microwave, pour boiling water over them and leave to soak for at least 2 hours.

2. Drain, then cook them in 1 quart of water for 25 minutes on HIGH.

3. Combine the lamb, onion and garlic in a casserole and cook for 5 minutes on HIGH.

4. Add the vegetables, dried apricots, spices, cooked chickpeas and tomatoes and microwave for a further 15 minutes on HIGH.

5. Set the stew aside while you prepare the

Step 4 Add the remaining stew ingredients to the precooked lamb.

Step 6 When the couscous has absorbed most of the water it will swell in size. Cook and then fluff up with a fork to separate the grains.

couscous. Place the couscous in a bowl with the salt and pour on the water.

6. Leave to stand for at least 5 minutes, until the couscous has swollen and absorbed most of the liquid. Cover the bowl and microwave on HIGH for 5 minutes. Remove the cover and fluff up the couscous with a fork. Serve the lamb on top of the couscous.

Cook's Notes

 TIME: Preparation takes 25 minutes plus 2 hours to soak the chickpeas, and cooking takes 30 minutes.

VARIATION: Chicken is often served in a spicy sauce with couscous. Use chicken breasts or boned leg meat which will cook quickly.

$ BUYING GUIDE: More and more supermarkets and most delicatessens stock couscous. There is no real substitute, although the lamb stew is also good served with rice.

CHICKEN TOMALE BAKE

SERVES 4

The diced chicken in this dish will take about 10 minutes to microwave and will be juicy and tender.

½-1lb cooked boneless chicken, diced
1 cup frozen corn
1 green pepper, chopped

Sauce
1 clove garlic, crushed
1 cup tomato juice
½ tsp ground cumin
½ tsp chili powder
1 tsp oregano

Topping
¾ cup polenta or corn meal
2 cups water
2 eggs
1 tsp sea salt
Pinch paprika

1. Combine the chicken and vegetables in a casserole.

2. Mix together the sauce ingredients and pour

Step 4 Beat the eggs into the cooked polenta.

over the chicken.

3. To make the topping, stir the polenta into the water and microwave on HIGH for 5 minutes.

4. Stir thoroughly then beat in the two eggs and the salt.

5. Spread the topping over the chicken and sauce mixture, sprinkle paprika on top, cover and cook for 10 minutes on HIGH, or until the topping is set.

Step 2 Combine the chicken, vegetables and sauce ingredients in a casserole.

Step 5 Spread the polenta topping carefully over the chicken and sauce.

Cook's Notes

 TIME: Preparation takes about 15 minutes, and cooking takes about 18 minutes.

 PREPARATION: This dish can be prepared ahead and refrigerated. Add 5-6 minutes to the final cooking time.

 SERVING IDEAS: This dish is almost a meal in itself, and needs only a green salad or a tomato and onion salad as an accompaniment.

CHICKEN PAPRIKA

SERVES 4

*Chicken portions are best cooked on medium for the tenderest results
and most even cooking.*

3¼lb chicken, cut into 8 pieces and skinned
3 tbsps sunflower oil
1 medium onion, finely sliced
1 clove garlic, crushed
1 red pepper, seeded and thinly sliced
1 tbsp mild paprika
Pinch cayenne pepper (optional)
½ cup chicken stock
8oz canned tomatoes, chopped
Sea salt and freshly ground black pepper
1 tbsp cornstarch mixed with 2 tbsps cold
    water
Low fat natural yogurt

Step 1 Cook the onion in the oil until softened.

1. Place the sunflower oil and onion in a large casserole dish and cook on HIGH for 3 minutes.

2. Add the garlic, pepper, paprika, cayenne pepper if using and salt and pepper. Cover and cook on HIGH for 2 minutes.

3. Pour in the stock and tomatoes and stir well. Add the chicken and cook on MEDIUM for 30-40 minutes.

4. Blend the cornstarch and the water and add to the chicken, stirring well. Cook for 6-7 minutes on MEDIUM or until the sauce thickens.

5. Allow to stand for 5 minutes. Spoon yogurt over the top before serving, if desired.

Step 2 Add the garlic, sliced pepper, paprika and cayenne and cook for a further 2 minutes.

Step 3 Add the chicken, pushing it under the surface of the liquid as much as possible.

Cook's Notes

TIME: Preparation takes 20 minutes, and cooking takes 36-47 minutes with 5 minutes standing time.

SERVING IDEAS: Serve with whole-wheat pasta, brown rice or boiled potatoes in their skins or jacket potatoes.

FREEZING: Freeze in containers or in the serving dish. Cover well and store for up to 2 months. To thaw and reheat, cook uncovered on LOW or DEFROST for 15 minutes, stirring frequently. Leave to stand for 10 minutes and reheat on HIGH for 10-12 minutes. Top with low fat natural yogurt.

SUGARLESS BAKED APPLES WITH DATES

SERVES 4

Although this recipe contains no sugar, the apples are delightfully sweet tasting. They can be eaten on their own or served with cream or yogurt.

4 large green apples
½ cup chopped, unsugared dates
4 tbsps sugar-free muesli
2 tbsps low fat spread
½ cup pure apple juice

Step 2 Mix together the dates and muesli and fill the cavities in the apples.

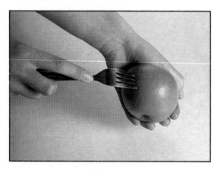

Step 1 Use a fork or small sharp knife to prick the apple skins in several places.

Step 3 Place the apples in a circle so that they are touching.

1. Core the apples. Prick the skins in several places, but do not peel.

2. Fill the cavities with a mixture of the muesli and dates.

3. Place the apples in a casserole so that they are touching.

4. Dot the filling with the low fat spread and pour over the apple juice. Bake for 3-4 minutes on HIGH, or until the apples are soft.

Cook's Notes

TIME: Preparation takes about 10 minutes, and cooking takes 3-4 minutes.

COOK'S TIP: Prick the apple skins with a fork or knife to allow steam to escape and prevent the apples bursting.

SERVING IDEAS: Top with natural yogurt mixed with a few drops of vanilla extract.

FRESH AND DRIED FRUIT SALAD

SERVES 4

Perk up dried fruit with fresh seasonal varieties — apples and oranges in winter, soft fruits or peaches in summer.

1½ cups mixed dried fruit
1 cup pure apple juice
2 dessert apples
1 orange

1. Combine the dried fruit and the apple juice in a bowl and microwave on MEDIUM for 8 minutes. Allow to cool.

Step 1 Cook the dried fruit in the apple juice and leave to rehydrate.

2. Wash the orange and cut four slices to use as a garnish, then peel and roughly chop the flesh.

Step 3 Combine the chopped apple and orange with the dried fruit.

3. Wash and chop the apples, leaving the skins on. Combine the chopped apples and orange with the dried fruit and apple juice and chill.

4. To serve, divide between 4 dishes and garnish each with an orange slice.

Cook's Notes

TIME: Preparation takes 10 minutes, and cooking takes 8 minutes.

VARIATION: Use whatever fresh fruit is in season and whatever type or combination of dried fruit you prefer.

SERVING IDEAS: Serve with low fat natural yogurt or fromage frais.

SUGAR-FREE FRUIT CAKE

Makes 1 large cake

A moist and flavorful fruit cake in just over 30 minutes? Anything's possible with a microwave oven in the kitchen.

1½ cups mixed dried fruit
1¼ cups apple juice
2 cups whole-wheat flour
2 tsps baking powder
1 tsp mixed spice
½ cup low fat spread
2 eggs, beaten
Reduced sugar apricot jam

Step 2 Rub the fat into the dry ingredients until the mixture looks like fine breadcrumbs.

1. Combine the fruit and the apple juice and allow to soak for at least 1 hour.

2. Mix together the dry ingredients and rub in the butter or margarine until the mixture resembles fine breadcrumbs.

3. Beat in the eggs and mix in the fruit and juice.

4. Line the bottom of a deep 6-inch round dish with wax paper. Pour in the cake mixture and smooth the top.

5. Let the mixture stand for a few minutes, then bake for 3 minutes on HIGH, followed by 13 minutes on MEDIUM, or until the center is just dry. Allow to cool slightly, then turn out onto a rack to finish cooling.

6. When cool, brush the top with reduced sugar apricot jam.

Step 5 The center of the cake should look dry when done.

 TIME: Preparation takes about 20 minutes, and cooking takes about 16 minutes.

 VARIATION: This recipe can be used for wedding, birthday, christening or Christmas cakes.

BANANA BRAN BREAD

Makes 1 loaf

*This teabread is the fastest ever. It also has all the goodness of bran
and whole-wheat flour.*

½ cup low fat spread
½ cup Barbados sugar
2 medium eggs
2 large, very ripe bananas, mashed
4 tbsps low fat natural yogurt
1 tsp baking powder
½ tsp baking soda
½ tsp sea salt
1 cup bran
1½ cups whole-wheat flour
½ cup toasted bran

1. Cream together the low fat spread and sugar.

2. Add the eggs, mashed bananas and low fat yoghurt.

3. Sift in the baking powder, baking soda, salt, bran and flour. Mix together thoroughly.

4. Turn the batter into a lightly greased loaf pan. Cover the top loosely with plastic wrap and cover the corners of the dish with aluminum foil, shiny side out.

5. Cook in the microwave for 10 minutes on HIGH. Remove the foil and plastic wrap, sprinkle on the toasted bran, replace plastic wrap, and cook for a further 2 minutes on HIGH.

6. Remove the plastic wrap and leave the loaf to cool in the dish for 10 minutes before turning out.

Step 3 Mix in the baking powder, baking soda, sea salt, bran and flour.

Step 1 Cream the low fat spread with the sugar until light and fluffy.

Step 4 If using a square or loaf dish, cover the corners with foil.

Cook's Notes

 TIME: Preparation takes about 20 minutes, and cooking takes about 12 minutes.

 COOK'S TIP: Covering the corners of cakes baked in square or loaf dishes prevents uneven cooking. The foil will deflect the microwaves, but use it sparingly.

SERVING IDEAS: This teabread is particularly delicious served cold, sliced and spread with low fat cream cheese.

PEACH COBBLER CAKE

SERVES 4

This marvellous pudding is simplicity itself to prepare and it cooks in less than 15 minutes. The brown sugar topping is absolutely delicious.

1½ tbsps low fat spread
2 tbsps soft brown sugar
14oz canned peaches, drained
Large pinch nutmeg
2 tbsps raw cane sugar
1 cup bran
½ cup whole-wheat flour
1 tsp baking powder
½ tsp cinnamon
Pinch sea salt
4 tbsps low fat spread
½ cup skim milk

1. Melt the 1½ tbsps of low fat spread in a 7-inch square or round dish for 1 minute on HIGH.

2. Stir in the brown sugar and spread evenly over the bottom of the dish. Arrange the peaches on top.

3. In a separate bowl mix together the dry ingredients and rub in the 4 tbsps low fat spread. Stir in the skim milk to form a soft dough.

4. Cover the peaches as evenly as possible with the mixture and bake, uncovered, for 12 minutes on HIGH, or until the center is just cooked.

Step 2 Stir the sugar into the melted low fat spread and spread evenly over the base of the baking dish.

Step 4 Spread the cake mixture over the peaches and the sugar topping.

5. Allow to cool for 15 minutes, then invert carefully onto a plate to serve.

Cook's Notes

 TIME: Preparation takes 15 minutes, and cooking takes 12 minutes.

 SERVING IDEAS: The cake is best served warm and can be accompanied with low fat natural yogurt.

 PREPARATION: The dish can be lined with wax paper to help ease the cake out of the dish.

 VARIATION: Other canned or cooked fresh fruit can be substituted for the peaches in this attractive and quickly prepared dessert.

FLAPJACKS

MAKES 8

*These favorite family treats are low in sugar and cook in less than
5 minutes. Two good reasons for making them often.*

½ cup low fat spread
2 tbsps clear honey
¾ cup whole-wheat flour
1¾ cups rolled oats
2 heaped tbsps sesame seeds
1 tsp cinnamon

1. Place the low fat spread in a mixing bowl and cook for 2 minutes on HIGH to melt.

Step 2 Mix the honey and dry ingredients into the melted low fat spread.

2. Mix in the honey and the dry ingredients. Pat the mixture onto a dinner plate which has been covered with wax paper. It should be at least ½ inch thick.

Step 2 Using a rubber spatula or the back of a spoon, press the mixture onto a plate lined with wax paper.

Step 3 Cut the mixture into wedges while still warm, but allow to cool before transferring to a serving plate.

3. Bake for 2½ minutes on HIGH. Cut into 8 wedges while still warm.
4. Leave to cool completely before serving.

Cook's Notes

 TIME: Preparation takes about 10 minutes, and cooking takes 4½ minutes.

 WATCHPOINT: Don't be tempted to sample the flapjacks before they are commpletely cool. The mixture gets very hot and can burn.

PREPARATION: Be sure to cut the flapjacks before they cool completely, or they will break apart.

 VARIATION: If you don't like the taste of honey, substitute the same quantity of corn syrup.

HOME-MADE YOGURT

Makes approximately 2 cups

*Yogurt made with the help of a microwave oven eliminates the need
for temperature testing and for cleaning messy pans.*

1½ cups skim milk
1 tbsps skim milk powder
4 tbsps low fat natural yogurt

Step 3 Boil the milk until slightly reduced in volume.

Step 4 Whisk in the milk powder and leave to cool to a hand-hot temperature.

1. Put the milk in a large bowl and cook uncovered for 2 minutes on HIGH.

2. Stir and cook for a further 2-3 minutes on HIGH until the milk boils.

3. Reduce the setting and cook uncovered for 8 minutes on DEFROST, stirring occasionally until the milk is slightly reduced in volume.

4. Whisk in the milk powder and leave to cool until comfortable to the touch.

5. Whisk in the yogurt, then pour into a wide-necked flask or divide between the glasses in a yogurt maker.

6. Cover and leave for 8 hours until the yogurt is just set, then refrigerate covered for a further 3-4 hours.

Step 5 Whisk in the yogurt which is needed as a starter.

Cook's Notes

 TIME: Preparation takes about 5 minutes, and cooking takes about 12-13 minutes. Setting time will be about 8 hours.

 VARIATION: Flavorings such as fruit, honey, spices, vanilla or chocolate can be added to the yogurt before it is left to set.

 WATCHPOINT: Make sure that the milk mixture has cooled sufficiently before adding the yogurt, otherwise it will curdle!

WHOLE-WHEAT BREAD

Makes 1 loaf

Speed up yeast cookery by using your microwave oven. Use it to prove the dough and then bake it in less than half the conventional baking time.

3 cups whole-wheat flour
1 cup all-purpose flour
1 tsp sea salt
1 cup milk
2 tbsps low fat spread
1 envelope active dried yeast
1 tsp brown sugar
1 egg, beaten with a pinch of sea salt
Oatmeal or bran (optional)

1. Sift the flours and the salt into a large bowl. Make a well in the center.

2. Heat the milk for 15 seconds on HIGH. Stir in the low fat spread to melt and the yeast to dissolve. Stir in the sugar, and pour this liquid mixture into the well in the dry ingredients. Stir to incorporate all the ingredients gradually.

3. Turn out onto a floured surface, and knead for 10 minutes.

4. Put the dough into a lightly greased bowl and turn over to coat all sides. Cover the dough mixture with plastic wrap or a clean towel. Leave to rise for 1-1½ hours in a warm place.

5. Alternatively, place the bowl of dough in a dish of hot water and put into the microwave oven for 4 minutes on LOW. Leave the dough to stand for 15 minutes and then repeat until the dough has doubled in bulk.

6. Shape the dough by punching it down and kneading lightly for about 2 minutes.

Step 7 Roll up the dough, seal the ends and place in a loaf pan.

7. Roll or pull the dough out to a rectangle and then roll up tightly. Seal the ends and tuck under slightly. Put into a lightly greased loaf pan, about 9 inches x 5 inches.

8. Cover the loaf pan loosely and leave the dough to rise in a warm place for about 30 minutes, or use the microwave rising method.

9. Brush the top of the loaf with lightly beaten egg and sprinkle on the bran or oatmeal, if using. Cook on MEDIUM for 6-8 minutes giving the dish a quarter turn every 1 minute.

10. Increase the temperature to HIGH and cook for 1-2 minutes, rotating as before. The top will spring back when lightly touched when the bread is done.

11. Leave in the dish for 5 minutes before turning out onto a wire rack to cool. If desired, oatmeal or bran may be pressed onto the base and sides of the cooling loaf.

Cook's Notes

 TIME: Preparation takes 1-2 hours and cooking takes about 10-12 minutes.

 COOK'S TIP: Using the microwave instructions for proofing bread dough will cut the time this step usually takes by half.

 WATCHPOINT: Yeast will die at too high a temperature, so test the milk and if very hot, allow to cool slightly before adding the yeast.